CAPE COD and the OFFSHORE ISLANDS

Books by Walter Teller

The Farm Primer

Roots in the Earth (with P. Alston Waring)

An Island Summer

The Search for Captain Slocum: A Biography

The Voyages of Joshua Slocum

Five Sea Captains

Area Code 215: A Private Line in Bucks County

Cape Cod and the Offshore Islands

CAPE COD
and the
OFFSHORE ISLANDS

by

Walter Teller

PRENTICE-HALL, INC.,
Englewood Cliffs, N. J.

Photographs by Josephine Von Miklos

Library of Congress Catalog Card Number: 73-97739
Printed in the United States of America *T*

Prentice-Hall International, Inc., London
Prentice-Hall of Australia, Pty. Ltd., Sydney
Prentice-Hall of Canada, Ltd., Toronto
Prentice-Hall of India Private Ltd., New Delhi
Prentice-Hall of Japan, Inc., Tokyo

To all who helped on the way

CONTENTS

Walter Teller
To
Elizabeth Beston
21 April 70

Introduction

In October of 1849, Henry Thoreau set out on the jaunt to be described in his *Cape Cod*. Whether or not Mr. Teller consciously intended to parallel Thoreau's enterprise and check up on some of the same scenes more than a century later, I don't know. But there are grateful resemblances beyond the obvious one that they covered some of the same ground and covered part of it on foot—which even in Thoreau's time was beginning to be a somewhat old-fashioned way of traveling.

Cape Cod is the most relaxed of Thoreau's books, and "relaxed" is the first word that occurs in attempting to describe *Cape Cod and the Offshore Islands*. Like Thoreau, Mr. Teller is not in any hurry to get anywhere (the road is always better than the inn, as Cervantes says), and neither is he grimly determined to prove anything. Weather, landscape, history (both natural and social), people, trades, changes and survivals—they all interest him as he proceeds with eyes and ears open. Moreover, he manages to inspire in the reader the same relaxed absorption. He talks to old-timers and also to recently arrived "developers." There are a number of life and character sketches of colorful people including Captain Slocum (upon whom Mr. Teller is the leading authority) and Nancy Luce, whose poems about her chickens are charming as well as pathetic in their gentleness and naïveté. There are even statistics: This is the cranberry capital of the world, and a productive bog may yield fifty barrels an acre. But all this variety is subtended within the undefined but clearly present field of Mr. Teller's interests, and it is thus given unity.

Like so many of the other picturesque areas in the United States, both the Cape and the islands are now dependent at least as much on the tourist and summer visitor as upon their year-round residents. Perhaps here the changes have been less devastating than in most similarly affected places. Authentic Yankee characters still stick to some of their old ways and hold to their old opinions. Undoubtedly the Cape Codders are more prosperous than they once were; they suffer fewer hardships, or at least fewer of the sort they once suffered. But there as everywhere, a price must be paid for prosperity, and as usual, when city dwellers go in search of elbowroom, they deprive one another of what they came seeking.

Mr. Teller is respectful of the past but not irreconcilable. "Today, Pilgrim Beach on Provincetown Harbour, west of the Truro line, is plastered with barrack-like bungalows. Shocking? Not really. This is America, land where our fathers died. Land where our fathers' world is dead." Old-timers and newcomers seem, as he reminds us elsewhere, to be getting along rather well together. And we should remember that the old way of life was not based on any Peaceable Kingdom: "The money and glory of whaling came from a brutal and bloody business."

This is a book of many truths, not only about places but about people. And Mr. Teller has developed a style that communicates very clearly the unity of his own mind and emotions. I don't know of anyone else who writes quite like he does.

—Joseph Wood Krutch

To imagine that things in this life are always to remain as they are is to indulge in an idle dream. It would appear, rather, that everything moves in a circle, that is to say, around and around: spring follows summer, summer the harvest season, harvest autumn, autumn winter, and winter spring; and thus does time continue to turn like a never-ceasing wheel. Human life alone hastens onward to its end. . . .

Miguel de Cervantes, *Don Quixote*

CAPE COD and the OFFSHORE ISLANDS

Chapter 1

AS FAR AS WEST BARNSTABLE

SPECIALISTS are many, generalists few. Geologists, archaeologists, naturalists, historians, folklorists, cranberry culturists, sociologists, writers of guide books and log books and cook books—all have their say. They are the specialists. What I have in mind is a general account, and personal too; one man's—a generalist's—response to Cape Cod and the offshore islands and the way they are now.

Cape Cod, a long narrow hook-shaped peninsula on the southeast coast of Massachusetts, juts eastward into the Atlantic Ocean, then swings north. It is sixty-five miles long and varies in width from one to nineteen miles. The opening of the Cape Cod Canal in 1914 between Buzzards Bay and Cape Cod Bay shortened the coastal passage for shipping. It also converted the Cape to an island—an inshore island, however, linked to the mainland by bridges. The offshore islands are the Elizabeth Islands, Martha's Vineyard, and Nantucket.

Although the Cape is a summer resort first of all, every year sees more people going there to live. Falmouth at the western end, known as the Upper Cape, has become Cape Cod's intellectual center. Hyannis, in the middle of the peninsula, is the business and social core. Provincetown, at the tip of the Lower Cape, may be called the Latin Quarter.

My first day on Cape Cod, I groped for a place to begin. I started walking from the triangular village green in Falmouth. I passed the white clapboard and steepled Congregational Church, 18th-century houses, and lofty bare branching elms, and headed out Main Street. Long narrow Main Street is studded with parking meters. Many a parking space this morning was occupied by an automobile, yet the red flags showed. An unwritten custom takes hold from a movable date in November to an unannounced time in May—months when tourists are scarce and space is no problem. Besides, who would then be feeding the meters? This time of year there are fewer travelers than native sons, but then, every year more come down for a whiff in all seasons.

The end of March is a lonely time on the Cape, a time of waiting— for sun, warmer weather, visitors, commerce and trade. Two liquor stores, large as furniture showrooms, displayed posters: Open April 1st. The signs told a story of six-months, which is to say, seasonal license. They also told of seasonal population swelling from fourteen to fifty thousand.

The ghost of summer never leaves Falmouth. Although it has a lived-in and year-round look, closed seasonal shops with Boston and New York names remind you that this is a summer-industry place, established, well-heeled, and busy. At a certain stage of growing up, its social clubs might make you believe that all the pleasures were here. Falmouth, second largest in area of Cape Cod's fifteen towns—"town" being the New England term for a territory elsewhere called a township—ranks second in population. In population density, Falmouth stands third.

Weather becomes a dimension to those who live alongshore. For Main Street customers and passersby, the bank provides a weather station. Downtown among Falmouth's motley collection of 19th-century two-story business blocks and houses remodeled to stores, you can take a reading: temperature, barometric pressure, direction and velocity of wind—and in the shelter of the bank, chart your course accordingly.

It was a blue sky morning, 50 degrees. "If the sun shines all day it will be the first in three months," said the man at the service station. House painters were spreading a coat of pink-lavender over a gray weathered building. If only the job they were doing had been as right as the day!

I drove to West Falmouth via Sippewisset, on the winding—maybe immemorial—road, the former Route 28, demoted now to 28A. The fact that it has been superseded gives this semiretired road a charm that was hard to see when I hurried along it intent on making the boat to the offshore islands. No one in a hurry should be licensed to use Route 28A. Here and there, through the leafless trees, I caught a glimpse of the wide straight and new divided-lane highway.

West Falmouth lies north of Falmouth—North Falmouth, further north. West Falmouth's post office, hardly larger than the proverbial postage stamp, tells what the winter traffic is. By a little pond stands a little house, and a barn conformed to the same snug scale—all by-passed now by the dual-lane highway. The single-track railroad that went through West Falmouth along a choice right-of-way gave up a few years ago. Why not convert abandoned trackage to walkways and jog-ways? A Cape Cod Walking and Jogging Way could rise from the bones of the New York, New Haven, and Hartford.

Chappaquoit Point, on West Falmouth Harbor, commands all of Buzzards Bay's grand open far-reaching sweep of green choppy water and lumpy tireless cold-looking waves. The never-ending wonder of water lies in the simple fact it is there.

As I walked on a long beach between Buzzards Bay and an empty stretch of parking area, I saw I was not entirely alone. In an old car with rusted-out rocker panels a couple sat gazing hypnotically, minding the gray-green water. They were the standard couple of the standard beach looking standard, apart and lonely: a man and a woman gone to the limit of the land.

Lunching in Falmouth, on Main Street, I found myself among auto-mobile dealers. Like the stuff they sell, they seemed to come in various sizes, shapes, and flavors. I overheard that Falmouth was bursting with business—the growing Air Force base a few miles north, in the town of Sandwich; the expanding Oceanographic Institution at Woods Hole in Falmouth's southwest corner; and several smaller commercial-cultural-researching ventures. The dealers spoke of businessmen leaving

Boston for Falmouth because Falmouth is large enough to be profitable, small enough to be pleasant. This tentative blue intermediate day had everyone with financial overhead smiling, licking their chops at the prospect of warmer weather and business.

Grand Avenue, as you might guess from the old-fashioned name, is the waterfront street of an aging resort, a slum-in-the-making beside the sea. The old-style summer houses, boarded up, looked lugubrious. The few that were open appeared drearier yet. Who lives in them in the last week of March? What goes on? They are a striking example of seashore blight, a place ripe for seashore renewal.

Just the same, the light on the water dazzled, and the view across Nantucket Sound of Martha's Vineyard stirred warm feelings. From the mainland, an island is good to see. My binoculars picked up the lighthouses, West Chop, East Chop, and Vineyard Haven deep in the cleft between. How many times have I sailed in, how many times sailed from that place. The ferry *Uncatena*, outward bound, charged by, full speed ahead. How superb and inspiriting was the new *Uncatena*, slicing through cold water.

At two forty-five in the afternoon, wind from the southwest was nipping and biting. Pale sky, pale sun: walking along Falmouth Beach I saw snow-covered sand in the lee of the jetty. I made a note because when July comes, snow on the sand may be hard to imagine.

Early evening: I traveled Main Street end to end looking for dinner or supper. Too late for the time of year. Those who foraged on Main Street had eaten and gone. Doors were locked, waitresses sweeping up. As I turned away, my eyes caught a bronze plaque on the edge of the common. Four Falmouth men fell in the Great War. Remember me: steady reality, and steady reproach.

Although Main Street restaurants were closed, the inn at Jones Pond, north of the village, was open. I went there, was shown to a place near a couple—fiftyish-fortyish, well groomed, trim, and wearing fine country clothes. A look of good manners, money, and not much to do—and waiting for what? Were they year-round residents, yachtsmen, tourists? Summer people off-season?

It was Sunday. The doors stood open, the congregants were walking in. The Congregational Church's bell was cast by Paul Revere. "The living to the church I call. Unto the grave I summon all." Seeking an alternative, I turned toward the lately enlarged Falmouth Public Library planted on Katharine Lee Bates Road, well back from Main Street.

Time for elevenses: at a cranberry restaurant and emporium I asked for tea, and was handed a pot and with it a chaser of cranberry juice, native beverage, and possibly, solace.

The Town House was closed; the Falmouth Diner, fortunately open. The one Yankee, the other Portuguese, and both the real Cape thing.

On the edge of the village green, almost in the shadow of the high-steepled weather-vaned Congregational Church, near the post office and the old hardware store—an enclave of the past on the fringe of the newer business district—stands the birthplace of Katharine Lee Bates.

Author of *America the Beautiful*, youngest of five children, Katharine Lee Bates was born in the two-story decent and plain frame house at 16 Main Street, Falmouth, 29 August 1859. Her father, William Bates, a Congregational minister, died within a month of her birth. She was raised by her mother, Cornelia Frances Lee Bates, a Mount Holyoke graduate. Few children in those days had mothers who were college women. Mrs. Bates, more unusual still, was a graduate who continued to study. Katharine began writing early; encouraged, I guess, by this intellectual parent.

When Katharine was twelve the fatherless family left Falmouth and moved further inland to the vicinity of Wellesley. At age seventeen she entered Wellesley College. "A plain girl, near-sighted, heavy of physique, awkward in movement," according to the college historian. "Yet hardly had she crossed the academic threshold when the personality that was to influence and delight . . . began to make itself felt." After graduation she taught in nearby schools, then returned to the English Department at Wellesley where she remained forty years. She never married. Except for a year of study in England, two other trips abroad, and her early years on Cape Cod, she spent her life at Wellesley. She died 28 March 1929.

Although Katharine Lee Bates did not write *America the Beautiful* on her native shore but rather thousands of miles away, the remembered ocean and English forebears got into it. In the summer of 1893, on her first trip west, as she looked out "over the sea-like expanse of fertile country" from the vantage point of Pike's Peak, the opening lines, she later recalled, "floated" into her mind. A minister's daughter, she sent the poem to *The Congregationalist*, a Boston publication where, fittingly, it appeared on the 4th of July, 1895, but in a form "more literary and ornate than the present version." In 1904 she rewrote it, "trying to make the phraseology more simple and direct." She made further revisions in 1911.

> *O beautiful for spacious skies*
> *For amber waves of grain. . . .*

In 1888, seven years before the first publication of *America the Beautiful*, another Boston journal, *The Parish Choir*, published a melody for another hymn, *O Mother Dear Jerusalem*. The melody, composed by Samuel Augustus Ward (1847–1903) of Newark, New Jersey, was called *Materna*. Sometime after Katharine Lee Bate's poem appeared, somebody noticed that "O beautiful for spacious skies" throbs to the same rhythm as "O Mother Dear Jerusalem." Somebody put the poem and music together.

Beautiful, and also rich. Proud, prayerful, simple-hearted—no one has combined the ingredients better than the Falmouth-born English professor. Although she wrote six volumes of verse, juvenile, travel and text books, she remains a one-poem poet—and one-poem poets are among the most durable kind.

Woods Hole, the village at the extreme southern end of the Town of Falmouth, takes its name from the tidal passage between Buzzards Bay and Vineyard Sound. Once important as a whaling and ship-building center, the village is famous now as the seat of the Woods Hole Oceanographic Institution, founded in 1930 for the study of oceanography—the science that deals with oceans and their phenomena. Oceanography integrates the marine applications of geography, geology, physics, chemistry, biology, astronomy, and meteorology. Woods Hole is also home port for the *Atlantis*, the Institution's sea-roving laboratory. Woods Hole is where Louis Agassiz incorporated the Marine Biological Laboratory late in the 19th century for the study of natural history, and where the United States Bureau of Fisheries has established a branch and an aquarium. Scientists and students drawn to this village have made Falmouth Cape Cod's year-round intellectual center.

At Nobska Point, southernmost tip of Woods Hole, stands a guiding light. A close-coupled sturdy New England queen dressed in white skirt and black bonnet, Nobska Point Light descends from ancient lighthouse lineage, from wood fires burning in braziers on antique towers to whale oil, electricity, and incandescent lamp. One of the older lights on Cape Cod, built in 1828, rebuilt in 1876, a fine example of 19th-century science and art of pharology, Nobska throws a fixed white light on navigable parts of Nantucket Sound. Toward Hedge Fence, and L'Hommedieu Shoal, however, she beams a red sector.

At Little Wharf in Woods Hole, chief port of the Woods Hole, Martha's Vineyard & Nantucket Steamship Authority, most of the Steamship Authority fleet is in—*Islander, Nantucket*, and *Uncatena*, but the latter two were ready to sail. Vessels about to depart look at you. They make you feel you are missing the boat.

At Quisset Harbor, snug and lovely recess in the Buzzards Bay coastline, I found very pale green-blue and clear water, pleasant beaches, a seawall, and rising behind it, tough-looking red cedars. I felt—I wanted to feel—like a discoverer. But then other discoverers in orange plastic helmets roared in. Having gone as far as they could go, they turned and accelerated out.

I followed, then came to the kind of post-World War II colonial style house that buyer, builder, and mortgage-holder feel sure of. In the front yard a woman was raking up remnants of winter. I asked about traffic. "We get some," she said. "You see, everybody is out exploring." No road, however small or obscure, is without traffic these days. All manner of people, restless with money, are hunting for clues to the good life and place.

Further north I looked in on Racing Beach: a harsh scene, as though the glacier had not yet completed its work, or had done it badly and man did the rest. Too many houses stand in close order, looking seaward, and even this early in spring I saw too many wheels—jeeps and automobiles. What would it be like in summer?

East of Falmouth, along the Nantucket Sound shore, tidal channels and fingerlike ponds gouge the outwash plain. Long skinny necks of land result, each neck strung tight with little streets and beaded with little houses. I passed by Great, Green, Bournes, then Eel Pond, wriggling inlets, harbors, sandbars, shoals, broad shallow waters. Colors, textures, watery shapes, and waterfront problems. "Because of a problem with raw sewage . . . ," reported the local paper, the *Falmouth Enterprise*, "the Woods Hole harbormaster has made known his intention of closing Eel Pond to boats with people living aboard to protect the shellfish from pollution . . . ." Indeed, days of dumping over the side and discharging all manner of refuse and waste, whether from a tanker at sea or a yacht in a pond or small harbor—those careless days and ways must go. Water unsafe for shellfish is also unfit for human use and enjoyment unless it be made clean again. We people and shellfish are in this together.

The road winds through scrub pine forest, then climbs, dips, and crosses little rivers—Childs, Mashpee, and Cotuit, rivers no larger than streams, weak and charming. Wherever you look, the glacier-scarred landscape charms. And why? Because it is manageable—the scale is human.

What Indians did the Pilgrims meet? Nausets, Pamets, and Wampanoags generally. The Wampanoag mode of life was similar to that of other northeast woodland tribes except for the quantities of seafood eaten. Like all American Indians, Wampanoags believed that land, being part of nature, belonged to those living on it, no more to be sold, transferred, divided, or individually owned than sea or air. Although a tribe occupied a territory more or less understood and defined, within those limits all was given by the Great Spirit for the common good.

Englishmen, like other early and practical-minded venturers, claimed the land, as they said, by right of discovery, exploration, or settlement. The fact that the land was the homeland of native inhabitants did not stand in the way of making grants or planting colonies. Indian right, if any, hardly figured. Although Indians, persuaded by various means, often signed on the dotted line, they lacked the concept of exclusive ownership and could not have really understood what they were signing away.

Mashpee: Some say it means "Standing Water," others are certain it means "Great Pond." Mashpee, home of present-day Mashpee Indians, descended from Wampanoags, is Cape Cod's least populated town. Its year-round residents number some 700, mixed native Indian, African Negro, Cape Verdean, and Portuguese.

Mashpee Center, away from the south shore riches of shellfish, commerce, and shoreside development, remains rural by Falmouth standards. Few seasonal people seem to have gone to the Mashpee ponds and groves. School, firehouse, and general store at an intersection of roads deep in the Cape's interior form the hub of the town.

I entered the store. A smiling and very ethnic-looking young girl was retailing penny candies to a young and unmistakably Indian customer. The girl's father, the proprietor, appeared. He stood tall, broad, and heavyset. Eyes alive and dark, hair black and straight, the man looked authentically first-American. By his round smooth cheerful beaming face, you would say he had been blessed by Kiehtan, the creator, and Habbamock, god of health.

Quiet season, quiet hour; a chance to talk. The proprietor said that as a young man he left his home town of Mashpee to work in a plant in Delaware. While away, he married a New Jersey girl. Later he brought his bride—and also some money—home to Mashpee. Since then he has prospered, and his wife loves the Indian town. They live on the shore of Santuit Pond. Their children attend the new school. He likes to fish, said he often closes the store and hangs out a sign, "Gone Fishing." He did not speak about being an Indian.

Like most, this Indian legend seems psychologically sound: Ahsoo, the Indian maid, is said to have been so plain that no man wanted her, yet her voice was so wonderful that when she sang, animals, birds, and even fish came to listen. Ahsoo lived beside a creek. She sang at evening, and when she did, an enormous trout, charmed by her voice and seeking to get closer to her, would burrow into the little creek. As Ahsoo sang and the trout burrowed and the evenings passed, the creek became the Cotuit River. The tribe was grateful for the river, and as a gesture of thanks to the trout, the chief transformed the Indian girl into a fish and set her in Santuit Pond. The trout then tried to tunnel to her, but died of exhaustion on the way. Ahsoo died of a broken heart. Today, the two are said to lie side by side in a burial mound called Trout Cave.

Bound west from Mashpee, cresting one of the little hills, I saw a single pine, black-green, a posturing beauty, and behind it, silhouetting main stem and branches, a flaming pink-crimson and purple-red sky, incredibly splendid and sumptuous.

A penciling of color remained on the northwest horizon. Blue deepened overhead. Stars—not many, but exquisitely placed—glittered yellow in the winey air. Have you ever imbibed well-salted air on an early spring evening? Winds were calm, traffic still. In the distance a bell-buoy sounded a slow-swinging *bong*. . . .

~~~~~~

Cape Cod is a watery country, shot through and riddled with ponds in almost 500 varying sizes and shapes. Pond waters cover a little more than one-third of the Cape. Driving over the contours of the moraines, as you come to a hummocky summit, the top of a hill, you see blue ahead, and you ask yourself, sky or water?

Driving through sandy Mashpee, outwash plain and flat Wampanoag country—in the semirural environment in the rear of perhaps all resorts—among the southern-looking pines and along back roads and back streets, you see white and Indian children playing. It looks like a very simple thing, yet I did not know what to think. Were these young ones lucky, living outside the traffic and without much money, or were they deprived?

On little clearings of sandy loam in the forests of scrubby pitch pine you come on little strawberry farms, every other farmyard a dump for rotting farm machinery and decomposing Cadillacs. Cape Cod's strawberry industry in Falmouth and Mashpee is said to comprise 700 acres all told. They say that sometimes 15,000 quarts are raised from a single acre. Wonderful yields, yet these little farms, farmhouses, and farmers look poor—and all the poorer by contrast with the close-by coastal and vacation areas.

The most profitable and Capely form of farming is cranberry growing. Commercial cultivation of the native wild cranberry began on Cape Cod more than one hundred years ago. When you come to the Cape you first notice the cranberry bogs in the towns of Sandwich, Falmouth, or Mashpee.

The specialist and professor in charge of the State Cranberry Station makes a proud boast: More than half the cranberries grown in the world are produced in Massachusetts. Cape Cod is one of the commonwealth's leading cranberry-growing areas. There are also cranberry bogs on the offshore islands.

The cranberry plant, a trailing vine with many upright branches and evergreen leaves that turn brownish in winter, likes the rich soils of swamplands. Thus most, but not all, cranberry bogs developed from swamps. You see many small bogs, very few large ones. (The world's largest is said to be on Nantucket.) The range is from one-half acre to ninety acres; the average size, ten to fifteen acres. The cranberry culturist knows the reason. "Other things being equal," writes Henry J. Franklin in Bulletin No. 447 of the Massachusetts Agricultural Experiment Station, "small bogs pay better than large ones. Long narrow bogs, after a certain size is reached, are more profitable than compact ones. The care of large compact bogs and the harvesting of their crops are disproportionately costly, because it takes more time to wheel sand to the center of the bog and to bring the berries from the center; also, most of the bog operations call for more tramping over, and consequent injury to, the vines on large blocky areas."

After a swamp has been cleared and drained, ditches dug in crisscross patterns, and the cranberry plants set in, about four inches of sand goes on them to insulate and help hold them in place. The roots go down to draw nourishment from the peaty soil of the former swamp. Thus cranberry bogs want not only rich peaty soil, but also suitable and easily available sand; Cape Cod provides plenty of both.

Well-managed bogs may yield fifty barrels of fruit to the acre. Rakings from the vines are often used by nurseries for ornamentals. Most of the Cape Cod crop is sold through a local cooperative. This organization not only markets, but also promotes the product. To date, all its studies indicate the cranberry is a health-giving fruit. The cooperative also distributes free cranberry recipes. On just the right cranberry intake, a man might go far and live who knows how long.

Green tinged motel grass. Although crocuses bloomed and daffodils were in bud, one of the co-owners and co-managers decided not to wait any longer. She brought out an armful of plastic blossoms and speared them into the flower beds. Also she brought me a real cake of soap—no more motel teensies—and a thermos of coffee.

Four kinds of April variable weather this morning and all of it welcome: gray, blue, sunny, sprinkly. Temperature 40, barometer 30.3 and steady, the air both salty and sweet.

Route 28, the winding and undulating road that passes ponds, crosses little rivers, penetrates the familiar pines and familiar commercial debris. I was heading east, bound for Centerville in the Town of Barnstable, to see Harvey Burns. A veteran of Boston, New York, Las Vegas, and World War II, he moved to Centerville not many years ago—one of the new men on the Cape.

Centerville lies south of the south shore highway, outside the line of through traffic. Forty years ago it was described as "quietly prosperous and dignified." It still looks that way.

I had been told to look up Harvey. Now that I did so, he explained a few things. He said he likes the Cape Cod pace, the feeling of being close to nature, the taste of the air, stars on clear nights, the smell of the fogs and the winds. Furthermore, he has found a present-day Cape occupation—what he calls "intelligent subdivision" and sale of land. As everyone who comes to Cape Cod must see, large tracts of land are being divided and laid out in building lots. Many layouts are bad, and some even worse. Harvey Burns said he can do the job better. (Can you, Harvey? How will the job look ten years hence?) But now on this variable April morning, Harvey, his dog, and I climbed into his four-wheel-drive station wagon. We headed out the Centerville-West Barnstable Road, on our way to Scorton Great Marshes and Sandy Neck.

Approaching Cape Cod's north shore road, Route 6A, very suitably named the Cranberry Highway, we passed the white clapboard West Parish Meeting House, said to be the oldest Congregational Church in America. The sky was gray, the light was level—the conditions right for taking pictures—and it seemed pleasant not to do so, just to let the landscape flash by the moving vehicle's window—onto the memory, into the mind, and not be historical-heavy about it. Since all materials bow to the law of gravity, what holds the West Parish steeple up is human construction—you might even say, human will. He who rides by can read the statement of the old anonymous architect-builders: birth, aspiration, and death are inseparable.

At Sandy Neck Road, by the Barnstable-Sandwich town line, Harvey pulled to the side of the road and stopped. He reached into a pocket and brought out an air-pressure gauge. We began letting air from the tires. Then, on tires deflated to twelve pounds of air—the lower the pressure, the greater the traction—we turned into the dunes behind Great Marshes.

Great Marshes, which yielded vast crops of salt hay to the early settlers, also rewards the latter-day pioneer. It is one of the unspoiled eastern United States marshlands, a growing marsh rather than one being smothered with refuse and junk. "Where shores are slowly invaded by rising seas, as the Cape-Island region has been, salt marshes replace drowned freshwater swamps and ponds," writes the geologist Barbara Blau Chamberlain in *These Fragile Outposts, A Geological Look at Cape Cod, Martha's Vineyard, and Nantucket.* "From small beginnings the marshes spread, stealing a little from the land and a little from the sea. . . ."

Forays by four-wheel-drive station wagon along graceful shore lines and into salt-water prairies are two of the reasons, Harvey said, he lives on the Cape. He picked up a trail—there are several to choose from but you must stick with one or another. Dune-hopping is not permitted on these Town of Barnstable public lands, for this would break down the life and growth in the dunes. They would then become loose, dry, and shifting, a prey to winds and erosion.

The trail Harvey chose showed marks of wheels in some places. Elsewhere it disappeared in loose sand. Then, brightening the edge of the not yet green marsh, appeared a chicken-sized, long-tailed, ring-necked pheasant, a cock with white neck ring, green head, and red ear patches gleaming. A native of China, he was surely at home on Cape Cod. And there stood American evergreen holly, a plant of moist soil and hardy as far north as Massachusetts. It also ornamented the scene. Deep inside Sandy Neck, however, the scape, barren-looking, would seem to resemble the moon's; a good place to leave as well as to visit. Harvey pushed ahead at an even speed. Never lose headway when driving through sand, he cautioned. We reached the north shore and a Cape Cod beach. Harvey parked his vehicle on firm sand. He and I and the dog disembarked. A brisk wind was blowing.

Overcoatless, leaning against his wagon, hands in pockets, Harvey, the man gone to live on the Cape, stood and studied the Bay. The dog went tearing along the strand, small pebbles flying. I clambered up a low-lying dune, the better to look over one of Cape Cod's finest harbors. Barnstable Harbor loomed large, the light uncertain. The water reflected a green-brown and gray, and the coastline enclosing Cape Cod Bay, after sweeping eastward, faded away toward the north. North of Wellfleet Harbor it grew very dim. *Fata morgana* or April mirage, or did I in fact raise Provincetown, twenty miles or so over the Bay?

We looked just so long. Harvey called the dog and then we converged on the wagon. By a different trail than the one we came out, we ploughed a way back to the Cranberry Highway.

At the edge of the pavement Harvey stopped and got out. From among all manner of gear stowed aft in the wagon he hauled forth a steel cylinder of compressed air. He was equipped to inflate as well as deflate. After he

fed the tires, we headed out the highway. He wanted me to meet a craftsman and friend.

One of the race of adroit little men, and sporting his product—he
makes leather belts—the craftsman looked middle-aged, homespun, and
very convincing. Besides working leather, he helps meet a growing de-
mand for Cape Cod nostaligia and cornbally stuff. He paints Cape Cod
scenes to order, *Sunset Over Great Marshes, Waterfowl on the Wing.*
He also built his own house.

Right after World War II the craftsman bought land, including an
old pasture. Down in the pasture he found a flat rock that he saw would
do for a hearthstone. How to haul the stone to the building site? With
block and falls, cedar logs for rollers, and a garden tractor for power,
he inched it along to its present location. The terrain was uneven, so the
journey of a few hundred yards occupied several days. With the stone in
place, he began building around it. Then a further problem arose: he
ran out of money. In the end, the craftsman lined out his workroom with
whatever lay at hand, including what he could salvage from an abandoned chicken house. I am not fond of mixed materials, but his workroom and indeed his house turned out well, a small but authentic addition
to culture and a reminder that everything, life itself, is a salvaging
operation.

Although one of the new men on the Cape—twenty years in Barnstable Town—the craftsman acting out his own style of life seemed part
of an older time.

The north side of Cape Cod—the bay shore side traversed by 6A, the
Cranberry Highway—is also the old-time side. More of the old and less
of the new is in evidence here than along the south shore. There may be
more looking backward, too. This is the side Henry C. Kittredge (1890–
1967), the Cape's historian, lived on.

But now Harvey wanted me to see an old barn farther east on the
highway. It stood on land extending from the highway north to Great
Marshes, a noble relic and remnant of an old farm. Haymow and loft
commanded a view across moor and marshland, and into Barnstable
Harbor. On a clear day you might see the sweep of the bay from Saga-
more bridge at the western end of the Cape to Wellfleet far to the east.
Harvey said he was keeping an eye on this barn and accompanying
tract, in his opinion a suitable candidate for intelligent subdivision. He

said there was just one way to buy it—through prior knowledge that it was up for sale.

A few steps from the barn was a pothole pool with ducks swimming in it. A pair of geese, hidden in unmowed grass, raised their necks when they heard us approach—up, up, looking us over. Harvey called to them gently. He crooned to them. He apologized for not bringing corn. It seems he loves water fowl and game birds—likes to admire, talk to, and feed them—and also to blast at them in the bird-hunting season.

We drove down Navigation Lane, a road that cargo once moved along when ships unloaded in Barnstable Harbor. In the course of traveling over Cape Cod you may nod much or little to history.

Before returning to Centerville, Harvey decided to drive to Cotuit Bay on the south side in search of fare that a man might move to Cape Cod for—oysters. Crossing the Cape, a matter of eight or nine miles, we made Cotuit and boarded the Cotuit Oyster Company. We saw but few bivalves in the company shack. The Portuguese lad in charge, dressed in black boots and yellow apron, said the bay is too rough for oystering. Harvey bought a dozen to take home as a treat.

Oysters belong to a large class of shellfish (mollusks) called Bivalvia because of their hinged double shells, or "valves." Marine invertebrate animals, they inhabit the shallow waters of oceans between latitudes 64 degrees north and 44 degrees south, from northern Labrador to southern Patagonia. Coastal waters or relatively shoal banks are their natural home. Oysters prefer slightly brackish water and often thrive in inlets.

From the early years of the nation to the end of the 19th century, oysters were one of the cheapest foods available. Natural beds of the American oyster, *Ostrea virginiana*, bordered the entire Atlantic coast. The beds were vast, almost beyond calculation; yet only a few generations of overdredging sufficed to ruin great areas and badly damage many others. Thus the uncontrolled exploitation that destroyed the oyster beds of the Old World repeated itself on a larger scale in the New. Today the American oyster consumer, like the European and Asian, depends on the oyster culturist, not on the oyster fisherman. Thousands of inshore sea-bottom acres have been converted to oyster farming, but a problem remains: the scarcity of seed oysters. Seed oysters are obtained from natural beds or by inducing larvae to attach to clean oyster or clam shells scattered on the watery acreage. Only a small part of the millions of eggs spawned reach the larval stage.

In its larval stage the oyster swims freely for two or three weeks. At the end of that time it sets—that is, cements itself to rocks, piles, clean shells, or other cultch spread over the oyster grounds by the oyster farmer. Once set, the oyster, a sedentary type, never moves again voluntarily. Larvae that fail to set, die. When all goes well, the American oyster grows to a length of six inches in as many years. Discharging industrial waste into coastal waters may destroy or adversely affect the growth of oysters. Dumping untreated domestic sewage into oyster-bearing waters may not kill them, but will almost certainly make them unfit for human food. In short, conditions that favor the welfare of oysters are also conducive to the well-being of man.

Cotuit. Hearing the name in the oyster trade does not prepare you for its combination of unspoiled bay with shores steeply rising, its curving headlands, deep inlets, and semicircular chain of bays dominated by big houses. These assertive places, swollen rather than stately, seek to pre-empt view and beach, and in high measure, succeed.

Until recent times, very limited numbers of city people had the means to visit around in the country. Instead, many city dwellers had the illusion that once they had time and money they could go to the open spaces, and that as citizens of the nation they had a right to something out there in the great expanses. The country, not really heavily populated even along eastern seaboard regions, gave off a feeling of being more loosely held than it was. Now, however, when growing numbers are traveling, who owns what is becoming abundantly clear. As the public increases, private land becomes increasingly out of proportion to public. *Keep Out. No Trespassing.* Peremptory signs multiply and keep pace with population, so these old-fashioned lord-of-the-manor places, such as one sees at Cotuit, get to look irrelevant and self-aggrandizing.

Small important things for which I was grateful: the not-infrequent town landings along these harbors and bays. True, they are very narrow landings—as though it has been a struggle to keep even such skinny strips of water frontage off the tax rolls. Still, they answered the question —where is the bit of beach I was free to walk? Or did they? Who knows the law of the seashore?

We drove past old money places crowding the shore. We took a turn along the back streets where those who serve the big waterfront houses dwell. We went down to Wianno, resorty and aggressive. It gave me the deadpan stare. Gross thick heavy houses really do blanket the air and take the wind out of your sails.

~~~~~~

Self-luminous white dwarfs to huge red giants, the stars are also suns, each shining by self-generated light produced by nuclear reaction. In the show overhead, the Big Dipper appeared upside down, but the two stars forming the outer edge of the bowl still drew a bead on Polaris, the Pole Star, not at the pole precisely, yet close enough, and at the same time fifty light years away. Polaris, Cynosure, the constant North Star— guide of the traveler through the turning hours. It is one of how many millions of stars in space. Yet space, they say, is very uncrowded; in fact, almost empty.

Empty scallop shells piled by the tide

Barnstable Harbor, a horizon bristling with masts

The roofline which is called "Cape Cod," but which in fact comes from 14th- and 15th-century Stuart houses in England. The long over-hang has never quite been explained, but one theory has it that it was designed to stiffen the horizontal timbers of the upper floor

Variations on a theme: gables on the Oak Bluffs Meeting Grounds

Meeting Grounds at Oak Bluffs

A cranberry bog near Harwich. The wooden crates
in the foreground are for shipping

"Long Pond," a kettle pond scooped out by the
glaciers during the last ice age

Chapter 2

ORLEANS AND CHATHAM

I F Cape Cod's old roads are beautiful, the new, in their way, are more so. Broad and unspoiled, they slice through where no trail existed before. They show remarkable morainal profiles; they reveal grand ice-molded contours. They pass through terrain you could hardly otherwise see. If you walked through it Indian fashion, you would not sense the surface, nor become aware of the bulk; you could not see the forest because of the trees.

The more I traveled the great Mid-Cape U.S. 6 Highway, the more commanding I found it. Limited access, generous right of way. Wide, open-armed, running high or cutting deep, this uncluttered new route unveils panoramas and sparsely settled pine-covered miles.

In the hilly country of the Buzzards Bay-Sandwich moraine, the east-west moraine of the Upper Cape, I found a bronze marker on a boulder. "A tribute by the people of Barnstable County to Thomas E. Adams/ Ervin A. Draber/Gordon King who were trapped, burned, and died fighting a forest fire April 27, 1938. Their supreme sacrifice should inspire us all to strive for the goal they sought—the preservation of our forests and wildlife." Fine words, fine bronze on fine native granite amid plantings of arbor vitae, pines, oaks and laurel—and behind the boulder, the seemingly inevitable whiskey bottle and beer can.

Barnstable County comprises all of Cape Cod. Cape and county are one and the same, not forgetting the strip of land that lies west of the Cape Cod Canal. There, as already noted, is Barnstable Town, the largest in area and population of all Cape Cod towns; and within the town there is Barnstable village, the county seat.

The name itself wants explanation. "In the northern states of America, the farmers generally use barns for stabling their horses and cattle; so that among them, a barn is both a cornhouse or grange, and a stable." So guessed Peter Kalm, Swedish scientist and traveler, in his 18th-century *Travels into North America*. More probably, Barnstable, like "Plymouth," is an importation from Devonshire, the maritime county of southwest England from which the Pilgrims sailed, a transmission of the English "Barnstaple."

From Barnstable town I rolled down Route 6 through the towns of Yarmouth, Dennis, Harwich, and Brewster to the only one with a French name, Orleans. Presumably, the town was named for Louis Philippe, Duke of Orleans, who visited New England in 1797.

In Orleans I reached the Lower Cape, that is, the part that runs north and south. The Lower Cape differs from the Upper Cape in having more wind, less traffic, and a greater feeling of space—buildings lower and smaller and main streets wider.

The old part of Orleans village looks 19th century, pleasantly frontier, unplanned and easy-going, yet it is studded with banks in new buildings, red brick and white clapboard—bankers' colonial. Red bricks and white clapboard for the Cape Cod Five Cents Savings Bank—six words that tell about Cape Cod values, life, happiness, and the pursuit of wealth.

The old center contains a little graveyard. Fenced with granite posts and galvanized pipe, it lies in a corner of Main Street and Route 6A, next to the movie house. Here rest a smother of Smiths. Also, Susanna, consort of Heman Doane; infant sons of Heman and Pamela Doane; Mrs. Mariad, wife of Leonard Young; Pauline Snow, wife of Josiah P. Young; John and Thankful Jarvis. A bunch of names—they bring to mind the everyday life of the past.

The old center you might say, resembles an old apple tree, its heart-wood gone, its heart-hollow expanding, yet continuing to grow at the circumference. Orleans has four shopping plazas built in chain-store colonial style. The most distant plaza includes a cheese store and calls itself the Village Center. Perhaps it is the new center, or will be in time. Parking areas become the new style of village square.

Wherever you can read sky and water and roofs can be a good place to begin the day. I looked out of a second floor room of a square, rather typical Cape-style house built in the 1920's, I judged, with a false central chimney. In earlier times New England houses were often attached to woodsheds, outbuildings, and barns. Latter-day houses such as this one may find themselves strung to motels. My room, ten feet by fifteen feet, faced Town Cove, a long deep irregular indentation in Cape Cod's east shore—its Atlantic Ocean coast, its backside, as it is called. From the opposite shore of Town Cove, a wooded ridge rises. At this point the Cove extends so far inland that it resembles a lake.

Fifty degrees at 7 A.M., the barometer was 30.1 and steady. South-east over the cove, a few tatters and tufts of cloud were flying. Northward, the sky appeared cleaned up and polished. The sun shone.

Hoofing along Route 28, the old highway, you sample not only Cape Cod but also rural New England. White elm, vase shapes, stood by the road, their blossoms more red than they were yesterday. Willow catkins were fading. Lilacs, bud-swollen, were coming on. A. F. Smith & Sons Hardware Store, a roadside perennial since 1875, displayed all manner of durable goods on the porch.

White elm, often called American elm, is what makes all New England elmy. No native tree is better known, and none, I think, more graceful. Wood-users know few woods are tougher or harder to split than elm. Fill your mind's eyes, friend, with beautiful elm—the tree faces extinction through Dutch elm disease even as a blight extinguished the American chestnut earlier in the century.

I walked to the Town Landing at the head of the Cove. An early morning random scene, pale yellow light rippling over shoal and not very salty water. There was no one about. Ducks resembling dark mus-covys, evolved from wild mallards, drifted by. Or were they wild mallards? It is hard to say. Mallards, the most abundant of all wild ducks, domesticate easily. They learn to eat all manner of things, vegetable or animal. So they may have been mallards, or possibly hybrid ducks. If you can't identify, speculate.

Wind northwest; what saith the anemometer? I went down to Nickerson's Lumber Yard to consult the anemographic devices hanging in their window. Winds blow and there are words for them. Words that indicate miles per hour.

Light 0–7
Gentle 8–12
Moderate 13–18
Fresh 19–24
Strong 25–38
Gale 39–54
Whole Gale 55–75
Hurricane—over 75 (or, you might say, from 76 to Kingdom Come)

A Main Street sign proclaimed "Sarah's Restaurant." I entered. Two women: one in the kitchen, one at the counter, and the latter, a big woman, round faced and smiling, obviously Sarah. She handed me freshly brewed rich heady coffee. A neat, self-respecting home-economics style lunchroom with, for mascot, a well-mannered collie. I ordered the works.

A mechanic came in, sat down beside me. "Good morning," he said, but then, as though not wanting to overstate it, added—"If it is a good morning." It was, in fact, cold and wet.

"A fine day," I said.

"Well, that's true," he said. "At least we're not shoveling it." Chaff between strangers.

The man turned out to be a mason and builder. Born in Maine, he had lived on Cape Cod since the end of World War II. Three times, he said, he had left and gone elsewhere, but each time the Cape called him back. The towns he likes best are Orleans and Brewster. I had come to the right place, he said—and if I found I liked the town and wanted to stay—well, you never know. He handed me his card.

Over bacon and eggs I heard the West Yarmouth radio station announcer report brisk winds on the Cape. Brisk, ugh! Did he mean moderate? Fresh?

Has any man seen all Cape Cod; does any man know all Orleans? It is one of the smallest towns on the Cape, thirteenth in size, ninth in population, seventh in population density. It strikes the mean value in the last-named department. Has anyone walked its disheveled borders, navigated its raveling coastlines, inlets, lakes, ponds, and arms of the sea? You cannot set foot where other feet have not preceded. Scattered cemeteries remind you that many have gone before.

What a relief that Orleans is less the colonial, and more mid- and later Victorian. The road to East Orleans and the Town Beach is bordered with lichened elms and graveyards, high wooden churches, manses and monuments. The mustached Union soldier stands immortalized in granite. "Erected by the Town of Orleans to the memory of those who died that their country might live/1861–1865." Then follow the indigenous names:

Isaac Y. Smith
Joshua Gould
Freeman A. Sherman
John W. Walker
James E. Studley
John H. Cowan
Joseph Moody
Lewis Eldredge

Rainy day in Orleans: daffodils bloomed and never is yellow so salt-butter yellow as in salt air and raw April rain. Old trees with gnarled trunks looked young in the branches. Maples and elms appeared rosy pink red and pubescent. Willows seemed painted. The greatest miracle of the spring is the miracle of old trees reborn. Nobody knows how weary a tree gets, how close to death in the winter. The older the tree the more of its character you can read in the bark.

Swamp maple and swamp birch incarnadined wetlands. These low-lands looked like cranberry bogs grown monstrous and wild. Apple trees glistened, their glittering bark resembling living wet skin. I drove close to Town Cove, then beside Salt Bay Pond. In the distance, through rain, I saw Nauset Marshes.

Rain, rain, rain—but the barometric pressure was rising. I complimented Sarah on her clam chowder. Smiling, she said that it is the best on the Cape. And her scallop stew! Her Indian pudding! What could be better for man on this cold rainy day good for trees?

"When you get to Cape Cod," a friend said, "look up George Redding. He lives in South Yarmouth." I telephoned Mr. Redding. He told me how to get to his place.

From Orleans, bound for South Yarmouth, I wheeled up the Mid-Cape Highway. Sun-lighted woods of pitch pine and oak flashed by. Last winter's oak leaves were hanging among the new buds. April is the month of full circle, old and new, death and life.

I crossed Bass River on Highbank Road Bridge. Fishermen lined the north side of the bridge, fishing shoulder to shoulder for flounder coming down from the freshwater ponds further up. Bass River rises in Follins Pond, only three miles from the Cape's north shore. Flowing south through a broad open valley, Bass River empties into Nantucket Sound. It marks the boundary between the towns of Dennis and Yarmouth, and the archaeologist says it is the route the Vikings took into Cape Cod's interior.

For those who fish in this part of the world, whether for livelihood or sport, the winter flounder, or blackback, plays an important role. Adult flounder spawn in the estuaries and ponds during late winter and early spring. While spawning, they do not feed. Their flesh becomes soft; they get poor. So why were these fishermen dangling hooks from the bridge? Were they fishing, perhaps, for the sake of fishing?

George Redding lives in a piece of woods close to the road but screened from it—a strategic location. His dooryard is forest floor duff. Even before you meet the man you know he is not a grass-mower. His house, seasoned, low-down, sparrow brown in color, squats on a bluff overlooking a marsh and Bass River's blue tidal water.

Tall, lean, and bespectacled, close-cropped and gray, Mr. Redding, wearing wool shirt and corduroy trousers, appeared and greeted me. He was smoking a pipe, and also holding another pipe in reserve by a leather thong on his belt. He looked exactly right in the part of retired professor which, in fact, he is. An early retired one, he told me. Said he has no use for dying with boots on.

The house, creosoted and woodsy outside, proved rustic and comfortable within, crowded with easy furniture, old rugs, prints, paintings, sculptures, and books. Would I join him in a beer, Mr. Redding asked. Indeed I would. He motioned me to a chair beside a window with view through the trees of the marshland and river below. What was I up to, he asked as we drank our beer. I explained.

"Oh. Come to see the Cape before it all goes under macadam," he replied, nodding vigorously. "I'm agin progress—not all of it, but a good deal of it. I like things let alone."

"Where will I find things let alone?"

"There are pockets of them, here and there." His own four acres, Mr. Redding said, is one of the pockets. He picked up an old-fashioned kitchen match, struck it with his thumbnail, and relit his pipe.

George Redding designed and built his own house, and it looks it—in the good sense of the phrase. It has an expression consistent with owner and builder, a house befitting a man who carves his own pipes out of rough chunks of brierroot, as Mr. Redding does, and who makes his own wine out of almost anything that ferments—cranberry, rhubarb, banana, currant, date, goldenrod, grape, parsley, potato, rice, oak leaf, carrot, honey, and apricot. Presently we visited his cellar, his winery filled with retorts and bottles of liquids whistling and working. Holding up a bottle and eyeing it closely, Mr. Redding said, "There is such a hell of a lot to see and touch and taste and smell that you don't do when you are all balled up with how am I doing and what am I getting done."

Mr. Redding spoke of the value of what he called demanding trivia, activities in which things take place and "shoots come up out of the goddamn ground." From a living-room–dining-room–kitchen window we watched a couple of myrtle warblers busy at one of his feeders. Small skinny and flitting like all the warblers, the myrtle is one of the most rewarding. A bird with a flashing bright chrome-yellow rump, it is simple to recognize, easy to get to know. In general, I am for birds clearly marked. The birds you acknowledge every day are the ones who seem to acknowledge you. The feathered vertebrate blending in—that is no friend, only a chance collision, something you add to your bird list.

Specialists estimate that the earth is 4.7 billion years old. Cape Cod, on the other hand, is young; 100 million years, they say. These are figures I neither grasp nor trust, but the concept behind them, eon on eon, layer on layer—endlessness, perhaps beginninglessness—the arithmetic seems to be an attempt to document some natural causes of the awesome majestic.

Recent drilling in the towns of Brewster and Harwich showed what was not before known so precisely: Bedrock lies about 435 feet below the surface. This seems to be the foundation supporting the capely structure of sand, gravel, clay, till, and other sediments stacked like a layer cake.

It is also said you can see hereabouts the remnants of a great coastal plain that existed long, long before the glaciers of the Ice Ages slid south, rearranged it—and built the present Cape Cod and offshore islands at the same time.

I find it a little difficult to pick up glimpses of that plain of a million centuries ago. This may be failure of imagination, but then I also find it hard to realize the Cape as it must have been only three hundred years in the past, two hundred, or even one hundred.

How slow went the changes through measureless epochs and periods. No individual life, when there was life, would have lasted long enough to detect the slightest difference. Today, however, change and erosion are observable year by year. Season by season you can see the reshaping both by the land developer and by his customer, the developed. From North Falmouth to East Orleans, getting the vibration, intimation, and price-range of the development style of living, I think I can hardly overpraise the way of a settler such as George Redding. I call him settler because he was born in the Midwest. He did not see South Yarmouth until old enough to get a job at a Cape Cod camp.

"The importance of demanding trivia," Mr. Redding explained on my second visit—we were walking around to the Bass River side of his house to inspect his herb garden—"is not only that it saves you from an accomplishment vacuum. Paying attention to demanding trivia keeps you from having to live by philosophy alone."

Mr. Redding's herb garden presents an unusual sight. Set in an irregular, small, and seemingly natural clearing among the oaks on the bluff overlooking Bass River, it employs unusual garden defenses. Planted among the various herbs are a number of liquor bottles, some with their labels on—whiskey, gin, vodka—uncorked emptied fifths, necks up, and canted in all directions. From whatever quarter the wind blows, some of the bottles whistle. Close to the ground, the sound of whistling is loud enough to annoy the long ears of rabbits. The sound keeps them out of the garden.

While I sat at the wheel and drove, the retired professor beside me smoked and offered Capely instruction. "Have you ever seen the Cape from the air?" he asked. "It looks as though it contains more water than land. Cape ponds are generally called either Long, or Flax. . . . Accent the second syllable in Nau*set*. All Indian names that end in *set* mean *by the water*. The Nausets and Wampanoags were long-headed Algonquins. . . . What is new on the Cape is not the tourists—we have had them for years—but the retirees. The banks are doing a good business, and so are the plumbers, the elite of the service people. . . . Right now the marshes are not looking their best. Come back in a month. Thank God the state passed the law: no more filling in of marshlands. . . . The postmaster in this village is a typical Cape Codder—born in Columbus, Ohio, and came here after the First War. The summer people love him. They bring their friends in to see him and hear him talk, and he obliges them—plays up the part. . . . Say, turn down this street. There's a house here with a slightly bowed roof. Built by ship's carpenters, they say. Architects come from all over to see it. . . . You know, some of my friends can't understand what I'm doing here. They say, 'How do you spend your time?' I answer by asking, 'How do you spend yours?' It's a nice question." Mr. Redding whipped out a friction match, struck it with his thumbnail, and relit his pipe.

I was covering ground too fast because Mr. Redding wanted to get back for the pre-evening-shift nap. Just the same, having seen something of Upper Cape towns, and getting an overview now of several others, I was ready to say that if you have seen one, you have not seen them all.

I sat at an Orleans lunch counter munching blueberry muffins and drinking villainous coffee. A townsman sitting beside me observed, "Too bad we couldn't have had these days the first of the week." He was speaking to the woman behind the counter.

"I know it," she replied as she handed him a plate of greasy potatoes and eggs. "And I don't like what they say about tomorrow, either. When that wind shifts to the east it takes the life out of you."

A second townsman entered and said to the first, "I got news for you. I got heat. How 'bout that?"

"Ain't that something."

"Yeah, and it took eighteen plumbers to do it."

I was fascinated. Eighteen! The elite of the service people.

Crystal Lake in the Town of Orleans—and Fisherman's Landing. I went down to see what they, fishers and fish, were up to. On the way, I read, "Attention all Fishermen. It is squarely up to you whether this area will remain open for your enjoyment. Do not abuse the privilege by discarding rubbish, refuse, or other waste material. All fishermen are requested to help in keeping this area clean and preserve our privilege of use of this land."

Farther down the path that leads to the lovely lake was more reading matter. "The use of this Public Landing Forbidden between 8 P.M.– 8 A.M. Reclaimed Trout Pond. Fishing permitted only during legal trout season. The use of fish, dead or alive, for bait is prohibited." Besides being illegal, fishing with fish is unsportsmanlike to the dry-fly fisherman.

From Orleans south the road traverses a rolling and wooded country-side. Below South Orleans, a post-office place, it bends around Pleasant Bay, undulates over low drifts, and then runs along Ryder Cove. This finger of Buzzards Bay-Sandwich moraine extending from Orleans to Chatham showed me I was more a moraine man than a man of the outwash plains. Terminal or recessional moraine, advancing or retreating ice, let me see glacial deposits!

Indeed, you readily see what Cape Cod owes to the glaciers. In the fullness of geological time, three successive waves of ice crept down from the north, presumably Labrador, to cover much of New England with a weighty blanket of soil and rocks. Where the great rounded mountain-ous masses of the ice sheet, the lobes, came to rest, they laid down moraine, a ridge of material, or piled it up ahead, or on either side. When the ice lobes rested, meltwater streams carried off sand and gravel to form the outwash plains. Each of the glacial invasions was followed by melting back and partial retreat. This slow-motion ice age crushing and building of only some 30,000 years ago left vivid remains; it modeled every natural feature and shape.

Orleans to Chatham, I suspect, is one of Cape Cod's most scenic pockets. After passing Pleasant Bay, I picked up Fox Hill Road. It leads to Nickerson's Neck, which is a kind of claw as well as neck, for it closes around Crows Pond. A knotty and hairy neck—big conifers and deciduous trees—and not too damnably overbuilt, surrounded by superb waters, Bassing and Chatham harbors. I should have been seeing them from a small boat.

A country club on the neck keeps a grand tract open—not open to traffic, but clear and unobstructed. You can look across it. As country-side everywhere builds up, country-club grounds achieve new importance. Many more open-land organizations are needed, not only for golf but for every manner of country enjoyment. Despite the excluding connotations, country-club acres give air and a feeling of space. You do not need to belong to enjoy it.

As I crossed the Chatham town line, I could almost feel the tempera-ture drop. Fog began rolling in. I would not be surprised if each of the fifteen towns breeds its own kind of weather. Approaching North Chatham, I ran again into big turn-of-the-century houses—not as many, however, nor as monstrous as those seen in numerous places further up-Cape. I am still amazed how the closed-down houses can fill the offscape and press around you.

Chatham is one of the Cape's smaller towns. It ranks sixth in population, fourth in population density. I heard some pronounce the name with equal stress on both syllables—Chat-ham. Chatham center, with its ups and downs, built, as geologists says, on knob and kettle topography —which means little hills among ponds and bays—seems a village unlike any other. Located on Cape Cod's southeast corner, it faces dangerous tide rips and shoals. Chatham is still a commercial fishing port. As sea-bound village and summer resort, and small-boat harbor, it appears dignified and long-settled.

Shore Road to the Lighthouse: stand on the bluff overlooking Chatham harbor, the tidal flats, the tail end of Nauset Beach, and the North Atlantic Ocean. With your back to Chatham Lighthouse and Coast Guard Station, turn your eyes southward where Monomoy Island, a sandbar and wildlife refuge, stretches eight miles. Then look eastward, straining your eyes for sight of Pollock Rip Lightship. A cool April fog blew from the southwest. The triangular red pennant, storm warning for small craft, was flapping. Face in mid-afternoon this view and weather. At first you feel tremendous excitement. You feel like shouting. But then, looking longer at shoals and deep water, feeling the wind, the fluttering beat of storm warning, your voice dies away—the inclination to use it dies away—and without knowing why, you turn away sad.

Chatham Light, on the west side of Chatham harbor, stands eighty feet above the sea, cast-iron chunky, white and hyperkinetic—four flashes every thirty seconds. A lighthouse seems to me female, not male. Female because it is a house and also because it guides and protects. To see a lighthouse as phallic is, I believe, to misread it. On Shore Road in Chatham you see the distinction. Juxtaposed beside Chatham Light is an obelisk, a lofty tapering cenotaph.

In memory of
William Henry Mack
of Cleveland, Ohio
1873–1902
erected October 1903
by his loving mother and sister

Engraved on the pedestal, a further inscription reads,

Monomoy Lifesavers lost March 17, 1902, in attempting to rescue
William H. Mack and crew of Barge Wadena.
Marshall N. Eldridge
Osborn F. Chase
Isaac T. Foye
Valentine D. Nickerson
Arthur W. Rogers
Edgar C. Small
Elijah Kendrick

The WPA Guide to Massachusetts misinforms the reader with a
gross error on page 591. "The monument," it states, "was erected in
memory of a life-saving crew, commanded by Captain Mack, that set
off in heavy seas to rescue the crew of a wrecked fishing vessel. All but
one were drowned, and old-timers say that he was so ashamed of being
rescued that he would neither discuss the tragedy nor accept commen-
dation."

It was just the reverse. Captain Mack was owner of the barge *Wadena*.
Marshall N. Eldridge was captain of the life-saving crew. There was no
"wrecked fishing vessel." Thus carelessness is added to death and disaster.

Cape Cod: Its People and Their History, by Henry C. Kittredge, published in 1930 and reissued in 1968, is one of the slender handful of
books about Cape Cod worth reading. Concerning this occurrence,
Kittredge writes, "Like so many other tragedies, it involved no more
impressive a vessel than the stump-masted coal barge *Wadena*, which
struck on Shovelful Shoal, south of Monomoy Station, on March 11 in
a heavy northeaster."

After the barge struck, Captain Marshall Eldridge and his life-saving
crew rowed out from Monomoy Station and brought all *Wadena* hands
ashore. For the next few days the barge held intact. During this time,
Captain Mack and his men, aided by wreckers from Boston, worked to
salvage their cargo. Wreckers are men employed in saving property from
wrecked vessels.

About the same time the *Wadena* drove onto the shoal, another barge,
the *Fitzpatrick*, ran aground close by. Her owners engaged two local
wreckers to try to float her. The local wreckers, Captain Elmer Mayo and
Captain Mallows, went aboard the *Fitzpatrick* the evening of March 16.
That night the wind increased to a gale.

Looking out next morning, the Monomoy lifesavers saw a distress signal flying from the *Wadena*. This is said to have been a surprise to Captain Eldridge, for he thought the Boston wreckers had taken everyone off the *Wadena* the night before in their tug.

After walking down to the end of Monomoy Point to study the situation, Captain Eldridge phoned for the lifeboat. When it arrived, he jumped aboard. Shipping a little water on the way, the lifesaving crew pulled through breaking waves to comparative shelter under the leeward side of the barge. They found five men had been left on board. All, according to Henry C. Kittredge, "had lost their nerve. . . . Worse still, they were in no sense of the word sailors, as appeared when their captain let go his hold of the rope by which he was lowering himself into the lifeboat and fell crashing aboard to the accompaniment of a smashed thwart."

Captain Eldridge ordered the *Wadena* captain and men to lie down in the bottom of the boat while he, in Kittredge's words, "braced himself for the return trip . . . as he leaned against his long steering oar to head the craft into the seas. It was a beautiful piece of boatmanship; some water came aboard but not enough to be dangerous. As soon as the trembling cargo in the bottom of the boat saw the top of the wave slop in over the side, however, they gave themselves up for lost, jumped to their feet, and seized the man at the oars around the neck. . . ."

In an instant the lifeboat was bottom up and everyone was in the water. Nothing more seems known about the *Wadena*'s captain and men. The Monomoy crew succeeded in righting their boat, but before they could pull themselves aboard, the waves turned it over. They managed to right it a second time but with the same result. After that, they could only cling to the bottom. "One by one," Kittredge writes, "benumbed and battered, they let go and vanished, until the only man . . . left was Seth Ellis, number one surfman of the station. Finding himself alone, he managed to wrap one arm around the centerboard which had floated up and protruded like a shark's fin from the bottom of the boat."

All this had taken place in fog. The local wreckers, Captains Mayo and Mallows on board the nearby *Fitzpatrick*, had not even seen the Monomoy men put out. But suddenly, through a hole in the mist, loomed the white bottom of a lifeboat and a body lying across it. Captain Mayo sprang to action. In a matter of seconds he stripped to his underclothes, got a twelve-foot dory over the side, grabbed a pair of oars, and started rowing toward Ellis.

Kittredge writes that Mayo, forty years old, "knew all that a man can know about dories and the Monomoy Shoals. He knew that the boat which carried him was a poor specimen . . . but even an indifferent dory is a remarkable sea-boat when handled by an expert. . . . Yard by yard he pulled her to the side of the lifeboat. . . . If Ellis had been another *Wadena* wrecker, both men would have perished. But numb and exhausted as he was, Ellis made not a single false move while Mayo helped him into the bottom of the dory. Then he headed for shore, came through the surf . . . and assisted Ellis to the station."

The Humane Society and the United States Government pinned medals on Elmer Mayo. Later, Seth Ellis, fully recovered, became keeper of the station.

So much for the story behind the Mack monument. Back of the monument itself lies a tiny fenced grassy plot containing one stone in memory of sailors lost off Cape Cod and washed ashore at Chatham: a nameless cemetery for nameless mariners.

Cranberries and fish, commerce and trade are a welcome sight at Fortune Landing. Then the Fish Pier at Aunt Lydia's Cove, Nickerson's Retail Fish and Lobster, the Chatham Sea Food Co-op, Old Harbor Fish Company. I descended to the wharf where the pleasure craft *Lori and Jean* and *Wee John* were tied up, and also a Coast Guard 44-footer.

A white-haired man sat on a bench and sunned himself in the lee of a shack. It seemed to be a public bench. I sat down too, at a certain distance, and gazed at the speed limit sign—three miles per hour in Aunt Lydia's Cove—and the unbroken water. Although the sun was no longer tepid, a northwest wind blew. Too windy to fish outside the harbor.

The man at the other end of the bench, of medium height and build, wore tan work clothes and tan cloth cap, but not the long-visored fisherman kind. His eyes were blue, his teeth yellow, and there were not many of them. Altogether he had an English face. Was he perhaps the wharfinger? No, the wharfinger had the day off. The harbormaster? No, the harbormaster was home working on buoys. He works on them all winter.

The man was George Ellsworth, age seventy-five. The son of a lighthouse keeper, he was a boy when his father, transferred from the Cape Ann light at Thacher Island, arrived in Chatham. When he became twenty-one, George Ellsworth joined the Lifesaving Station at Monomoy where Captain Marshall Eldridge, and first surfman Seth Ellis, had preceded him. The Lifesaving Service, he said, was one of the local availabilities. He meant, naturally, for someone like himself.

After serving seven years at the Lifesaving Station, George Ellsworth turned to another local opportunity—working for the rich. He helped build the golf course on Nickerson's Neck. Later he acted as year-round caretaker for a Chatham estate. He has fished, and taken out fishing parties, and guided duck hunters. At present he works the hoist—a few hours a day—for one of the fish companies. He counted his wages and blessings. In addition to what he earns, he receives a pension from the Lifesaving Service, that is, from the Coast Guard, for the two merged long ago—and social security. Twenty years ago he bought a small house in South Chatham. He and his wife have lived there since. Furthermore, the house is paid for.

"Mr. Ellsworth," I said, "you have triumphed."

"I think so," he said, his face corrugating with pleasure.

Men who spend their lives in the high confusion and civilization of cities tend to romanticize those who pass their days in villages and small harbors. The latter, sometimes, are thought to be more their own men; to chart their own courses, to live more resolute lives. But is it true? What are the chances in a place like Chatham? What is the future in working for summer people, or in inshore fishing? Village life may be wonderful if you can take it at your own price.

Meanwhile, an old man sitting on a bench on a wharf in the lee of a fishing shack, face turned to the April sun, is a sight with deep-down pleasure in it. Little harbor and village lives appeal strongly to the outsider. What is their great attraction? They suggest that in the more simple existence, one may find the good life.

Chapter 3

CHILMARK DIARY

APRIL Monday morning: a broad band of red light lay along the horizon. Overhead, the sky was mantled in gray. Red sky, in the morning, sailor take warning—that is what they say in New England.

Rain mixed with snow as, wheeling through Falmouth, I hurried along the west flank of Cape Cod. I was bound for Woods Hole in the southwest corner of the Cape, and the ferry to Martha's Vineyard. As the ferry runs, the island of Martha's Vineyard stands eight miles south of this coast.

In Woods Hole, snow and a wind hauling east. A dozen cars, and scarcely more than a dozen souls, boarded the *Islander*, two thousand tons gross and almost two hundred feet long. She is licensed to carry 788 persons, May to October, in daylight hours within ten miles of shore. October to May she may carry 242, the number of places available in her lifeboats.

41

The ferrying *Islander* made it again through the tidal passage, the narrow waterway called the hole. Off to port, Nobska Point Lighthouse was sending her beam, flying her small-craft warning pennant, and sounding her horn—neat little Nobska doing her work. Through a pelting spring storm, crew and passengers dieseled across the Sound. Roofs of unheated summer houses crowding East Chop loomed white with snow.

A disembarking in Vineyard Haven: more snow on the island than on the main—and this was unusual. Clinging wet snow that scarcely seemed cold. But I knew the fair-weather house I was bound for would be cold indeed. A stop at the hardware store to buy an electric heater. Sold out. Across the street the Cape & Vineyard Electric Company brought forth the last one in stock. Now a stop for groceries.

Wheels slavering through slush, I headed up-island. Behold a spring landscape plastered with watery flakes. Reds of spring smothered in coarse-meshed snow had turned into ice-cream colors, red tips of birches like cranberry sherbert, greens of the pines like frosted lime.

Mushing through Tisbury, West Tisbury—then the roadsign "Entering Chilmark," the town where I had spent many summers and where I have a house. Although the house was not designed for all seasons, the passing years, and the changes years bring, have made it, for me, the place where the heart feels home.

And so I arrived on a scene which however familiar must never be taken for granted. From a hillside I gazed at an inner and outer pond, Quitsa and Menemsha, arms of the sea joined by a miniature strait; and all of it held in a network of moors and encircling hills. You see at the same time, but farther off to the north, Vineyard Sound and some links in the chain of Elizabeth Islands. Turning eastward, through a slot in the hills, you glimpse the flat gray ocean. A wide-ranging, yet not too distant view, not at all a view to get lost in.

I was writing now at the kitchen table, sitting with my back to the fireplace, feeling the heat from the oak logs stacked to the tops of the andirons. The fire had been going five hours. At the other end of the room, the electric heater turned out to be a boy trying to do a man's job. Never mind that end of the room. By the fireplace I soaked up the open-hearth warmth. You do not know how good a fire can feel until you need it—and make a big one.

Nine o'clock. Snow and rain slacked off. I had dined well—Scotch whiskey, hamburger, raw onion, boiled potatoes. The wind hauled northwest, the sky was clearing. And it was cold, 35 degrees. This beautiful bed of coals and logs—may it last through the night.

At 5:15 A.M. a fair day looked in. The mercury clung to 35, barometer 30.2 and rising. I poured logs onto the fire. The snowy white moors of yesterday were today a not-quite winter brown. The green tinge, although faint, was there. In clearings among the moor's tangle of vines and tough plant materials, swatches of meadow-grass green appeared. Down by the pond shore, domestic greens started into view on a formal summer-house lawn.

Some houses humanize the scene, others disturb it. Among the latter, some disturb more than others—there is, you might say, a disturbance scale. At one end are houses whose owners have scraped away the indigenous growth, laid on topsoil, cultivated grass, manicured, suburbanized, and then crowned the whole effect with trucked-in somehow emasculated boulders. At the other end of the scale are the houses that work with what is there and blend in.

He was back, the marsh hawk—migratory like myself, and seasonal resident of how many years. He is lighter colored than she. Good to see him at once and have that settled and not be left wondering where he was.

As the yellow rump patch announces the myrtle warbler, so the white rump band makes known the marsh hawk, or harrier. Eighteen to twenty-four inches long, round head, hooped beak, long squared-off tail, you cannot fail to recognize it. Harriers, say specialists in falconiformes, are a separate genus of hawk: slender, long-legged, and with long-angled wings. Flying over open ground, meadow as well as marshland, the harrier hunts the rodents, reptiles, and insects it feeds on—all in all a steady sort, the kind you like to have around.

Noon: 58 degrees, the day setting a standard by which to measure perfection. When the marsh hawk quarters, you see his shadow. Buoyant, unhurried, he skirted the edge of the shore, glided on the wind, and then disappeared, perhaps to perch on secluded ground between house and pond. It was hard to believe in yesterday's wintry landscape—now that all traces of snow had vanished. The heavens were for us.

Squibnocket Beach, the Atlantic Ocean. Water yellow and turquoise, surf gentle and very inviting, and the beach, end to end, clean as on the Third Day. Herring gulls, scavengers of the longshore, stood at their separate stations. One rock, one gull—plenty of elbowroom—and all facing into the wind like boats at their moorings. The better to hear? Smell? Hardly: the olfactory organ is poorly developed in birds, and the question remains whether a bird possesses much power of smell, or indeed any. Or do gulls face into the wind to keep their feathers unruffled? Since birds have virtually no intelligence, their instinctive behavior may be all the higher.

A good day for sketching, good for walking the beach. I saw prints in the sand where a herring gull walked, and also a periwinkle; not the plant of course (although the word is the same) but the small marine snail that in Europe is used as a food. Winkles and red tips of sea grass poked through the wet.

April showed landscape alive without leaves. Driving farther up-island, along the state road to the westernmost and Indian town, Gay Head, I saw stone walls and swales invisible during the season; and in the woodlands were scattered little old houses which in summer I did not know were there.

Skunk cabbage marked the roadside wet places with flashes of early spring green. The leaves were four inches high. It is said that bears enjoy the juice and flesh of these early perennial herbs, and they did look good enough to eat—or would by another name. I seem to have missed the skunk cabbage flowers that precede the show of leaves; flowers as strange and hard to imagine as the Jack-in-the-pulpit (a family relation) if you had never seen one.

Five o'clock light: cooling air. Looking over the moors—and if you are in a glass-paneled house as I was, you cannot help looking—you see a great change has occurred since morning. Patches of untamed shrubbery that not many hours ago were fuscous and brown were turning to silver and lavender.

Pale crimson western horizon. Then night rose blue and glittery— good omens. I was ready to say tomorrow would be a fair day. I should have, but did not, for I had listened to the radio and heard a different forecast. So there went courage, faith, and weather conviction.

On awakening, frost! By noon, however, the temperature reached 50 degrees. The day was fair. An unclouded sky, truly azure—and an azure-reflecting ocean; deep water of tidal ponds, also azure. On the shoals the color shades from glaucous to light greenish gray.

Bill King appeared in his pick-up truck with a welcome cargo, fireplace wood sawed to 30-inch lengths, most of it split but some 10-inch backlogs included as well, and every stick of it oak—as good-looking fireplace wood as you want to see. Stacked on the porch it made a beautiful sculpture—expendable, which is part of its beauty—and while it lasts it reassures. And so, April, prima donna of months. Spring in New England can be a wild season.

Bill King of North Tisbury, native son, studied the fireplace masonry built of drilled and split granite. He asked who laid the stone. I answered, George Cook, Gay Head Indian, builder of boats, master of many trades and perhaps jack of none. Bill King asked further, "Where did he get the stone?" I have never been sure. From the ruins of his grandfather's house, from foundations and doorsteps of burned out or tumbled down dwellings, some old curbstones salvaged from dumps. Some may have been stolen. Bill King shook his head. "Not stolen. Not stolen. Let us say, requisitioned."

To those who knew him, George Cook, not many years dead, is already a legendary figure. Someone may someday write his story—a story of a style of life that has gone. Skills and crafts no longer learned, an unschooled artist's love of native materials, an innate simplicity and understanding of the economy of means, and zest for enjoying the pleasures of life.

During the night I replenished the fire twice. At 6:30 the temperature outside read 38, only ten degrees higher inside. A translucent gray light shone overhead, smooth and cold.

This rectangular house of recent design, its four corners pointing to the four directions, confronts the northeast. Today it had the wind in its face, a glassy modular face, and the wind blowing hard and gusty. Eastward I saw the white horses.

Bill King's hot-burning oak logs pulled me through. I hauled the kitchen table closer and sat backside to the blaze. Pure pleasure to feel at your back the heat from the hearth. However, internal warmth would be wanted by evening. West Tisbury, Chilmark, and Gay Head—the up-island towns—are dry, which means a trip down-island.

This seems as good a place as any to say a word about the shape and size of Martha's Vineyard. An irregular triangle, deeply indented, notched and eroded, some appendages and wavering lines—20 miles long, 9½ miles across at its widest, its perimeter 100 miles of shoreline, its area 106 square miles. It comprises six towns—the aforementioned up-island three, and three down-island: Tisbury (which includes Vineyard Haven), Oak Bluffs and Edgartown. Edgartown takes in Chappaquiddick, a small island separated from the Vineyard proper by a narrow bay.

I drove the fifteen miles down-island to Edgartown. At this time of year you meet very few cars on the road. Vineyard roadsides gladdened the eye: fencerows sympathetically trimmed, hedgerows lovingly contoured and molded, a total absence of billboards. To drive down-island is not a chore; the drive itself is pleasing.

Edgartown, county seat of the County of Dukes County (to call the latter by its full legal name), is one of the two Vineyard towns that are wet. I went there to make a purchase. "You're like the robins," said the seasonal licensee, putting out a big hand as he welcomed me in. "You give us something to look forward to." Namely, the returning wave of summer, when the population of Martha's Vineyard rises from an estimated 6,500 persons year-round to a crest of 40,000 or more.

Home again in Chilmark I found the barometer falling. The wind continued to rise. Some might call the day bleak. I, however, did not, since weather like most matters is somewhat subjective, the exterior atmosphere usually modified by the climate within. The day seemed exhilarating. The light remained even, lines and edges of landscape clear and sharp.

Forty degrees at five in the evening. I was holding off the low temperature with oak logs, hot tea, and whiskey. (Had given up on the electric heater.) And I was making plans for a tighter and snugger house come another off-season.

They said this was an exceptional April. I have never known one that was not. There was no perceptible change in the foliage—spring did not move, it stood still.

I had felt nothing like it since the last hurricane. The house kept jumping all night, big expanses of plate glass bellying and straining like sails. I kept the fire up and slept beside it.

Thirty-seven degrees at 6:30 in the morning, gale-force winds, "gusting to 60 and more miles an hour," said a local radio station. Winds north northeast, slashing rain mixed with snow, high seas and pounding surf. The seven o'clock sailing of the ferry, Vineyard Haven to Woods Hole, was canceled. I was intending to leave. Would I be able to do so?

The nine o'clock sailing was canceled, and then the eleven. The ferry, one of the charms of an island, can also be one of its problems. Winds, came a report, are holding at fifty. Winds and seas, rather than fogs and rains, are the elements that halt the service.

I headed for the general store and post office, an informal meeting place in West Tisbury, Albion Alley & Company, Dealers in Almost Everything. Established in 1858 as the S. M. Mayhew Company, it is said to be the oldest continued store on the Vineyard and one of the oldest general-merchandise operations in Massachusetts. Albion Alley, born in the down-island town of Oak Bluffs, went to work up-island in West Tisbury at age eighteen. That was in 1920. Twenty-six years later in 1946, he bought out his employers. He then went on to triple the business, but he also kept the original storefront and building, the original floor, and the counter. Half the people who come in during the summer, he said, come to see what an old store looks like.

When he began keeping store in 1920, he sold not only meats and groceries, but also harnesses and grain and farming tools, rubber boots, foul-weather gear, and all manner of yard goods and notions. These lines have been replaced with a wide range of hardware, electrical fittings and fixtures, gardening equipment, furniture, even imported baskets. Dealers in Almost Everything today means a gamut of goods from kerosene lamps to hot coffee dispensed by a vending machine.

In 1964 Albion Alley turned over the business to three of his children in partnership. Since then, Jimmy, Phyllis, and John have added a laundromat, a U-Do-It car wash, and a real estate agency. Also, Jimmy succeeded his father to the postmastership of West Tisbury. The oldest son, Albion, Jr., is proprietor of one of the Vineyard's first garage and gasoline stations. "All our enterprises," said the father with quiet pride, "are on this street."

Customers come from all the towns on the island. Albion Alley remembers when they came from Gay Head in ox carts. Unlike the supermarkets and chain stores, the Alley family's store extends credit. Sometimes it carries Vineyarders six to eight months, more or less through the long off-season. Not everyone speaks well of summer people, but Albion Alley does. "I never lost a penny from a summer account," he said.

Graying, bright-eyed, and cheerful, Albion Alley has the air of a man who has done his job well and also been rewarded. While the younger generation of partners were minding the store, the Dealer in Almost Everything had time to retail the news and to talk. During the night, he said, gusts of wind were clocked at 82 miles an hour, that is, winds of hurricane force. The biggest blow of the winter, he said, and in fact the biggest since 1954.

West Tisbury village, centerpiece of the island away from sight and sound of the ocean, was a favorite place of retirement with Vineyard whaling captains. Here you find the wind in the tops of the trees, which is different from whipping over the water. As befits a one-time agricultural center, the setting is open, rather level and pastoral. If sheep were still being raised in West Tisbury, this late April storm might have been the lambkiller.

On Music Street, beside a dwelling of maybe 150 years, old orchard grass put on young green. A great woody lilac, antique-looking as the house it was standing beside, produced a new crop of buds. A robin hopping along the ground made a pass with its beak, hauled forth a worm, swallowed it down. Classic and cliché: it happens every spring.

The large North American thrush called the robin seems to enjoy the presence of people. Perhaps in order to live more among them, it spends a great deal of time on the ground. I would not be surprised if in, say, ten thousand springs, the robin became a ground dweller. Meanwhile it has made itself so familiar that it qualifies as a yardstick bird. (The other yardstick is the sparrow.) When describing birds for which we do not have a name, all of us say it is larger or smaller than a robin or sparrow.

The rain slacked off, but the two o'clock sailing was canceled just the same. Winds continued to blow. Seas swept over the breakwater outside Vineyard Haven harbor. A topsail schooner, pride of the seafaring nostalgic rich, dragged her anchor and went aground, stern first, onto the beach. You may as well take her for a reminder that time was when the coasting trade was handled almost entirely by schooners. Fleets of them once rode through Vineyard Sound. With a shift in the wind, Vineyard Haven harbor would fill with vessels finding the wind against them, and there they would wait for a favoring change.

At Squibnocket Beach, the wind whipped a long spray from the tops of the combers. Tides were not only high but raving. The clear beach of two days ago disappeared under roweling gray-brown waters. At Menemsha, the waves stormed over the riprap. Sand blowing off the Menemsha Creek dunes blasted at the human intruder and car.

The four o'clock sailing was canceled, the seven as well, which completed the schedule. Feeling of an island cut off. Then clouds broke away, the sky opened. A sunset arrived, brief and delicate. Gale warnings were still flying; the storm, however, was blowing out.

The wind hauled east and continued at 40 knots, but when morning came, the ferry sailed for Woods Hole. Crossing Vineyard Sound, bound in, I caught up on the papers. "Raging Sea Sinks Ship, 6 Die," headlined a Boston sheet. "No real hope was held out for the six men, including the captain and the owner, who comprised the crew of the 94-foot *Deep Water*, which left New Bedford Friday. . . . The *Deep Water* disappeared 100 miles south of Martha's Vineyard. . . ."

Two days later, newspapers reported two trawlers, captained by father and son and believed missing in an Atlantic storm, had turned up safe. "The father's ship, the 91-foot *Elizabeth N*, drew into New Bedford. . . . Sixty-year-old Captain John A. Edwards and his crew of five were safe. But the 94-foot *Deep Water*, captained by his son, George, 34, was still listed as missing. . . .

"Then a Coast Guard search plane spotted the *Deep Water* . . . all six aboard were in good condition.

" 'Oh my God, it's too good to be true,' said Mrs. Lorraine Edwards, wife of the younger captain, when she learned her husband was safe. She was about to call his parents when she saw them drive up to the house.

" 'We got out of the car,' said the elder Mr. Edwards later, 'and the daughter ran out to us screaming, "He's safe. He's safe." My wife fainted in my arms, knocking me down, and we both went sprawling in the grass.' "

So ended the storm of the year, and also April.

Duck pond near West Tisbury on Edgartown Road

Cemetery in North Tisbury

Two nineteenth century gravestones in the same cemetery, commemorating those whose bodies were lost at sea

Menemsha Blinker, seen through drying fish nets on the pier

Menemsha's fishing village, framed by the piles of one of its piers

Wire lobster basket on a Menemsha pier

Textures

Another pier, another vista

Chapter 4

TO BREWSTER AND EASTHAM

CROWS calling at daybreak, country sounds from far down Town Cove: rural sounds from a rapidly semisuburbanizing Cape Cod. Who does not know the American crow when he hears it, one of the few birds the human voice is able to imitate? But then listening further I could not be certain the sound did not come from the throat of the smaller, tidewater-loving fish crow.

The big change since April was in the deciduousness. Leaf buds radiated lavender haze. Poplars were dropping red catkins on Route 28. What kind of poplar I cannot say, but the species was unmistakable; it had the populus look. You recognize family traits.

Although round-shouldered and dwarfed by a windy environment, Norway maples displayed their usual green-yellow blossom. An introduced tree, its origin European, hardy and able to withstand exhaust fumes, dust, drought, and insects, the Norway maple grows fast and does its work well, shading the hard edge, city or country, concrete or macadam. Little branches of elms were filmy with tiny leaves about to unfold. The only expanded leaves I saw were the soft-looking, handlike, and fingery organs dangling from stems of horse chestut trees.

Grape hyacinth opened its spikes of blue flowers. A home owner with mower attacked his lawn. Bullfrogs, tailless amphibian songsters, belted out their characteristic sounds, first of the season. I love to hear them. While bird song is often overrated, frog song tends to be ranked too low. Why not another nature manual, *A Field Guide to Eastern Frog Croak*?

Hard against the Orleans town line, yet wholly within the Town of Brewster—its main gate opening on Route 6A, the Cranberry Highway —lies an ornament of the Cape—Nickerson State Park. A splendid tract of Buzzards Bay-Sandwich moraine, it was given to the Commonwealth of Massachusetts in 1937 by Mrs. Addie Nickerson and Mrs. Helen Nickerson Sears as a memorial to Roland C. Nickerson, husband to one, brother to the other. The park is rich in kettle holes, hollows caused by ice broken from one or another of the retreating glaciers, and now holding water. Kettle holes and plentiful groundwater, water found in the earth's upper crust, are the source of most Cape Cod ponds. The Park is also well supplied with glacially transported boulders from who knows how far away, the kind geologists call "erratics."

Since 1673 and one William Nickerson, a Yarmouth man whom the historian Henry Kittredge called the "greatest speculator in wild lands the Cape ever saw," Nickerson has been a name of the region. Blood relationship, if any, between William and Roland C. is a question for the genealogist. They do, however, seem to have shared an entrepreneurial kinship.

Roland C.'s father, Thomas Nickerson, born in Brewster in 1810, was one of a maritime family. For many years he followed the family tradition. After the Civil War, however, he saw which way the country was moving. Although Thomas Nickerson was then about sixty, he quit Cape Cod shipping, went west, and into railroading. In 1874 he became president of the Atchison, Topeka and Santa Fe.

The son, Roland C., followed his father down the same iron track. When he returned to his native town a rich man many years later, he was able to buy quite a piece of it. For his own reasons he bought up 1,775 Brewster acres including nine charming freshwater ponds. The shore, apparently, did not lure him—he had become an inland man. Although he may or may not have intended to save and bequeath the tract, who has done more for home town than Roland C. Nickerson, helped by widow and sister? A rare gift not only for Brewster and Barnstable County, but also for state and nation.

Large parks are almost always impressive achievements—especially those that preserve a wilderness, self-contained area or reasonable facsimile thereof. Nickerson State Park is no exception. From the moment you enter you feel a quiet of space, a sense of a large irregular hummocky tract, not really wild—how could it be?—but mercifully only half-trammeled. The first pines inside the gates cast their spell. They are not primeval trees to be sure, but they are much larger than the run of the roadside. There is air among them and depth to the pinestraw beneath.

At park headquarters I stopped to inquire, and also to pay respects. The lodge (if that is the word), in which I seemed to be the only visitor, felt very much like a summer camp in the stage of opening up or closing down. I met Robert Hooper, Park Supervisor, a lean, patient-looking, sandy-haired man of indeterminate age. Supervisor Hooper has been twenty-five years on the job. He spoke quietly and whereof he spoke rang true. A camping family at Nickerson used to average 3.5 persons, he said. The camping family today, however, adds up to 4.4. Experience tells the Supervisor that from the end of June, when school lets out, until the last days of August, prospective campers will be queuing for campsites. The Park does not accept reservations. First come, first served is the rule.

Where do the campers come from? Forty-six percent from Massachusetts, 15 percent from New York, 9 percent from Connecticut, 8 percent from Canada, and the rest, you might say, from hellangone. A party assigned to a campsite may stay two weeks. In the unlikely event that no one is waiting in line, camping time may be extended up to another two weeks. The fee for tentsite is $2 a day.

I had a question for Supervisor Hooper. Do we, the citizenry, breed a better camper than heretofore, campers with a sense of the wholeness of nature in which man is a part, campers whose actions bespeak a concern for the overall out-of-doors, or who simply love the park? We do not, Mr. Hooper said; in fact quite the contrary. For one thing, few use wood for fuel—almost all are equipped with gas. And then so many things come in throwaway packages. Of course the trash barrels are there, but so are the people who will not use them. The park force is busy picking up refuse all summer long, yet can hardly keep pace with the discharge. Mr. Hooper said, "At the end of last summer we filled two trucks with debris from the beach and shore of Flax Pond." Flax is one of the ponds in the park. Mr. Hooper does not take the throwaway culture personally. "They have the same problem at the National Seashore," he added quietly.

If, as Mr. Hooper observed, few are using wood for fuel, then many are losing touch with the woods. Few will be on intimate terms with trees. Few will know an ax, or the feel of the helve in their hands. Not many will have the art of building an outdoor wood fire. Not many will watch it, smell it, get smoke in their eyes, cook over it, or lie down beside it.

On high wooded ground overlooking Flax Pond, I found tiers of beautiful camping sites, each marked with a number and furnished with fireplace, tables, and benches. Looking amphitheatrical, the furnished sites stood in the early May weather waiting. The park appeared to be resting up, the scrub oak not yet awake from its winter repose. What was this low-growing plant with needlelike leaves? Looked like moss phlox but it was yellow.

In a two weeks' hitch in the camping season, a visitor might get somewhat acquainted with Nickerson State Park, its five large ponds and the four smaller ones, marshes and bogs, swales, boulders and hills, and tour the four hundred camping families as well. Out of season as I was, what I did instead was start up the slender open steel stairway of the Fire Tower. As I neared the square aerie at the top, a trap door opened above my head. "You can come all the way," a hearty voice boomed. I followed instructions.

The man with the hearty note in his voice was, I learned, Ranger Glenn Miller. Gray-haired, crew-cut, and husky, a veteran ranger who looks the part, he wore the uniform of the Massachusetts Division of Natural Resources. Fire towers, Ranger Miller informed me, face the four directions. I got my bearings. Wellfleet Harbor lies due north, and much farther west than you might imagine, the hook of Provincetown. South, beyond Chatham, I got a narrow view of the wide Atlantic. Although it was only noon, the day was losing distinctness. A blurring of clouds filled the sky. Far to westward, forty miles off, lay a vague mass which, said Ranger Miller, was the mainland, the land beyond the Cape Cod Canal.

Looking out from his tower and seeing smoke, a good ranger, said Mr. Miller, can pinpoint it within a quarter mile. In his tower, Ranger Miller is tuned to five radio bands, two fire departments, two police departments, and the Park's own system.

From the height of the fire tower, the country appears deceptively undisturbed. You see miles of pine trees, and bear and scrub oak. You can count seven different kinds of green. And where are all the houses? "Yes," Ranger Miller allowed, "you don't see the houses but they are there." I knew what he meant. Although the woods are still there, they are in fact retreating.

~~~~~~

Brewster Center spreads out along the Cranberry Highway. There, on 6A, you seem to be in the old New England. What you see are fossil remnants, bones of old ports and hinterland villages, artifacts of the old slow places killed by fast-moving technology. The artifacts survive because Cape Cod's north-shore resort expansion has been less massive than on the south side.

Incorporated in 1803, Brewster is Cape Cod's newest town. Seventh in size, thirteenth in population, and twelfth in population density, it is one of the quieter, less built-up places. The town was named for the Pilgrim father and Elder of the Pilgrim Church, William Brewster, "so named," Thoreau wrote, "for fear he would be forgotten else." In his book *Cape Cod*, Thoreau asks: "Who has not heard of Elder Brewster? Who knows who he was?"

I would go further. Elder Brewster is a name composed of forbidding sounds, two of the most frightening words in American history, associated with Calvinistic strictness and with doctrine of total depravity. The official seal of the town that honors him immortalizes Elder Brewster's uncomfortable-looking straightback chair.

Brewster is a distinctive town. It has no natural harbor at all, no yacht club. Years ago the town built a long rock breakwater to serve as a harbor, but only a ruin remains. I traveled out Breakwater Road. Shoal bay water under a cloudy sky rested in a state of stasis. Should I also go down to Brewster's pond beaches? The charm of water was not wanting here. You can enjoy it every day. Brewster boasts seven public beaches, and choice of freshwater or salt.

Sheep Pond—another of the Cape's five hundred, another of how many trout ponds qualified as reclaimed. Beside the pond, at Fisherman's Landing, a sign clinched to a tree advertises: "Landcourted Waterfront Lots for Sale." Apparently everyone knows what the adjective means, namely, title unscrambled in land court, possession registered, wrested, and wrung. From whom, Indians? The view over Sheep Pond was blue-hazy placid. There were only two houses in sight, and one of them an old woodsy job, laid up of logs with a cobblestone chimney. I watched the wind scoot over the water. It was shifting to south with a feeling of rain.

The lane to Fisherman's Landing is narrow, flanked with woodland littered with bottles and beer cans—no paid attendants to clean up. This is no supervised Nickerson State Park. Here the citizen is on his own, and the place looks it. What kinds of lives and inner feelings fling their trash here at Sheep Pond Fisherman's Landing?

Walking cross-country 110 years ago on his fourth and last Cape Cod excursion, Thoreau may have come this same way. "After passing Sheep Pond," he wrote, "I knocked at a house near the road from Brewster to Chatham to inquire the way to Orleans. . . . I kept on through uninter-rupted wood by various paths. . . . At length, seeing no end to the woods, laying down my pack, I climbed an oak and looked off; but the woods bounded the horizon as far as I could see. . . . This gave me a new idea of the extent of Cape Cod woodland."

The woodland still looks extensive—from the crown of a scrub oak tree or the top of a fire tower. And it looks extensive to a person on the ground. Today, however, almost any road that leads into what seems uninhabited woodland will almost certainly show the way to a network of new little sandy streets and very small one-story houses.

Picking up Stony Brook Road, I headed for the highlands of West Brewster, Stony Brook, and the Herring Run. Stony Brook is the largest stream of fresh running water on the eastern half of the Cape. From the mid-17th century to the mid-19th it provided water power for grain, weaving, and knitting mills.

The old grist mill, converted to a museum, still stands. It is a choice example, oozing nostalgia and history. The waters from Walkers and Upper and Lower Mill ponds in the hills above rush down beside the old mill. The waters pour over the fishway, down concrete ladders, through resting pools built in the hillsides, then through a valley of ancient cranberry bogs, broad tidal marshes, Paine's Creek, and so down to Cape Cod Bay. The route by which the waters go down is the one the alewives come up—in their season.

Specialists in ichthyofauna say that at about the time of the vernal equinox, alewives in coastal waters from Newfoundland to the Carolinas foregather at inlets and tidal estuaries. Like the salmon and shad, the alewife is a running-upward, an anadromous fish, ascending rivers to spawn. It lives in salt water but lays eggs in fresh. At the moment when fresh water becomes slightly warmer than the salt water into which it flows—a movable date, early as mid-April and late as mid-May—the the run is on. Although the fish are alewives, everyone speaks of them as herring, and more often, herrin.

Cousins to herring, alewives are bigger, coarser, and fatter. The origin of the name *alewife* is uncertain. Some say it is a corrupted Indian word, others that it comes from an English dialect. Some think it refers to the fish's rather large belly.

Be that as may be, they were indeed running—as anyone driving on Stony Brook Road, and slowing down as the road crosses over the brook, could see. He could see if advance troops were coming upstream, or if the big run was on. I arrived in time to note a heavyset, middle-age man coming from downstream, smiling. He carried a huge net flopping with fish, which he dumped into a bushel basket. His expression of cat that swallowed the canary made me wonder. Was he a herring pirate?

I walked downstream along Stony Brook to the place where the man had been scooping them up. A remarkable sight: The brook boiled with fish. It was almost solid with alewives battling the down-rushing water. Little by little they made their way upward, fell back some, then went forward again, up over the concrete ladders and into the resting pools. They pushed on in incredible numbers, heavy solid-looking foot-long fish, staring, persisting, dark and driven—strange manna ascending from the sea.

Herring Brook Rules and Regulations: No herring may be taken Friday, Saturday, or Sunday. On other days, residents of Brewster may take forty-eight herring (12-quart pail) per week.

Upstream there is another sign. "Fishway Area Closed for Protection of Marine Fish Seeking to Spawn in Fresh Water . . . the fishway and fish ladder for the protection of fish coming from coastal water to spawn or returning thereto. . . ."

Walking upstream on the Stony Brook bank, I reached the kettle hole known as Lower Mill Pond in its lovely setting of glacial erratics, great jewels of uncut stone. There the herring who get to the top of the ladder enter calm water. As you might expect, those who climb to the top are the largest and strongest and perhaps the most motivated as well—pushing and shoving and going uphill all the way. From the shore of the pond I looked out, and down to the distant marsh, through which the brook winds and snakes toward the Bay. Down there I saw flocks of herring gulls earning their name, swooping onto alewives fallen beside the way or trapped in the shallows.

You cannot help committing the pathetic fallacy of projecting human feelings on forces of nature, and I think it is all right to do so. Why should man hold himself aloof and apart? In this instance I was for the fish, but I also saw that Brewster is an excellent town for a gull, or for a man with a taste for alewives—fresh, dried, salted or smoked—or a taste for pondering the overall scheme. Why do fish that live in salt water want to lay eggs in fresh? Is the urge perhaps part of a universal migration, the mysterious tendency to want to go home, back to the place of beginning?

Starting from the low forties, the day began to warm up. Skies were sunny, but the wind! The word from the man at the gas station—paradigm of the man who lives close to the traffic—was that there will be no weekend, no weekend for business, that is, because of the northwest wind. Tourists will not fight a headwind. And another thing; they listen to weather reports—every few minutes. Although they could see the sun was shining today, what they were hearing was "50 percent chance of rain tomorrow." Since nobody knows just what those words mean, people felt doubtful and stayed home today.

A solo traveler hears a great deal about business. The season is late, they said, and yet everyone knows that in New England the warming up process goes slowly, slowly—especially along the coast. So these early May mornings when spring hangs in the wind, and birds are singing, you are hearing a low-keyed plaint.

I moved north into Eastham (pronounced East Ham), one of the oldest settlements on the Cape. Once a large town but reduced by partition, it now is one of the smallest. Eleventh in population, Eastham ranks tenth in population density.

Here in Eastham, just north of Orleans, the Cape is less than three miles across, and windswept from backside to Bay. One can get in the lee of very few natural objects. Few woody perennial plants become trees when beset by winds, salt air, and thin sandy soil. In such circumstances many a scrub oak reaches no higher than a man's knees. I stopped to salute an old-timer fantastically shaped, bent, twisted, and half-wrestled down by the side of the highway, a sturdy venerable unknown tree, eloquent of the elements and of battling them every day. From this point of the persevering tree, Route 6, Grand Army of the Republic Highway, is the only road leading north—that is, down-Cape to Provincetown.

Pitch pine with gnarled irregular crowns told another windbound story. They grow as though battened down. I passed by Depot, Jemima, Widow Harding, and Herring ponds—beautiful ponds whose simple names tell of the everyday life. Words follow character, and you can almost hear the names spoken in the old rude flat nasal tone.

A hazy gray morning, but not without color. Leaves were busy putting forth. Since yesterday they had filled in a great many spaces. From the highway, just west of Eastham Center, I saw the "Old Windmill"— indeed, could not miss it—left over from the end of the 18th century, and also from the mid-1930's. The later time saw it restored. I got the message. What the mill says is that crops of Indian maize were once raised in Eastham. Some declare that as late as one hundred years ago, hogs were fattened in Eastham on homegrown corn. I passed up the windmill as, for the most part, I passed up the bygones of the Cape. I found enough in the way it is now.

Except for a couple of new and monstrous motels—and what a pity they were not zoned out—the town retains a windswept and low-growing scale. There is an absence of steeples and the usual sea captains' houses.

Eastham is a distinguished town. The Cape Cod National Seashore Park headquarters building and main entrance stand in Eastham. Authorized by Congress in 1961—and not a moment too soon—the National Seashore Park embraces 27,000 acres. It includes a good slice of Eastham and the larger parts of the towns farther down the Cape, Wellfleet, Truro, and Provincetown.

The park envelops public and private lands. "The Secretary of the Interior," says Public Law 87-126, "is authorized to acquire by purchase, gift, condemnation, transfer from any Federal agency, exchange, or otherwise, the land, waters, and other property, and improvements thereon and any interest therein, within the area . . . or which lies within the boundaries of the seashore. . . ." These acquisitions will take time, understandably; indeed, the lifetimes of many life tenants. But in the proverbial one hundred years—and all to remain open for the ages. For the present, however, while the park is still in its beginning, it makes this announcement: "Four Areas Only Are Open to the Public: Private Property Must Be Respected." Today and tomorrow the most significant aspect of Cape Cod is, and will be, the National Seashore Park. The park concept is big. No town could have established it, nor the fifteen towns together.

There is dignity in a government doing its rightful work. I felt it as I walked into the Vistor Center, which serves free educational snacks—illustrated talks concerning local natural and human history. My hunger, however, was for the road and the shore. I was about to slip out when a park guide in uniform graciously asked would I not like to see the showing of slides given in the auditorium. It would take seven minutes, she said as firmly, and courteously she led the way. She uncovered two more customers, and now the show went on. Nice little sequence, but rather too boastful concerning the past, too passive about the present. Never a word about realities, the writing on walls, the litter of beer and soft-drink cans, the problems of being a park, and why only a few people love them. Many use them but do not love them.

I left the center and went down to Coast Guard Beach, as the backside beach north of Nauset Harbor is named. Widely known and considerably written about—Henry Thoreau called it the Great Beach—you expect to be disappointed. All the more remarkable then that I was not. On the contrary, words blow away in the wind. Unbroken, the beach extends fore and aft as far as the eye can see.

An east wind, an onshore wind was blowing. An east wind makes a man nervous. To the eye of the nervous beholder, the running waves appear nervous, and so does the gray uncertain light on the water.

Nauset Light: small-headed, handsomely high-collared, decked out in red and white, and rigid as cast iron. Short-bodied, only 48-feet tall, Nauset Light stands on high dunes midway between Chatham Light and Cape Cod Light further north. Nauset's identifying characteristic is three flashes every ten seconds. Three is Nauset's historic number. Established in 1838, the first light consisted of three stone towers, 15-feet high, 150-feet apart—Three Sisters of Nauset, they were called. In time, three beacons became three flashes.

In 1853 Ralph Waldo Emerson visited Nauset Light. He wrote in his Journal, 5 September: ". . . to Nauset Light on the back side of Cape Cod. Collins, the keeper, told us he found obstinate resistance on Cape Cod to the project of building a lighthouse on this coast, as it would injure the wrecking business. He had to go to Boston, and obtain the strong recommendation of the Port Society."

The back side of Cape Cod was a graveyard for mariners and ships, especially before the Cape Cod Canal went through. In earlier days it was a green pasture for wreckers. Although mariner and wrecker must at times cooperate, their basic interest must conflict: What is good for one may not suit the other. The lawful business of the wrecker consisted in searching for or working on foundered vessels, in saving property and sometimes lives. For a legal wrecker to turn illegal, that is, to encourage and cause shipwreck, is no more difficult to believe than the case of the cop turned robber or the man who first sets the fire and then runs to help put it out.

Stories of lights hung out on deserted beaches to lure vessels onto Cape Cod's back side are still being told. Mooncussing was the word for it. A mooncusser was one who cursed the moon as a drawback to this activity.

On a knob in Eastham east of Route 6, the Captain Edward Penniman House rises. House and grounds on the edge of the new and already famous Cape Cod National Seashore Park, are property of the United States Government. Unlike the mass of sea captain's houses, the Penniman house gives domestic expression to wildness. Penniman was an Eastham whaling master who made five voyages out of New Bedford in the 1860's to 1880's. Foursquare on its granite foundation, superbly proportioned, decorated with jigsawed curvilinear abstract design, walls painted bright yellow, windows white-trimmed, tall shutters intensely green, shingled mansard roof improved with broad horizontal stripes of red and brown, Captain Penniman's house adds the color of far-away places to the prevailing Puritan culture. So although it stands empty, its time has by no means passed. For some reason I liked it.

North and east of the Penniman House lies Nauset Marsh and the National Seashore. From what must have been the back yard of the house, I picked up a new park trail. Arrow-shaped signboards pointed a way to something called Skiff Hill shelter. It sounded inviting. I walked through rank heavy-textured meadow that years ago had been pastured. Remnants of early stone fence and later barbed wire travel the rims of these fields. Once they prevented cattle and horses from wandering off into the marsh. By the size of the volunteer cedars, and the total absence of dung, you know that the livestock left some time since.

I arrived at the shelter, and indeed it was that—a hefty successor to the wigwam, but open-sided. An admirable place, I would guess, to sit on a rainy day watching the life of the marsh. Today, however, I was grateful for sun. In the distance rose Nauset Beach Coast Guard Station, white-sided and red-roofed. My field glasses raised the beach buggy trail that leads along the inner side of the dunes.

At Skiff Hill shelter a sign proclaims, "Nature Trail." Another informs that the time required to cover the distance is thirty minutes. Life is crowded, the sign seems to say, take half an hour for nature.

Do not be put off by the blacktopped beginning as the trail descends to a swamp. Were it not for the blacktop, the rains and the wear and tear of thousands of feet to come would gully that slope. The blacktop extends to the edge of swampwater. You cross the swamp on a sturdy freeform meandering boardwalk. Where the boardwalk ends, you step onto lowland duff. Both boardwalk and duff make light walking. I sauntered along, not working at all at studying nature but simply enjoying the path hacked and cleared through thorny greenbrier. Call it by any of its names—catbrier, bullbrier, horsebrier—to right and left of the path it forms an impenetrable tangle. Although swamp maples tasseled out in full crimson bloom, the trees were still leafless. Sunlight poured down. A redwing was calling—and now I saw him.

The swamp cast its warm May afternoon spell. A strangely placed swamp, to the eye it seemed a place of seclusion—but not to the ear. The northwest wind carried the noise of traffic. Nothing in Eastham can be far from the highway. I came to another clean stretch of boardwalk laid over brackish water. The water stood in a clearing rather than woods. Although it was Saturday afternoon, I did not believe there would be other walkers. I lay down on the planks so that my face felt the sun.

When I awoke I saw that the light had changed and the air become cooler. To my left, on dry ground among dead leaves, something was stirring. Raising my head from the boardwalk, I glimpsed a brown bird, not a woodcock nor a short-billed marsh wren. But all nature trails lead to little brown birds, so let this one pass.

I rose and continued down the trail where I found the most common of graceful and elegant things—gray birch with its neat triangular leaves; smaller, poorer and darker-skinned than canoe birch. Gray birch, like scrub oak and pitch pine, is a denizen of sandy soils. I also saw wood anemone or windflower, tripping as far as the eye could see into the ravel of brier, five-petaled white wildflowers growing close to the ground. Wonderful commonplace fiddlehead ferns poked through the wet woodland floor, just the downy scroll showing.

Out of the swamp now, and into the salt-laden air of the pasture with the ocean in view, I saw serviceberry in bud. This woody plant, be it tree or shrub, is also known by the name of shadbush. It blossoms in May when shad ascend rivers to spawn. And there stood a runt of a pear tree, a fruit tree gone back to the wild. The pear may have sprung from seed dropped by a passing man, or perhaps by some other animal. It could have been an escape from an old farm orchard. Some plants, like some people (and nobody knows how many of either) seem to want to avoid cultivation.

Not until I returned to where the car waited and saw in the sandy road the trademark of the prevailing culture did I realize I had been down a beercanless trail. I mention this only because the moment may prove unrepeatable. The trail, the work of the South Wellfleet Job Corps, completed in 1966, was still new. Obviously very few people had as yet stumbled along it.

A beautiful mercifully windless evening: I went to the eastern end of Long Pond in the Town of Harwich. Long Pond on the Harwich-Brewster line is Cape Cod's largest, more than a mile in length. I hear it covers 743 acres and that it is 66 feet deep. I arrived in time to look down the long dimension, west toward the vanishing point and horizon, and a rather tentative sunset of pale pinks and pastel blues. Spring sunsets are the least confident kind. Their lack of assertion is part of their charm. While configurations and colors developed, then slowly recomposed themselves, a fisherman at the adjacent town landing, dressed in hip boots, hooked a small fish. A small boat with stepped mast rode at its mooring. A pair of ducks floated on the water. In the foreground stood a horizontal branched pine, and beside it a tupelo or sour gum tree, in characteristic hair-streaming gesture. Night came as blue on blue. Edged stars and a young moon shone. As the temperature dropped, the air turned crisp. These early May nights were still hard at the center.

Chapter 5

HENRY BESTON

O N the back side of Eastham in the National Seashore Park, a mile or so above the public entrance to Coast Guard Beach, stands the hut in which Henry Beston lived and wrote his book *The Outermost House.*

In his time, no building rose between him and the old Coast Guard Station at Nauset. This is no longer the case. Walking beside the inner face of the dunes, I passed a line of nondescript camps, a line, however, that will not lengthen, thanks to National Park regulations. Jeep tracks stretched ahead. I walked on until I came to the weathered and wren-plain cabin perching on posts in the lee of the dunes, twice hauled back from the edge of the sea. A low grassy dune rose east of the little house. Beyond lay the beach and horizon of water. Westward, the view across Nauset Marsh, across salt meadows, extends to the center of Eastham.

I circled the forty-year-old cabin, untenanted now and anonymous-looking, then read a bronze plaque beside the locked door and wrote the inscription down. " 'The Outermost House' in which Henry Beston, author-naturalist, wrote his classic book by that name wherein he sought the Great Truth and found it in the Nature of Man. This plaque dedicated October 11, 1964, by a grateful citizenry, at a ceremony denoting The Outermost House a national literary landmark." Three names followed: Endicott Peabody, Governor of Massachusetts; Stewart L. Udall, Secretary of the Interior; The Massachusetts Audubon Society.

The Outermost House, subtitled "A Year of Life on the Great Beach of Cape Cod," published in 1928, has been in print ever since. It appeared in England and was translated into French.

"Having known and loved this land for many years," Henry Beston wrote in the opening pages, "it came about that I found myself free to visit there, and so I built myself a house upon the beach." Constructed by local carpenters from Beston's own sketch, the house "stood by itself atop a dune, a little less than halfway south on Eastham bar." It was only twenty feet long by sixteen wide, partitioned into two rooms. If, as he wrote, his house showed "a somewhat amateur enthusiasm for windows"—there were ten—that would be all right, for Henry Beston aimed to see what winds, waves, and birds were up to.

The summer of 1927 was waning when he moved in, thirty-nine and single. He intended to spend a couple of weeks, but he "lingered on." Autumn came, and something of moment happened: "The beauty and mystery of this earth and outer sea so possessed and held me," he wrote, "that I could not go. . . . The longer I stayed, the more eager was I to know this coast and to share its . . . life. . . . I had no fear of being alone, I had something of a field naturalist's inclination; presently I made up my mind to remain and try living for a year on Eastham Beach."

And so he stayed—alone—and transcendentally watching. "The sand here has a life of its own," he noted. He saw "land birds and moor birds, marsh birds and beach birds, sea birds and coastal birds, even birds of the outer ocean." He discovered need for "a wiser and perhaps more mystical concept of animals." He listened to the "awesome, beautiful, and varied" voice of the sea. He learned firsthand that "it is not good to be too much alone, even as it is unwise to be always with and in a crowd."

He lived very simply, heating his house with a fireplace "crammed maw-full of driftwood," cooking meals on a two-burner oil stove, writing in longhand at the kitchen table. Water came from a pipe driven into the sand. Using a knapsack to carry his groceries, he made weekly trips for "fresh bread and butter." Day and night the Coast Guard patrol would stop to converse and "mug up," for Henry Beston always kept a pot of coffee on the hearth. "The world today," he wrote then, "is sick to its thin blood for lack of elemental things, for fire before the hands, for water welling from the earth, for air, for the dear earth itself under foot."

After seeing his house and outermost site, I reread Henry Beston's book. What was his Great Truth? To say, in the words of the bronze plaque inscription, that he found it in the Nature of Man seemed to beg the question. "Some have asked me," he wrote in his closing pages, "what understanding of Nature one shapes from so strange a year? I would answer that one's first appreciation is a sense that the creation is still going on, that the creative forces are as great and as active today as they have ever been, and that tomorrow's morning will be as heroic as any of the world. *Creation is here and now.* . . . . Poetry is as necessary to comprehension as science. It is as impossible to live without reverence as it is without joy."

Twenty years after writing those words, in a new foreword for a new edition of *The Outermost House*, Beston wrote, "Once again, I set down the core of what I continue to believe. Nature is a part of our humanity, and without some awareness and experience of that divine mystery, man ceases to be man. When the Pleiades and the wind in the grass are no longer a part of the human spirit . . . man becomes, as it were, a kind of cosmic outlaw. . . . Man can be either less than man or more than man, and both are monsters."

Having read the book and surveyed the scene, I wanted, while there was time, to see the man. He was, I knew, getting on. Born 1 June 1888 in Quincy, Massachusetts, Henry Beston was the son of a physician who had studied in France. His mother was a Frenchwoman, member of what he described as an "old military and Bonapartist" family. He went to Harvard, received his B.A. and M.A., then turned to teaching. During World War I he served in the Army, afterward spent a year in the Navy in "the curious world of submarines." He published his first book in 1919. Several children's books followed. Then came the climactic year as observer-philosopher of the beach. In 1929 he married Elizabeth Coatsworth, and soon after bought a farm in Maine. There he raised his family and, as it turned out, made the farm a lifetime home.

I met the author of *The Outermost House* in the New England parlor of his 19th-century farmhouse. A noble-large, courtly, well-favored man, Henry Beston looked younger than his years. Although he no longer got around easily, his complexion was ruddy, his moustache and hair iron gray. I asked him how he accounted for the present-day interest in his book.

"The interest in nature is growing. People see it's a kind of impossible world and they have to have something else. I wish people would get on more peaceably," he said smiling. A big man with a gentle smile.

Why had he gone to the beach, I asked. "During the war [World War I] and afterwards," he said, "I saw so many people writing in New York I was anxious to see what a year, more or less alone in the midst of great natural beauty, would mean. Cape Cod has good people—hospitable to wild and unexpected things—so I decided to go there alone. I wanted to be solitary and to have nothing between me and nature."

Was this the whole plan? "I had no particular plan," Henry Beston said. "I thought it would be a gorgeous place to live—with the roar of the surf and a wonderful view to north and south. And to the east, the Gulf of Maine, you would find lobster buoys on that beach that had drifted down from Matinicus Island. I had a little money. I used a handful to build the house. Everything went ahead. It developed in its own way."

Had he been influenced by Thoreau? "No, I think not. I admire Thoreau but don't care much for him. He wasn't warm enough."

What books had he taken along? "I had a good clutch of books. There were Shakespeare's plays, the Bible, W. H. Hudson, and Longfellow, whose poems of rain and sea have always appealed to me. I had Forbush's three-volume *Birds of Massachusetts*, wonderful reference books. And the Sherlock Holmes stories. And the Rubaiyat—a great favorite."

Henry Beston showed me a photograph of himself taken at the time. "I was 6 feet 1½ inches tall, weighed 190—strong as a bear," he said. "I was a good deal out of doors and a good deal indoors. I wrote every morning from nine to twelve. I didn't put in any fake stuff. I told everything truly.

"It was a lonely life out there. Nobody patted me on the back, but the life had great appeal. The most solitary time was on certain wild nights. Sometimes I would be inside when a single wave would crash on the beach and shake the whole house. I always had a fire going—kept fire on the hearth. I was an old-fashioned person—always liked a hearth fire. I had a teacher who used to say hearth fire was the only fire fit for a human." Henry Beston paused and summed up, "It was a very happy year."

Five years after *The Outermost House* appeared, Henry Beston, replying to a reader, 11 September 1933, wrote, "I have just returned from a long walking trip . . . and found your most kind letter waiting for me here. Nothing in the world gives me more pleasure than a new sign that 'The Outermost House' has fallen into friendly and discerning hands for it is more than a book to me, it is part of my life and the corner stone of all the teaching I wish might find its way into the heart and mind of this disordered, wrong-headed, violent, and so profoundly unhappy age. . . .

"The walk . . . was just the kind of thing I like, a Borrovian adventure along quiet roads, and through a countryside where one still pauses at a wayside spring and talks to anyone on anything. But now that autumn is here, and the skies have cleared and gone cold, it is the great sound of the surf I hear in my inner mind and not the pleasant talk of brooks and the stir of overhanging leaves! . . ."

Fifteen years later, in 1948, in reply to another admirer, Henry Beston wrote, "As I view my contribution to the writing of our times, it seems to me to consist of a double affirmation, saying first that an awareness and experience of Nature is necessary to Man if he is to have his humanity, and saying in the second place that same awareness must have something of the religious quality, the Latin *pietas*, if you will."

On a postcard written to the same correspondent, 16 January 1956, Henry Beston said, "The young man in his 30's who walked the great beach has long ago vanished over the edge of the world, but he retains his eager interest in the spectacle of the world and in its wonder and color."

Although there seemed to be parallels between his experience at Eastham Beach and Thoreau's at Walden Pond, Henry Beston appears to have felt greater kinship with the Englishman, George Borrow (1803–1881), author of *Lavengro, The Romany Rye, The Bible in Spain*, and *Wild Wales*, a walker as well as writer. In any case, *The Outermost House*, an inner life story, is told with dignity, courage, and above all, a point of view.

Henry Beston died on the 15th of April, 1968. The passing years that have changed Cape Cod and taken their toll of the cabin have also enhanced the values built into his book. If the Cape that Henry Beston knew is diminished, the importance of his point of view grows. Never has it been more needed.

Scrub pine, found everywhere along New England's beaches, hard and tough and nourished only by the minerals in salt water and the sparse amounts of organic matter drifted into the sand

View from the Visitor's Center at the National Seashore in Eastham. The body of water in front is called "Salt Pond" and is fed
directly from the Atlantic Ocean in the distance

Nauset Beach, the National Seashore, Eastham

Seagrass bends with the winds, digging a small furrow around its roots—still another plant that likes to put its roots in sand

A scallop, probably pried open and eaten by a starfish, lies in the shallows on a surfless day

The ubiquitous seagulls

Chapter 6

CHILMARK DIARY

A mid-May morning. Trip No. 7, Woods Hole to Vineyard Haven, $10 one way for automobile and driver. This was the full-season rate, financially a sad change from April. Although the air on the water costs more in May, it is superlative, especially to a person on the *Islander*'s boat deck, in the lee of the wheelhouse, basking in sun.

Further signs of a changing season: down-island, in Vineyard Haven, hustle and stir. In Menemsha, up-island, Bill Seward's seasonal post office and seagoing grocery store was open—and had been since the first of the week. At the Chilmark dump a new trench gaped, wide and deep-mouthed, engineered by the dumpmaster. The dump, you might say, was open for business. A longtime summer resident, apparently pleased to have an excuse for coming down early, waved as he passed. I heard Captain Donald LeMar Poole, commercial lobsterman, scion of whaling families, thirteenth generation in Chilmark, was painting his boat. And my fairweather house, a doubtful shelter in April, did nicely now, its glass walls drawing in solar heat.

Spring rose. The temperature climbed to 60 degrees. White-petaled flowers of common wild strawberry, Virginia strawberry, revered little ancestor of all cultivated varieties—one of the low-growing herbs that everyone knows—bloomed on the hillside above Quitsa Pond. Hairy wild strawberry growing all over the region is the progenitor of the favorite small fruit. The domesticated and marketable kinds, large in size and rich in yield, are excellent in their way, but they lost the woodsy flavor of the *fraise des bois*. Windy spring. South to southeast winds blew. Wild apple trees were displaying white buds.

At Erford Burt's boatyard in Vineyard Haven my eyes confirmed what I had heard earlier. Captain Donald LeMar Poole was indeed painting his boat, the *Dorothy C.*—that is, he was supervising the job. Copper red to the waterline, topsides Cape Breton green, a green so green it made your eyes ache; a color Captain Poole said he is very fond of. Smiles, handshakes, greetings. Captain Poole knocked the ashes from his pipe, asked me what I was smoking, then refilled from the pouch I proffered and lit up.

"Did I tell you, Walter, we went down to Maine last fall? Went to Cumberland Center. That's where we get our lobster pots. It was Fair time. Dorothy wanted to go. They had something there I would like you to see—a stone-dragging contest with ox teams. When the winner was announced, they said he came from New Vineyard, so when I heard that I went out to meet him. I think I may have told you that New Vineyard was settled by people from Martha's Vineyard. 'Any Pooles in New Vineyard?' I asked him. He was a man of but very few words. 'No,' he said. 'Any Smiths?' 'No.' 'Any——?' " Captain Poole named a Vineyard clan of lineage as time-honored as his own.

" 'Just one family. Sons-of-bitches.' I told my wife what the man said," Captain Poole chuckled. "It was worth the whole trip," he laughed. (An island in joke, side-splitting.)

As for the *Dorothy C.*, although he has fished from the craft ten years, she has never quite suited. Captain Poole said she is too lightly built, that in a heavy sea you can feel her working. So he thinks of having a new boat built to his specifications. He said he has reached the time of life and estate where he can afford to make a damn fool of himself. "Then why not have what you want," I asked.

"Yes," he said, "but am I entitled to have what I want?" So the captain has reached that stage of philosophy, too, when one learns to do a lot with longing.

Towhee or chewink? Towhee is the song; chewink the call. Indians named birds by song or call, or both. Towhee and chewink are the same bird, and one of the few that retains its Indian names or at least a facsmile thereof. On the other hand, "Drink your teeeee, drink your teeeee," is what the English-speaking birdwatcher thinks he hears. He refers to the towhee-chewink as the ground robin.

The towhee is one of the common warm-weather birds of the region—noisy, gregarious, evident, clear, delightful, and also annoying. Again, my thanks to all common, easily recognized birds, especially those who live close aboard. Birds who hang around and seem to like you are the ones you depend on.

A further likeable thing about the towhee is that it belongs to the likeable family—or call it firm—of Grosbeak, Finch, Bunting, and Sparrow. All of them are easily known by the family characteristic of short stout canarylike seed-cracking bill. And most of the family, including the towhee, seem to rejoice in strong color.

Barn swallows keep pace with the spring, and with sociological change. This is another everyday sort that seems to like to live among people. As fast as civilization fanned through New England, barn swallows gave up nesting in crannies and along the ledges and cliffs. They early saw the opportunities in barns, sheds, bridges, wharves, and boathouses. As the barns and sheds disappear, they adapt to the new forms of summer houses.

The mud nest barn swallows were building here was taking shape, although still in the wet stage. I suppose the mud came from down in the swale where a trickle of water ran over sand and clay. The question is how have they carried the mud. Ornithologists disagree; some say the birds make pellets, which they haul on top of the beak and against the forehead. Others say they fetch the semiliquid in their capacious mouths and throats. One thing is certain: The mud was in transit. The nest was growing, globule by globule. And the mud was so wet that water ran down the grain of the siding to which the barn swallows plastered it.

Both male and female worked at constructing the nest. There were, however, three builders here. Two females and one male, or was it the other way round?

The male Baltimore oriole, from a distance, appears orange, black, and white. But close up he is more splendid than that. As he crosses your bow, you see that his rump is bright yellow. The combination is yellow and orange, and black and white, and the yellow makes all the difference. The male Baltimore oriole not only gladdens the eye, he also makes glad the ear. Smaller than a robin, he can really pipe and whistle his tune; one you enjoy hearing over and over.

I did not think of it at the time, but the oriole cutting in front of me at windshield level was flying too low. Coming up Abel Hill, passing Chilmark cemetery where in these latter years you begin to find names of deceased summer people as well as old island names, I saw a bit of red in the road. I stopped, got out of the car, walked back, and picked up a male scarlet tanager, evidently struck by a passing automobile. The birds were feeding too low in the roadside thickets, and the reason was the cold weather. This cool late spring made them weak and dopey.

I never before held a scarlet tanager. A small bird, sparrow size, it is really small when dead—and mostly feathers—and the colors are not like the plates in the bird books. The scarlet is washed with yellow and orange, the black of the wings trimmed with white, a touch of yellow-green at the wrists, and gray on the upper tail coverts. No need to believe it until you see it. I recall that Audubon shot the birds he wanted to study and paint, the one use, I suppose, for a bird in the hand, unless you are going to eat it.

Rain fell before daylight. At seven, a mighty clap of thunder, then long reverberations rolling across the pond. A hard shower followed, and lightning.

At the post office I ran into Cyril Norton, retired schoolteacher and native son of the town. His house, protected by a stone wall, stands close to the junction of the Menemsha Cross Road, the Middle Road, and the South Road. Beetlebung Corner, as this four-way intersection in Chilmark Center is called, was named for the stand of tupelo or sourgum trees that occupies one of the corners. Beetlebung, local nomenclature, probably derives from the fact that beetles—heavy wooden hammers or pestles—and bungs—stoppers for bungholes of casks—were carved from this very hard wood. Cyril Norton spoke of the early morning thunder and lightning. It was, he remarked, quite a tempest.

"The best place to be in a tempest," he said, "is a rocking chair with your rubbers on and your feet off the floor. I was visiting friends one afternoon in Edgartown—oh, some time back—when a tempest came up, but we were expecting it. We were sitting in the living room with our rubbers on and our feet in the air when we saw a ball of fire roll across the floor. It went out the door, crossed over the yard to a fence post, and followed that post right down into the ground—and that was the last we saw of it. We waited a while, and when we were about sure the tempest had passed, we looked around the room for damage but all we could find was a slight track burned down the middle of the carpet." Eyeing the sky, and noting the mares' tails, Cyril Norton said he believed we might get another. "Rain before seven, clear before eleven. Between one and two, we'll see what 'twill do."

Next month he would go to his fiftieth class reunion, Harvard 1917. Cyril Dexter Norton, born 7 August 1893, Chilmark, Massachusetts. "I still ride a bike, swing a hand scythe, have a large vegetable garden, cut a few figure eights on the ice in winter, and go swimming in the surf nearly every day in summer," he wrote for the fiftieth-anniversary yearbook. "Reading any and all histories is a favorite pastime with me. I'm a hard-shell Republican but split my ticket at times. . . . I refuse to be categorized. . . ."

A reader of history, Cyril D. Norton cares about the fine edge of what really happened. Whenever he thinks it necessary, he sends a letter to the local paper and straightens the journalists out.

Two or three weeks ago the *Vineyard Gazette* reproduced a photograph of the up-island stage of perhaps sixty years earlier. The rig, owned and driven by one Fred A. Mayhew, apparently made a daily run from Chilmark to Vineyard Haven, some twenty-five miles round trip. The names of Mayhew's horses were given as Kitty and Julia. A write-up accompanying the photograph said, "On the last day of his life Fred Mayhew drove Julia in a cart to the pond marsh to gather seaweed. As he loaded his cart, he dropped dead. Neighbors went looking for him when he failed to return home, and they found him where he had fallen, and faithful Julia stood beside him, where he had halted her to load his cart. 'She wouldn't leave him,' the searchers observed."

Nothing pertaining to the island is unimportant to an islander. The weekly *Gazette* is closely read. The piece on Fred Mayhew was not overlooked. "The following is an account of Fred Mayhew's death which I am personally cognizant of." So begins Cyril D. Norton's letter to the editor.

"Fred harnessed up Julia and her team mate," Cyril Norton continued, "hitched them to his truck wagon, and told his wife, Ruth, that he was going up to the shores of Menemsha Pond to get some seaweed for his stable of horses. He also took along a pail and hoe, to dig out a mess of clams. That was the last time Ruth saw him alive.

"Fred reached the pond shore, loaded his truck wagon, and started digging clams. After digging a few he had a heart seizure, and fell on his back, still grasping the hoe handle. Ernest L. Mayhew, on his way, in his small power boat, up Menemsha Pond from the 'Crick,' saw the team of horses, but no Fred, until he had swung over to get a closer view. He found Fred, as described above.

"Then, he shoveled out most of the seaweed, lifted Fred into the truck wagon, drove across the hills to the State Road, down it, and into our yard. Ernest called on my mother, Mrs. Malvina M. R. Norton, who joined him, to drive over to Fred's house, to break the news to Ruth (formerly Ruth Jernegan of Edgartown).

"There were no searchers. Oscar Flanders, who happened to drive into our yard, while Ernest was there, joined me as we trooped behind the truck wagon to Fred's place, where we assisted Ernest in carrying Fred into his house and depositing him on a bed in the downstairs bedroom.

"Meanwhile, Ernest Dean had gone after Dr. Fairchild, who, at the time, was at Allen Flanders'. Upon the doctor's arrival, he pronounced Fred dead, and the above is the unvarnished truth of what took place."

The unvarnished truth concerning the death of the one-time stage driver, Fred Mayhew. So what? Simply that the dead are not dead until they are forgotten. There is no way to tell what will stick unforgettably in a boy's or man's mind. To remember and want to say just what happened may be to understand it. In any case, vivid and detailed memory is the most enjoyable kind.

Sunny Saturday afternoon brought on the first busy spring afternoon in Menemsha. People drifted into the fish market on the mole at the Basin where the next generation of Pooles carries on. They shook hands with the proprietor, Everett, son of Captain Donald, asked how he had been, and if lobster would be as high this year as last.

Saturday night, six o'clock. I arrived on the hour at Captain Poole's to partake of Mrs. Poole's home-baked beans. Saturday night, beans are *de rigueur*, or as the Captain put it, "Something of a fixture—like a knothole in the planking." His wife Dorothy bakes yellow-eye beans to perfection, he said. Not much time gets lost in preliminaries; everything is ready. We sat down to the beans, and to salt pork, cold lamb, frank-furters, bread and butter, pickles and mustard, bread pudding with ice-cream, and coffee.

After supper—dinner is Captain Poole's word for the midday meal —we moved to the living room. Bookshelves at either end harbor the Captain's library. Captain Poole brought out the last of his Christmas cigars. As we drew on them he showed me the latest additions to his collection on whaling, literature of the sea, and Arctic exploration. "When will you take up your cross," he asked, "and write the story of the Vineyard whaleman? The Vineyard whaleman has not received his due."

Later, through the living room windows, we looked out on Quitsa Pond clearly defined on this not very dark spring night. Captain Donald LeMar Poole pointed to the cove where the moorings he set out for small pleasure boats are riding. "Twenty-three in all," he said, smiling with quiet satisfaction. "The tub is full of salt cod, the pump brings us water, and the goose hangs high."

So the long slow time of early spring, the melancholy prelude passed. The wild goose honked high—good weather coming. In fine weather geese fly at greater heights. The goose hangs high; propitious omen.

Chapter 7
DENNIS

THE Buzzards Bay-Sandwich moraine, I learned, thickens in Dennis. I decided to go there. Beside Scargo Lake, facing Scargo Hill, near the Cranberry Highway, and east of a granite marker saying thirty-eight miles to Provincetown, I found a cottage.

"Cottage" is what its owner called it, and the word was all right. Three little rooms, and a screened porch seven feet by ten—homemade and looking the part, obviously something he built himself—with a view not only of lake and hill, but also a pointed stone tower. Just the same, I called it a camp. I recognized the genus by the odor of raw and indoor weathering wood—lumber with all its pores open, absorbing moisture, giving forth exhalations, some of them rather poignant these first days after the long winter hibernation.

Randomly designed and constructed, it smelled like a camp and also showed other characteristics. The batten door to the bedroom could not open all the way because the battens, placed on the wrong side, struck the jamb. The door to the bathroom swung on a very short arc, then banged against the toilet. You could not stand squarely before the wash-basin because the shower stall overlapped it, so you stood offside. Although the sweated joints of the copper tubing looked uncommonly good for a job of unlicensed plumbing, the faucets were wholly convincing. Hot and cold were reversed. Two shades of violet paint garnished the wood trim and skinny rafters.

I was his first tenant of the new season, my landlord informed me. He said there were only three places for rent on Scargo Lake—his and two others. The fact that he had a hunting and gunning lodge on this site when zoning went into effect enabled him to parlay the former lodge into —lo!—this camp.

Scargo Lake in the Town of Dennis is shaped like a Ping-Pong paddle. At its widest axis, its shore line sweeps close to the highway. On its opposite shore, Scargo Hill rises wooded and clothed in colors of spring. One hundred sixty feet high, one of the loftier hills on Cape Cod, its round summit resembles a prostrate earth-figure's belly, head to southwest and long legs extending north. The belly is covered with a deciduous growth, the legs with pitch pine like coarse textured hair. Tobey Tower, a round chunky stone castle, a veritable rook misplaced from a giant chess set, stands on the earth-figure's navel. Where the face ought to be, a good-size conventional summer house rears and blanks out the ancient's expression.

Half a mile long, a quarter mile across at its broadest, Scargo Lake looks as though scooped from the woods. Legend says Scargo was a chieftain's daughter who had a small pond in which she kept fish. One summer the pond dried up. Scargo's fish died, and the Indian princess mourned. The tribesmen then built her a new and much larger pond. The earth they moved raised Scargo Hill.

June differed from May as bud haze from leaf bloom. Horse chestnut trees flowered in massive clusters. Old oaks, wind-blasted and lichen-covered, decked out in gay-looking tassels of yellow-green catkins. Young oaks unfolded yellow-whites and pink-greens. Tactile spring was amazingly new and downy: honeysuckle blossoms, and tiny wild white rambler roses; old and young pitch pine, all of them scraggly, standing at ease in this lake shore yard, displayed their new twigs, pinky-green, brownish.

In the world of plants, pines constitute a great well-known and leading family. White pine was the most important timber tree of North America. The colonists felled it for masts and shipbuilding. Later generations cut it mercilessly. White pine is a loftier, nobler, more finely textured tree than pitch pine—and on Cape Cod very much rarer. Very few first-rate stands of white pine remain in any part of the country. The eye knows the difference between white pine and pitch. If it doubts, the arithmetical test will tell. The needles—that is, the leaves—grow in clusters of fives on white pine; on pitch pine, in clusters of threes. White pine cones are long and pendant; pitch pine egg-shaped, with the large end toward the point of attachment. Here on the shore of Scargo Lake you see a great many egg shapes.

One of the three towns spanning the peninsula from Cape Cod Bay to Nantucket Sound, Dennis ranks eleventh in size, seventh in population, and eighth in population density. It has run a more or less standard Cape gamut of history—from fishing, farming, and shipbuilding to summer theater.

Out Nobscusset Road and along Whig Street and side roads leading through dunes to the Bay, festooned now with white flower clusters of beach plum, stand a few old houses and little barns, still very Capely because not yet overhauled. Age and infirmity showing, rich in qualities of time, they approach the climactic beauty of ruins. Reverend Josiah Dennis, for whom the town was named in 1793, lived in this part of it.

Dennis, Brewster, and Bourne are the Cape Cod towns named for ministers. "Titanic figures," Kittredge says vaguely. "Theirs was the task," he writes, "of setting a spiritual and intellectual standard that should permeate every phase of life. Righteous themselves, they demanded righteousness in their followers. . . ."

Consistent with this description of the type, Josiah Dennis' house seemed to me as remorselessly ugly and New England gothic as the traveler will find from Falmouth to Orleans; a house with a stiff and inhibiting gesture. Old is by no means the same as good. The Town, however, has done its duty: It recently bought the esteemed reverend's house for the future home of the Dennis Historical Society.

Five villages to follow down the historical track—East Dennis, Dennis, Dennisport, South Dennis, West Dennis. Zoning and civic pride are in evidence. Names of all places of business are given on uniform white boards lettered in black and hung in a single display at the head of each road. No billboards or other forms of competitive signs; very few roadside beercans.

The Union Church cemetery, looking its historical part, does not lie out back but is displayed up front. A daily reminder. . . .

Italians emigrating to Dennis from Boston and Taunton played a historic role. Hence the names New Boston Road, Taunton Avenue, Lombardi Heights, Angelo Lane. I am told the older generations came to build the roads and the railway. Later they built their houses, not Cape Cod weathered shingle, or clapboard, but Mediterranean plastered and painted pale pink or blue—a leavening influence.

The Cape Playhouse on Route 6A in the village of Dennis announced, Open June 21st. Summer waited in the wings. Dennis keyed into and mirrored the beauty of an exceptional day. The town is still in scale and proportion. Its houses, for the most part, are small; its trees, among the Cape's largest. Along the highway, and on roads leading north to the shore, staghorn sumac swelled to a size that is almost tropical.

A fullness of spring lay on either hand: to the right, yellow hawkweed —dandelionlike flowers—and blue lake water; to the left, the old road, old stone walls glinting in sunlight, a few pickets and cut-granite hitching posts with remnants of iron rings rusting. Old trees. . . . Hard by the Cranberry Highway stands a large craggy specimen I thought was a rock chestnut oak, but if not that, then swamp white oak. Both belong to the group of white oaks in which the leaf lobes are rounded. Beside it bloomed a red-flowered English hawthorn.

A white English hawthorn, another of the 1,200 species of haw—what hero counted them?—frothed in full blossom in Dennis village, in Herbert L. Sears Square. Herbert L. was a local lad killed in one of the 20th-century wars.

An earlier war, the American Revolution, brought an earlier Sears to public attention. "Captain John Sears, of Dennis, his wits sharpened by the high price that salt was beginning to fetch because of the British blockade, tried the experiment of letting the sun do the work of evaporation. . . ," writes Henry Kittredge, historian of Cape Cod.

Salt from the sea looked like such a good thing that presently many Cape men were encouraged to become "at least part-time salt-makers." But when, in the 1840's, salt from mines in the West, and abroad, began pouring in, Cape Cod salt could no longer compete. The Cape Cod industry at its peak had 442 salt-works going. Of all that, scarcely a bleached board or timber remains. Sesuit Neck where Captain Sears hailed from, once sprinkled with salt-works, is peppered with summer houses today.

~~~~~~

Last night I awoke, heard the village church bell toll three, then lay and listened to the silence: no sound at all, a blessed stillness, a soothing balm. At daybreak I heard a small wild creature running lightly over the roof.

In a camp such as this, the second thing in the morning is a walk out the flimsy screen door, down to the lake, out to the end of the little dock, and look around. A hard-eyed sun glared across the water. The water rippled, and then it broke. Little fish leaped up, their silvery sides flash-flashing in the sun. So the day began with little fish, and also with pollen dust, the microspores, fertilizing element of the prevailing flat-leafed plantain. Pollen filmed the porch of the camp, my gear, and my shoes.

One of the family of woodpeckers and semitame here, the yellow-shafted flicker, close up, seems huge. Larger than a robin, the male flicker carries a patch of red on his head and sports black whiskers. A pair of flickers poked through the wire grass, jabbing at the thin sandy soil. They were looking for ants and finding them. Overall brown but dotted with black, black at the throat, white at the rump, they lifted off on golden-lined wings.

My landlord heaved into view and drew alongside. "Have you seen any ants?" he asked. He meant, had I seen any in the camp? The answer was no. "Cape Cod is the second worst place in the world for termites," he allowed, and added, "The worst town is Brewster." That figures, since Brewster is the next door neighbor.

~~~~~~

A well-paved road, newly built by the Town of Dennis, leads up and over Scargo Hill. A newly macadamized parking area surrounds stone Tobey Tower. Tossed over the edge of the pavement and into the oaks, the beer cans begin to arrive.

Thirty-nine steps to the top of Tobey. The wood stairway and rail are pockmarked with names and initials of persons, some of whom are doubtless already dead. In spite of notched names, they may be forgotten.

Alone at the top of the tower, I looked all around. Then a car arrived down below. Two men remained seated in it. Two women got out and approached the tower. Voices echoed in the stairwell. "Do you want to go up, Ellie?" Ellie did not.

So they missed a good view, not a great one. Panoramas of low-lying shorelines tend to look much alike. Here, the near view holds too many houses—too many to be sublime, too few to inspire awe. And then, looking down on Scargo Lake involves you less than living beside it.

I returned to camp via the east side of Scargo Hill where subdivisions follow the new roads. The view would be different next time I saw it. Down on old 6A, the Cranberry Highway—it had its endearing stretches —Oriental poppies blazed bright scarlet. Lavender wisteria, white bridal wreath, pink laurel, yellow laburnum, and masses of iris were blooming, remnants of perennial gardens planted how long ago.

A swim in the lake confirmed what I sensed on the tower. The real view is not from above and outside, but from down and in. The swimmer's view is not merely seen but felt. A woody margin of shore appeared wilder as you move into colder water. From warmer shoal water, however, the shoreline looked tame.

In the Revolutionary War, it is said, Scargo Hill served as one of the relay points for signal fires. From hill to hill, Cape Cod to Boston, bonfires transmitted messages concerning the movements of British ships. A bonfire blazing on the dark broody hill, lighting up the sky—you must try to imagine the sight.

My landlord sat in his picture window reading the morning paper when I came in. His first weekend guests had gone and he was glad of it. "We get ten weeks of this," he said, "so we don't want to start too early."

His wife may or may not share his view. It was hard to tell. On the walls of his office and paying-guest breakfast room hang his Lodging House License (Town of Dennis); his Room Occupancy Excise Registration Certificate (Commonwealth of Massachusetts); extracts from regulations governing Innkeepers, Operators of Overnight Camps, Cabins, Motels or Trailer Coach Parks; fish and game laws; tide tables; and a framed color photograph of his dog. Also a couple of slogans to live by: "The opinions expressed by the husband of this house," reads one, "are not necessarily those of the management." The other: "The arbitrary opinions of the entrancing female of this house are not necessarily shared by its male occupant but on occasion are tolerated by him." The latter, my landlord said, hung for a week before his wife noticed it.

Seventy-seven degrees at 9:45. Barometer 30.3 and rising. Prevailing opinion said early spring was too cold, while these latter spring days, it said, are too warm.

Warm weather brought out the little greenish flowers of plantain, a beautiful weed. My landlord, however, did not like it. This dooryard weed wanted to live and grow. He wanted to root it out. For all its modest and rather amusing expression, plantain is tough—tough as things all over.

A south wind blew and exacerbated all manner of pent-up feeling. The public beach at the north end of Scargo Lake, although it may be an asset, is also a problem, said my landlord. An adjoining public-spirited landowner gave the beach to the Town, but now the Town has to hire a college boy at $125 a week to patrol it. Why? Because of the out-of-town truckloads of children and corned-beef sandwiches people bring to it. They come and wash themselves in the lake, and also their clothes. And they leave their litter. My landlord said that the college boy whose job is to limit use of the beach to residents of Dennis, accomplishes little. The out-of-towners soon learn his schedule. As soon as he leaves, convoys of them drive in. My landlord can see them from here.

The citizen who gave the beach to the Town retained a cranberry bog alongside. One night when the beach he formerly owned filled up with visiting automobiles, an overflow of fifteen cars and trucks parked on top of his cranberries.

***

I drove to Yarmouth, the adjoining town west, which extends from the Bay to the Sound like Dennis and Barnstable.

Yarmouth, fifth largest of Cape Cod towns, stands third in population and second in the revealing ratio, population density. The densest part of the town is South Yarmouth, the Bass River village on the line between Dennis and Yarmouth. South Yarmouth with its saltier air, and heavier traffic, seems all little streets and little houses. And the charm of the houses seems to be inversely proportional to their size: the smaller the house, the more charming. An old Friends Meeting House, a white clapboard steepleless building, stands there quietly hugging the ground. If a temple more in the Spirit exists on Cape Cod, I have not yet seen it.

South Yarmouth, on Route 28, lies in the thick of the vacation business. Four miles to the north, on Route 6A, the village of Yarmouth clings to the nostalgia antiquarian trade.

Not many American towns are older than Yarmouth, incorporated in 1639. The Indian name was Mattacheese, the tribesmen living there, Mattakees. Homesickness was perhaps the motive for changing the name to Yarmouth. But once you know it was Mattacheese, Yarmouth does not look right.

By all accounts, an unbroken forest confronted the first Yarmouth pioneers. Setting to work with axes, they swiftly and almost completely destroyed it. Trees fell to clear land, build houses, ships, provide naval stores, feed the home fires, and also the fires of local industry. Less than two hundred years later, tree-planting became a necessity. Early in the 19th century, Amos Otis, Edward Thacher, and Oliver Hallet, three men who deserve the world's thanks, set out saplings along Route 6A, the Cranberry Highway, and Main Street of Yarmouth. Their trees became, and are to this day, Yarmouth's long cathedral of elms.

Traveling Yarmouth, I got the feeling that not very much has been going on here for maybe one hundred years—since the Civil War— when the merchant marine began to fade and the fishing industry moved away from Cape Cod towns such as Yarmouth and concentrated in Boston, Gloucester, and Provincetown.

About halfway between Yarmouth and Yarmouth Port, Centre Street leads to the Cape Cod Bay shore. At the head of the street I read three signs: Town Landing, Native Lobsters, New Homes. On the way to the shore I passed the Ancient Cemetery, as it is called—chock-a-block, and has been for years. These old orchards of the dead gain in beauty and at the same time preserve open space for the living—space that cannot be used, an especially valuable kind. Farther out the sandy street, tall blueberry bushes hung heavy with unripe fruit. And now I came to Gray's Beach picnic area, equipped for cookout and softball. And here was Chase Garden Creek and Bass Hole. A narrow boardwalk slung on posts, a kind of rustic viaduct, bobbled its long way over the marshy flats but collapsed before it reached the beach. Very lightly peopled, the scene evokes mid-19th-century American landscape paint-ing—Martin Johnson Heade's *Salt Marshes*, or Worthington Whittredge's *Old Homestead by the Sea*.

At the Town Landing a gray-haired man, strongly built, dressed in clothes that have known salt water, hauled on a lobster trap. He reached in and brought out a lobster, dark green and mottled, and held it up for inspection by the customers standing beside him: a beautiful gleaming wet crustacean of the Atlantic coast, genus *Homarus americanus*, a marine animal with stalked compound eyes, two pairs of antennae, five pairs of legs, the first pair modified into large unequal and dissimilar pincers, and some abdominal swimming legs. Its tail, however, is the lobster's chief swimming organ. With fast hooking motions of its tail, it sprints backward. As for the lobsterman, was I looking at the last one in town? In any case, he seemed to account for the sign, Native Lobsters. Concerning the other sign, "New Homes," it was only too easily explained. New Homes—you cannot miss the houses.

Native lobsters, and hence native lobstermen, are becoming fewer, and in fact have dwindled steadily since the latter part of the 19th century. Exploitation of the lobster fishery from Nova Scotia to North Carolina is one of the familiar stories of waste that become increasingly shocking and inexcusable as the years pass. Protective laws probably saved the lobster from extinction, yet too often fishermen have removed the eggs from egg-bearing females instead of returning them to the sea to perpetuate the species. Government hatcheries have launched millions of tiny lobsters, but the results of this effort have not been impressive.

Lobsters grow slowly. An individual twelve-inches long is presumed five years old. Just how old or big a lobster can get is not known, but a lobster is thought to keep on growing as long as it lives, somewhat like an old oak. A lobster grows by breaking out of its shell in a kind of molting process, which occurs frequently in early life and less often later on. A molting or shedding lobster is extremely vulnerable to natural enemies, such fish as cod or tautog. The lobster's external framework supports as well as protects it, for it lacks a skeleton.

Like most inhabitants of the deep, the lobster preys on others. Scavenging the sea floor, the lobster with its smaller and more slender claw— the cutter—slices dead fish, its favorite food (as lobster-hunters know). With its larger—the crusher—the lobster breaks the shells of smaller shell fish. Claws of captured lobsters are pegged not only to save the lobsterman's fingers but also to keep the lobsters from tearing each other apart, for the breed is strong and fierce.

At home in the sea, the lobster can survive considerable mutilation and grow replacement parts. It migrates a little—to shallows in spring, to deeper water in winter. In either location it seeks the rocks where it finds its food, and dodges the sea's ever-present dangers. But once inside a lobsterman's pot, an oblong cage with slat sides and a funnel-shape net, it lacks the mental equipment to find its way out.

The Historical Society of Yarmouth Port invites the passerby to walk
in its fifty-acre tract of woodland, pond shore, and fields marked with trails.
The point of beginning lies behind Yarmouth Port post office. Things
being the way they are—walking land hard to come by—I accepted, and
gladly.

Midday and muggy. I went down the trail, through abandoned uneven
farmland, cropped-out soil, and sandy New England desert, good for
mosses and lichens and trailing bearberry with its little evergreen leaves.
The gray-green tapestry of lichen growing on many a Cape Cod tree may
look parasitic, but it is not. Although it grows on other plants, the lichen
is not a parasite but an epiphyte, an air plant, one that takes the moisture
it needs from the air.

Further inside the tract, the ground rose. A feeling of woods, of cover
for deer, some denseness of second-growth trees—the ubiquitous scrub
oak and pitch pine. Nothing resembling timber. Perhaps what I saw was
a healing of time, the farmer gone to his reward, the flora returning to
its own, the indigenous wild plants left alone now and beginning to look
undisturbed.

A white flower with deep green stellar leaf, the star flower, one of the
primrose family of spring and cool woods, seemed an auspicious find.
There were many here. But then I came on a woodland plant with a
power of suggestive beauty that buckles your knees. A cool pink, deeply
cleft pouchlike shape, its cheeks veined with hot pink, floated on a slender
stem sprung from low basal leaves. It is the orchid called lady slipper,
or moccasin flower.

I discovered another, a slipper of larger size, solitary beside an oak,
this one magenta with ruby veining, a superb variation of reproduction,
unlikely and wholly unimaginable. I looked around and counted seven
of these flowers, woods-haunting and Indian quiet, untransplantable and
as rare as they looked. I had not seen a moccasin flower since boyhood.
Not knowing when I might see another, I stayed with them a while.

On the move again, I came to Miller's Pond, small and weedy, a basin
for frogs and water lilies. A place where you might study pond life but
neither swim in nor drink the water. I parked myself on a conveniently
placed wood slab. A small spotted turtle sunning on a half submerged log
gave me the eye reptilian, then deftly plopped in. No structure, clearing,
cultivation, or person subverts what the pond itself wants to be doing.
No one lives here. But then it would be a poor place to live. Too static—
fine, however, to pause beside, idle the mind, get a feeling of, and then
press on.

Fifty-eight degrees at eight o'clock. Wind from the northeast. Sooty gray clouds, changing shape as they went, marched across an unpolished sky. A bleak morning.

In Barnstable village, on the steps of the County Court House, I heard the decision. "More like October all of a sudden again," said a denizen of the courthouse row.

Barnstable village in Barnstable town is the county seat, hence this grim-looking gray granite courthouse on Route 6A, with the pair of small War-of-1812 cannon out front. Just to look at it makes you feel under suspicion. And I knew what the verdict would be. Nevertheless, I mounted the steps. They command a good view of Barnstable Harbor on Cape Cod Bay. Then looking around, I saw where there was a better view. Back of the courthouse, on higher ground, rises Barnstable County Jail and House of Correction.

The jail and correction house must enjoy as handsome a view as any of Cape Cod's institutions. Their situation reenforces a point: View is always subjective. A high chain link fence, topped with strands of barbed wire, surrounds the brick buildings. Little tin signs hanging on the fence say, "Jail Grounds. Do not talk with the inmates." They are like little signs you see at a zoo. Below the jail grounds, a pastoral scene unfolds— young cattle grazing, brown and white Guernsey heifers. They looked serene and gentle. It is not surprising, after all, that to some men cattle are sacred. And there is a well-tended truck garden. Peas were in bloom, and so were wild phlox in the fence row.

From its Main Street, 6A, the Cranberry Highway, Barnstable village looks rich—and feels it—in an old Boston way. Only a rich town has call for a blacksmith today. Barnstable has its Village Smithy. I do not know if the smith is making a living, but he seemed to have plenty to do at the forge. He was not shoeing horses but making andirons, old style latches, and HL hinges.

Cumaquid. Is it Town of Barnstable's smallest village? Its post office looked like a children's playhouse. And in Cumaquid, on the Cranberry Highway, a dwelling is lying so close to the ground that platter-faced poppies standing in front of it looked right into the windows.

North of 6A stretch the lowlands of Salten and Calves Pasture Points on Barnstable Harbor. Westward you can see the Great Marshes.

Late in the 17th century the salt hay marshes of Barnstable Town, the most extensive in Massachusetts, attracted a cattle-raising pastor, a minister who divided his time between his herd and his flock. Then a second minister, bringing his followers, came to town and ousted the first. Apparently in all Barnstable from Cape Cod Bay to Nantucket Sound, there was not latitude at that time for two points of view.

Although more crowded now—not to be compared to the way it was three hundred years ago—Cape Cod seems to have far more room for individual thought and style. If the old days were good, the new are probably better.

Near the end of the book he wrote forty years ago, Henry Kittredge asked, "And what of recent religion on the Cape? . . . Quakers, Baptists, and Methodists broke down the bars. . . . The Church of Rome came with the Portuguese fisherman to Provincetown. . . . Finns. . . have presented the Cape with various sorts of Lutheran theology. . . . Some of the old Congregational churches. . . went Unitarian. . . . Here and there are Christian Scientists; the Swedenborgians have a number of representatives. . . . South Yarmouth echoed not long ago to the enthusiastic activities of the Holy Rollers. . . . A group of Dennis men. . . created. . . the Free Independent Church of Holiness. . . ."

A Friday evening, eve of the Sabbath. I inquired the way to the Cape Cod Synagogue, the Cape's first and only synagogue. The place of meeting, a simple frame structure, ceiling and rafters painted the traditional blue and white, is on Winter Street in Hyannis. Organized about twenty years ago, the synagogue includes about one hundred families. Although most of the congregants live in or close to Hyannis, the hub of Barnstable town and county, seat of the Community College, and social-commercial capital of the Cape, they also come from the corners and coves—from Sandwich and Bourne to Provincetown.

Sitting among fellow Jews in history-proud Barnstable town and county, reading from the old teachings, I thought of the strong Hebraic influence on Puritan and Pilgrim. Some of them called themselves Christian Israelites. Modeling ethic and law on those of the ancient Jews, they also excluded Jews of their time, along with Catholics, Turks, and all manner of dissenters. Although the first known Jews in the Bay Colony arrived in the middle of the 17th century, Jews seem not to have settled on Cape Cod for another two hundred years. Still another hundred would pass before this synagogue could rise, the first Jewish public building in Barnstable.

A portfolio of Massachusetts fences: split rails and barbed wire in a
seaside pasture, built to guard cattle that vanished long since

A sturdier gate frame, erected from slabs of granite blasted loose
by dynamite

Nearer to civilization, fences are built to keep boundaries neat, or simply to be proud of. This one is more ornament than barrier

An even lovelier design, better for attracting roamers than keeping them away

The venerable picket; behind, a pair of evergreens—arborvitae—
planted in front of a newlywed's house: an old New England custom

108

High, upright, and emphatic; but discreet and stately nonetheless:
Hyannis

A rare curved fence in front of a West Tisbury Church

Balustrade on the stoop of a house on Edgartown's Main Street

Chapter 8

NANCY LUCE

"LINES composed by Nancy Luce about poor little Ada Queetie, and poor little Beauty Linna, both deceased. Poor little Ada Queetie died February 25th, Thursday night, at 12 o'clock, 1858, aged most 9 years. Poor little Beauty Linna died January 18, Tuesday night, most 2 o'clock, 1859, aged over 12 years. She lived 11 months lacking 7 days after poor sissy's decease."

Poor little Ada Queetie has departed this life,
Never to be here no more,
No more to love, no more to speak,
No more to be my friend,
O how I long to see her with me, live and well,
Her heart and mine was united,
Love and feelings deeply rooted for each other
She and I could never part,
I am left broken hearted.

O my poor deceased little Ada Queetie
For her to undergo sickness and death,
And the parting of her, is more than I can endure
She knew such a site, and her love and mine,
So deep in our hearts for each other,
Her sickness and death, and parting of her,
I never can get over, in neither body nor mind,
And it may hasten me to my long home,
My heart is in misery days and nights,
For my poor deceased little Ada Queetie,
Do consider the night I was left,
What I underwent, no tongue can express.

Poor little Ada Queetie's last sickness and death,
Destroyed my health at a unknown rate,
With my heart breaking and weeping,
I kept fire going night after night, to keep poor little dear warm,
Poor little heart, she was sick one week
With froth in her throat,
Then 10 days and grew worse, with dropsy in her stomach
I keep getting up nights to see how she was,
And see what I could do for her,
I bathed and birthed her stomach,
And then give her medicines, but help was all in vain,
Three her last days and nights
She breathed the breath of life here on earth,
She was taken down very sick,
Then I was up all night long,
The second night I was up till I was going to fall . . .
The third night I touched no bed at all . . .
She died in my arms at twelve o'clock at night . . .
I could been heard to the road, from that time till daylight,
No tongue could express my misery of mind.

So begins *Poor Little Hearts,* a great American naive poem. Ada Queetie and Beauty Linna were not, as you might suppose, Nancy Luce's children. They were bantam barnyard hens. In Nancy Luce's wail and long lamentation, vernacular verse and genre writing, is the voice of the folk and indigenous poet.

If Nancy Luce's life was provincial, her condition, at bottom, was wrong. Denied the fundamental existence a woman has the right to expect, her chickens became her family, her poetry, her love-making and communication. Femininity flowed in the lines she wrote.

> *Poor little Beauty Linna, departed this life,*
> *My hands round her by the fire, my heart aching.*
> *I wept steady from that time till next day.*
> *I took the best care of her, days and nights,*
> *I did everything could be done,*
> *I did the best I could do,*
> *I sat up nights with her, till it made me very lame;*
> *Then I fixed her in her bed, warm, close by the fire,*
> *Put warm clothes under, over and around,*
> *And left fire burning and lay down with all my clothes on,*
> *And got up very often with her, and sat up as long as I could;*
> *I never took off none of my clothes for 18 days and nights.*
>
> *Poor little heart, never can call me back any more,*
> *When I go out of the room;*
> *She did it as long as she was able.*
> *For eight months after Poor Sissy's decease,*
> *She would not let me go out of the room;*
> *Called me straight back, as soon as I went out.*
> *I fed her with a teaspoon in her sickness,*
> *Good milk and nutmeg, and good porridge,*
> *And so I did Poor Sissy.*
>
> *I made fire days and nights,*
> *To keep poor Beauty Linna warm;*
> *The day before Poor little dear was taken away,*
> *She opened her eyes and looked up into my face,*
> *For the last time, O heart melting . . .*

About forty years old when she wrote *Poor Little Hearts*, Nancy Luce was born in West Tisbury, midland town of Martha's Vineyard, in August, 1820, day of the month unknown. She was the only child of Philip Luce, a farmer, and his wife Anna Manter Luce. At the time of her birth her father was already forty-nine, her mother thirty-nine. Philip and Anna had been married nine years.

Nancy Luce was born in her father's small farmhouse on Tiah's Cove Road, a mile or so southeast of the village, close to a Tisbury Great Pond inlet. The house that she lived in all her days and where she died is still standing. Outwardly it has not changed much since her time. Set back from the road, it shows the same shy narrow-windowed shingled facade and narrow red-brick central chimney. Pines have sprung up beside the brook that passes east of the house and flows into Tiah's Cove. Trees on the opposite side of the road have grown tall and cut off the view Nancy probably had of the Cove.

Since Philip Luce owned a recognized earmark, one presumes he grazed sheep on the common lands. He owned several tracts—some salt meadow at Quansoo and land at Tississa and Great Neck Bottom, and at Tiah's Cove. He also owned the "third wall pew east of the pulpit" in Tisbury Meeting House. At one time he was collector of taxes for the "first precinct of the Town of Tisbury."

While Nancy was still very young, however, her father developed an "affliction." Something went wrong with her mother, too. "My poor father used to own English meadow," Nancy wrote later in one of her homemade notebooks, "but his sickness and my mother's sickness a number of years caused him to sell all his English meadow and part of his wood-land and clear land and sheep and creatures etc to get money to pay a number of doctors and folks. . . year after year, the most of it when I was a little girl. See what sickness is." Sown areas of upland meadow were called English meadow; the crop when harvested, English hay.

In spite of her parents' illnesses, Nancy must have had some schooling. She learned to write a beautiful hand, and she must have been quick with figures. By the time she was thirteen she was doing business on her own, buying on consignment from Timothy Coffin, merchant and trader in Edgartown, and selling the goods in West Tisbury. On the return trips to Edgartown she carried West Tisbury farm produce and piece work knitted by farm women. She bought her own furniture—a four-poster and a bureau—and for her aging parents, as she wrote later, "3 barrels & a half of flour every year. & over a hundred weight of cheese, every year, that my folks eat. & mutton, & beef in plenty. & part of father's clothes."

Concerning her West Tisbury girlhood, Nancy wrote, "There never was such a slave as I used to be. . . . I sot up nights, & knit, after my folks went to bed. . . & then I got up mornings, as soon as I could see, to get my clothes on." Her pleasure came not from making money—whatever she earned went to paying expenses, doctor's bills, or paying off debts —but in riding a horse. In her struggle to maintain herself and her parents, "the cream of it," as she later wrote, "was, in having a horse to go at market." In her poem *No Comfort*, she remembered:

> *I have had horses to run with me,*
> *So that the ground looked*
> *All in black and white streaks.*
> *There never was a horse*
> *That ever started me from their back . . .*

When she was about sixteen, to judge on the evidence of the handwriting, she copied on an old legal document the well-known drinking song, *The General's Toast*. It appealed to the future poet. It begins with a salute to a girl of about her age:

> *Here's to the maiden of blushing fifteen*
> *Now to the widow of fifty*
> *Here's to the flaunting, extravagant queen*
> *And then to the housewife that's thrifty . . .*
> *Let the toast pass*
> *Drink to the lass*
> *I warrant she'll prove an excuse for the glass.*

Up to age twenty, Nancy managed her business. She spun, knitted, took care of farm and house chores, and whenever she could, rode. But then all this left her. Five years later she was writing, "I'm strained, & that is dreadful to undergo, & dangerous. . . . I undergo more than tongue can express, by spells, everyday, for about 3 or 4 months at a time, or thereabouts, & then I get a little better, for about as long a time, & that is the way, year after year, with one of my worst complaints. . . . Dr W H Luce, has cured many very bad complaints for me, & helpt many more of them, slowly, & patched along many more of them. It seems as if, 2 of my worst complaints cannot be cured, only patched along, & helpt very slowly. Discouraging."

What happened to Nancy Luce between ages twenty and twenty-five? I consulted Joseph Chase Allen, author of *Tales and Trails of Martha's Vineyard*, and *The Wheelhouse Loafer*. Mr. Allen was born in Chilmark in 1892. He had heard about Nancy Luce, he said, from a Chilmark farmer of an earlier generation, Moses Norton, who was also a cartwright, boatbuilder, and harnessmaker. About 1906, Moses Norton told a then-young Joe Allen that Nancy had been a beautiful girl and a horsewoman who would jump stone walls and fences, an unusual accomplishment among young women of her day. She attended social gatherings all over the island, for she had her own means of transportation. Mr. Allen recalled Mr. Norton saying, "She would dress up to go to a dance and I can see her now with her handkerchief wrapped around her sleeve to protect it from the horse." Mr. Norton said several times how very nice looking she was. Apparently he admired Nancy. Had he worked on her bridle and gear?

According to Joseph Chase Allen's information, Nancy expected to marry a young man, who sailed on a whaling voyage but did not return. During these years of waiting her parents declined, and then Nancy herself became sick. Later on, Mr. Allen said, when Nancy turned to her hens, she would not keep a cock. When she wanted to raise chicks she bought fertile eggs. Nancy, an unusually enlightened keeper of poultry, doubtless knew that the way to get maximum egg production was to keep roosters out of the flock. She must have known hens are more docile, manageable, and even affectionate when cocks are not running among them. But it also seems that deprived as she was, she did not want to face romance in the barnyard. With her hens and a cow, Nancy in effect established a kind of nunnery.

From horses to hens seems to tell both the outer and inner story of her life. The horse stands for aggression, power, and sex. The hen, on the other hand, symbolizes withdrawal. It represents mother, a fussy and worrisome mother, or a small hen may signify a child.

Nancy, not a nostalgia writer, tells how it was on the old Philip Luce place on Tiah's Cove Road in the mid-1840's. Her father, apparently a dirty old man now, did not milk the cow right. "When I take milk in my mouth," Nancy wrote, "I cannot help having to puke, when I cannot watch father, & see him milk, & tell him what to do, & what not to do. I suffer with nastiness. I cannot stand nastiness."

She lived in constant fear of pauperage. "If every bit of property father has was sold, & layed out in victuals, & clothes, it wouldn't last them but a little while. & then we should be all 3 of us throwed on the town, and that I cannot endure. I won't be here on earth to be murdered alive. . . . People that are on the town, are always barbecued, & can't help themselves. & can't live respectable. & can't have anything handsome. & can't have anything for themselves. & can't have the leastest comforts of life."

By the mid-1840's Nancy had lost mobility. "You cannot realize how dreadful hard it is to me," she wrote in one of her little hand-stitched journals, "because I cannot ride somewhere. Every time I have seen a horse going on a canter, since I have been out of health, it has damaged my health, & brought me back ever so far, because it is so dreadful hard to me, because I cannot ride so. Understand me, it hurts my feelings at such a rate, to see horses cantering, because I cannot ride so, that I cannot help crying about it, & that damages my health, & that is double misery. . . . Understand me, the handsomer I see them look, & the smarter I see them, the more it hurts my feelings. . . ."

On 1 January 1847, Philip Luce, "in consideration of services rendered to my perfect satisfaction," deeded Nancy his "homestead lands together with a house. . . a certain tract of meadows land. . . . Also one cow." On May 1 he died, age seventy-five.

The next year, 1848, when Nancy was twenty-eight, the selectmen of the town voted to petition the Judge of Probate, "representing that Nancy Luce. . . Single Woman, being in possession of some estate, but through Insanity and imbecility is liable to become chargeable to the Town. . . ." They asked the judge to appoint a guardian.

A second petition followed on the heels of the first. Signed by twelve townsmen, half or more of them Nancy's cousins, it stated that "the undersigned Inhabitants of Tisbury humbly represent that Nancy Luce. . . is in our opinion fully suitable to manage or superintend her own affairs without the assistance of the Town. . . . " The two physicians living in the town also signed.

Several months later the judge ruled in Nancy's favor. No guardian was appointed. Three years later, in 1851, Nancy's mother, Anna Manter Luce died. From then until her own death thirty-nine years later, Nancy lived without another human in the house.

Her parents gone, Nancy picked up. In 1852 she was able to knit again—and trade. She bartered socks and butter for coffee, bicarbonate of soda, and tobacco. In 1855, like her father before her, she was selling off land to meet expenses. She was having the house repaired. That year she wrote Dr. Luce asking for port wine in exchange for blue mixed stockings if the doctor thinks wine will do her good; also for "a small tite barrel to catch water in," in exchange for garden truck.

In February, 1858, Ada Queetie, one of the little hearts, died. A small aging hen and close companion to a 38-year-old woman on lonely Tiah's Cove Road, passed out at midnight in the dead of winter.

Later that year, in October, at the annual Agricultural Fair in West Tisbury, Nancy sold her cow, perhaps the one she inherited from her father. The event called for a poem:

Poor Sarah Wilbor must be hurled a way off,
In the 15th year and a half of her age,
After she had been here 13 years and 5 months,
Only I did do it,
She always behaved well with me,
And never tempted to hook nor kick me,
And always minded all I said to her,
She was carried off the 27th of October,
Susannah Allen was brought the 16th of November 1858.

The following year saw Beauty Linna die in the small hours of a January morning. Nancy buried her in the graveyard surrounded by a seven-foot board fence that adjoined the east end of her house. Two marble headstones with which she honored her hens—much finer stones than the one she herself lies under—eventually traveled further than tombstones usually do. After Nancy's death they went first to the West Tisbury Public Library, then to the grounds of the Dukes County Historical Society in Edgartown where they now rest.

The doctor who helped and patched along Nancy's complaints, William H. Luce, was a neighbor and native Vineyarder, an 1840 graduate of the Medical School of Bowdoin College. In the early 19th century Luce was the surname most often encountered on the island. If all who bore the name shared a common ancestor, there nevertheless were Luces and Luces. William H. Luce and Nancy Luce belonged to separate families.

Dr. Luce, six years older than Nancy, had his home and apothecary's shop in West Tisbury village, less than two miles from Tiah's Cove. All her adult life Nancy took him her problems. From time to time she would ask a neighbor to deliver a letter to him. In 1860, when she was getting ready to declare herself—that is, have her poems printed—she consulted him about an important matter.

Dr W H Luce
I want to know how your health is.
Another thing is, you willing to be so kind as to let me know how to spell the names of my poor deceased friends, do you know certain how

to spell them to be on sure grounds to always have them sounded out on a, just as I used to speak them, if I put a to the end of their names as I used to do, they will sound them on r, that must not be. I used to spell them Ada Queta, Beauty Lina, now I spell them Ady Queety, Beauty Linny. I ain't suited yet, to spell them right, to have them sounded out on a. If you know, do be so kind as to write them to me on this paper.

Nancy Luce

Nancy, not surprisingly, had an ear for speech as it was spoken. She knew Tiah's was Tyer's to most Vineyarders; Martha's pronounced as if spelled Mather's. Ella was Eller; Celia, Cely. A poet, Nancy cared about words and especially about the names she invented. Dr. Luce, as requested, replied on the same page.

If you wish to sound the a *long* you must put the mark over it so—a— that indicated that it is sounded as in day bay etc & not like r—as in short a. Or you can add the y or—ie—is very fashionable now as— *Addie Queetie, Beautie Linnie*, the *ie* here sounds like long e——

In haste
W H Luce

Poor Little Hearts, sixteen pages printed at Nancy's expense, did not appear until 1866. In addition to the title poem, it contained seven shorter pieces in verse and prose. Nancy drew the device for the title page and wrote the caption, "This heart with a little one in it/Is to give you to understand/That hearts can be united."

Copies of *Poor Little Hearts* are exceedingly rare. I know of two only —one in the library of the Dukes County Historical Society, the other in the Harris Collection of American Poetry at Brown University in Providence.

In 1871, and three times thereafter, Nancy got out what she called *A Complete Edition of the Works of Nancy Luce, of West Tisbury. . . .* This 32-page booklet, also rare, included her prose treatise, "Hens— Their Diseases and Cure." Nancy called herself a "doctor of hens."

"Human, do understand how to raise up sick hens to health," she begins. "Some folks do not know how to doctor hens, they doctor them wrong, it hurts them, and it is dreadful cruel to let them die. It is as distressing to dumb creatures to undergo sickness, and death, as it is for human, and as distressing to be crueled, and. . . to suffer. God requires human to take good care of dumb creatures, and be kind to them, or not keep any. Now do understand, and I will tell you exact." And she does. Specific home remedies and instructions follow for treating some gallinaceous ailments. Gapes, for example.

"Gapes—If a hen or chicken gapes a great deal. . . and complains of her throat, make pills of black pepper, cream, white flour, and. . . make her swallow it. . . the black pepper kills the worms. I cure them so." Although Nancy's subject was doctoring hens, her theme was the same you find in her poems, feeling and friendship for the race of dumb animals. While speaking of hens she includes some first-rate advice concerning the feeding of cows. And she also inserted a paragraph about birds.

"Birds—When I step down to the door, the little harmless birds come fly down on the ground, only one yard off my feet, and some of them a half yard off my feet. I give them oats and dough to eat; they eat it. Will they come to anyone else? So few folks have feeling." St. Francis, tradition says, preached to the birds. Nancy Luce, by her own account, fed them.

In *Martha's Vineyard Summer Resort 1835–1935*, in a chapter entitled "A Woman and Her Hens," Henry Beetle Hough wrote that Nancy "was an attraction in summer life ranking with the Katama clambakes, the illuminations, and the meetings in the Tabernacle." According to Mr. Hough, camp meeting people visiting Oak Bluffs in the 1860's heard of her "largely through the influence of livery stable keepers who took their fares on the long drive from the camp ground, through the village of Holmes Hole [Vineyard Haven], over the road up-Island. . . to the home of Nancy Luce. The drive was an adventure, and the woman of the hens was a 'character'. . . ."

Nancy's booklet of poems and photographs of her were on sale at the Oak Bluffs camp meeting grounds down-island. Up-island, she sold them at home, twenty-five cents a copy for either.

Among the papers Nancy Luce left, and which the town sold after her death to pay for her burial, is a photograph of her. Seated in a high-backed Windsor chair, she looks melancholy, haunted, and haunting. On her lap she holds a white hen. An inscription she printed in fanciful letters embroidered with hearts reads, *Miss Nancy Luce*, and below her name is the name of the bird, T. T. B. Pinky. A heart and its conventional representation are Nancy's key word and emblem.

> *Poor Tewedle Dedel Bebbee Pinky*
> *Died June 19, 1871.*
> *at ¼ past 7 oc. in the eve.*
> *aged 4 yrs.*
> *Poor dear little heart*
> *Sore broke in her*
> *I am left broken hearted*
> *She was my own heart within me*
> *She had more than common wit*
> *She is taken from the evil to come.*

Although playing her role as poet and character brought Nancy some cash, it also added to her problems—problems that doubtless were already there. They would be for anyone so deviant. An anonymous contributor to the *Atlantic Monthly*, October, 1892, reports a visit to Nancy in 1887 when she was sixty-seven:

"I see again the old gray-shingled front of her dwelling, startlingly set off by the green door and window casings, and attracting further attention by this sign, close to its entrance:—

'I forbid all persons coming here on the Sabbath.

Nancy Luce.'

"On the right a high board fence is set thickly with three rows of nails that suggest a question which is answered by many tales afloat on the island. We were told that Miss Nancy underwent malicious teasing which sometimes amounted to torture; not from her neighbors or any of the islanders, it is justice to say, but from strange visitors. . . . "

The writer stated that Nancy no longer appeared "as represented in the frontispiece of her odd pamphlet, or as, in her best days. . . . She is a grotesque figure. . . . Over her head, down on her forehead, and close under her chin, so that not one strand of hair is visible, is drawn a thick woolen hood. This accents the unusual length and pallor of her face. . . . Her dark, heavy eyes, unshaded by lashes, are eloquent of pain and reproach. But it is her hands that bear chief witness to her sufferings."

Not only the hands gave testimony but also what the hands wrote, and the changes in the handwriting. Ridicule can kill the creative impulse. Like many a poet, prophet or oddball in her own country, in this case an insular New England town, Nancy Luce was dishonored. The "teasing which sometimes amounted to torture" was not the work of "strange visitors"—as Vineyarders by and large must have known—but rather the work of homegrown young persons of both sexes. In fact, baiting

Nancy was quite a popular sport. You could serenade her with pots and pans, as she noted in her diary jottings, or bang on the side door, rattle the pantry window, heave rocks and logs over the fence and into the graveyard for hens, gather up cow dung and plaster it around her front door, or stand in the yard or road and just cuss her out. She recorded these encounters with "murderers," "gross sinners," and "stone hearts," as she called them, and the records survive.

Cousins on the distaff side proved solid friends. Nancy's mother had been the daughter of an early George Manter and his wife, Sarah Athearn Manter. Through her mother, Nancy related to two of Tisbury's leading tribes. She may have been kin to Jenny Lind Athearn, a 19th-century Vineyard lady and inhabitant of Scrubby Neck, who belted out hymns at the pasture gate to call the cattle home.

"A Well-Known Person Dead," read the headline in the *Vineyard Gazette*, 18 April 1890. Spelling her name in the fashionable way Dr. Luce referred to many years earlier, the long obituary said, "Miss Nancie Luce, who died on the 9th inst., was the daughter of the late Philip and Annie Luce. When quite young she manifested a desire for business, and for a while she bought and sold dry goods. Her principal amusement was horseback riding. 'The comfort of life,' as she called it. . . .

". . . During the last thirty years hundreds of people have visited her. . . .

"Miss Luce has been in very feeble health for the last two years, yet she lived alone. She positively refused to leave her home or have anyone to tarry with her. Her neighbors have been very kind in attending to her wants; but it so happened that no one came in from Saturday morning until Monday noon, and in the meantime she had fallen and was unable to help herself. After her situation was discovered she was carefully attended to, but soon went into an unconscious state and died on the following Wednesday. She lived a moral life, the Golden Rule being her motto. . . . "

North of West Tisbury village, at a bend in the road, one finds Nancy's grave. She lies under one of the plainest stones in the cemetery's three acres. "Nancy Luce. Died Apr. 9, 1890, Aged 79," says the inscription. It is incorrect. Since Nancy was born in 1820, she was 69, not 79, when she died—not as old as her townspeople thought, or as she evidently had looked.

Nancy's will said, "To my neighbor Mary Vincent. . . my Yellow Bureau. She has been kind to me when murderers were murdering me. . . . To George W. Manter of Tisbury, who is the man to see to my graves, all the rest and residue of my Estate both Real and Personal. . . ." The real estate, however, had long since been deeded to Dr. Luce. The residue of personal property consisted of unpublished poems and photographs not included in the papers sold by the town.

Among the Manter memorabilia is a moth-eaten photograph of Nancy seated outside by the open front door of her house. On her left, head down, stands an ill-favored cow. Built like a beef breed more than a dairy cow—body short and thick, coat rough, and udder misshapen, she looks like a piney woods scrub. Is she, perchance, the cow named Red Cannon by Nancy, and to whom she wrote on a scrap of brown paper, *Red Cannon's Failings*?

> *Loud noise. Keep their noise going.*
> *Won't eat blackgrass hay.*
> *Raven for company*
> *Won't come to be milked.*
> *Go dry half their time when with calf.*
> *Kick. Fluk.*
> *Give little milk. Thin milk.*
> *Rank milk. Hold up her milk.*
> *Milk sour quick. Milk hard.*
> *Horns long forward or turn back.*
> *Horns large. Horns sprawl out to sides.*
> *Hook me. Red cow.*
> *Cream go up top in one night, milk not fit to use.*
> *One part of cow large.*
> *Skittish.*
> *Jump. Hook down fence.*
> *Mash down fence.*
> *Run head through fence.*
> *Meet cattle to fence and hook it down and won't come away.*
> *Can't be governed when she has unclean spirit in her.*
> *Short teats,*
> *Bloody milk.*

Few poets down the ages have sung about cows. Few have celebrated the wit and laughter of hens. Nancy Luce's original, and in that sense primitive view, her subtle syncopation, her discordant grammar but concordant style, may leave a small but enduring trace in a land where time seems always past, and the epitaph is vanishing.

Chapter 9

CHILMARK DIARY

A July-foggy morning, wind south-southwest. Rain came and it hypnotized. I looked at landscape through streaming-down water. Misty hills and headlands appeared Japanese. The rain slacked off, then came pelting again.

An afternoon of exquisite grays followed, gray-white and silver and green-gray breakers. Very few went to Squibnocket Beach today, but those who did found it pleasant enough. A few children showed up, and young men with surfboards and female companions.

I walked down a long stretch of yellow-gray sand, past windrows of glistening wet seaweed. Returning, I saw in the dunes a pink-lavender beach pea in bloom; by a roadside wasteplace, a cluster of violet night-shade. You tend to see what you know the name of. Old friends salute; unknowns pass by. A year-round resident, noting that I had been swimming, expressed surprise. Or was it horror or even disgust? "I shall go

125

swimming in September and October," she called out, "when the water's warmed up."

Sixty-six degrees in the morning, and breezy. Cyril Norton, on parking-duty at Squibnocket Beach, said that the small black flies which day before yesterday "raised hell" with him, today had gone with the wind. While speaking he carefully inspected his forearms.

On Squibnocket Bight, a short piece east of the beach, the ocean breaks against a tumble of boulders lying on the edge of the strand and extending into the water. I focused on a particular rock. A wave rolling shoreward struck and then curled around it, then another wave came, another, another. Water that shapes, stone that withstands—the beholder also resisting, and also, inevitably yielding.

Warm sand at my back, sweet air in my face, the ocean as far as the Bay of Biscay before me—and down the beach, a few people, a few souls humanizing the sand, and a couple of swallows, bank swallows, or maybe rough-winged—they also leavened the impersonality of the unfinished shore and water. Life here is measured by great moments, which might last several hours—until you become too hot, cold, hungry, or thirsty. Most likely the last comes first.

Foggy rain, the kind that only a few like to walk in; south wind and varying fog. Over Squibnocket Beach the fog-beset air was lemonade yellowish-green. Wading at low tide among the rocks, I found them festooned with seaweeds and slimy secretions, and encrusted with snails and barnacles in their uncounted thousands. The calcified, permanently attached acorn or rock barnacle is a different crustacean from the goose barnacle, often encountered on floating logs and ship bottoms, fastened by a leathery stalk. It was, all in all, a primeval scene, but modified by several pieces of scantling drifting ashore. I hauled them onto the beach, then carried them home—for the satisfaction inherent in salvage, and also because I had use for them.

"Squibnocket Beach reserved," said the sign, "for Chilmark residents, property owners, their guests and lessees." Property owner is by no means the same as resident. Property owners in Chilmark are many, residents rather few. One may or may not be both. The distinction is that only residents vote in town meeting. A difference in season plays a part, too. Town meeting is held in the other phase of the cycle—not in July, but in February.

Cyril Norton, standing beside the sign and guarding town interests, consulted his stem winder. "One o'clock," he said, and added, "by the old time." He meant Eastern Standard, not Daylight Saving. Some find this confusing. He did not.

At nine in the morning—eight by the old time—a hot yellow sun glared through mist and fog, ghastly as the eye of the Ancient Mariner.

As I came from the Quitsa Pond shore, I saw in the southwest corner of the meadow two saucer shapes, succulent looking and each of them four or five inches across. I could almost taste them sautéd—the brown-gilled horse, or meadow mushroom, *Agaricus arvensis*, cousins to the common market variety but very much bigger, meatier, and gamier. As I approached, I saw, alas, not the genus *Agaricus* but rather the genus *Amanita*. *Amanita muscaria*, the fly amanita or false orange, cousin to the destroying angel, is poisonous and very beautiful. Bright yellow-orange warty caps—and some little ones, buttons, coming along. They brightened the corner and kept me from being unduly affected by nature, slushy about it, and that way misunderstanding it.

Oh, the nifty bobwhite—the quail, that is—looking like a small ruddy chicken gone wild and smart. Few birds are called by the sounds they make. As a job of naming, bobwhite was careless. Should have been "bobwhoit," or "poor bobwhoit," but its voice agrees with the way it looks. Its clean clear-edged call fits the shape and size of the bird and makes all July days delightful.

Swamp rose, pasture rose, northeastern rose with bristling canes, and sweetbrier, all wild and all pink, were blooming. Spires of hardhack or steeplebush rose in ungrazed pastures. The season was pink. On sheep laurel other pink flowers clustered. Sheep laurel, also called lambkill, is said to be lethal for sheep but fine browse for deer. Is it either, or is it part of the folklore, the unscientific approach to wildflowers? Certainly nothing could look more innocent than the small cup-shape flowers of lambkill.

I do not find rare plants more pleasing than everyday sorts, but rather the other way round. On a knoll a thousand feet back from the North Road in Chilmark, I found a colony of Conrad's Broom-Crowberry, *Corema conradii Torrey*, alleged to be the rarest plant on the Vineyard. Ground cover resembling a minature shrubby evergreen, it is a charming variation, and more of it would be more so. Upwards of twenty thousand kinds of plants and wildflowers grow in America, say the botanists. Clearly, one is not called upon to know or love all, but only some.

Fog, the thickest kind of vapor. Damp tobacco, damper matches. Fog-moistened floor. My shoes stick to it.

In his fisherman's shack on the mole at Menemsha Basin, Captain Donald LeMar Poole sat on an old sea chest, an heirloom, and looked out the open door. The worst July weather he can recall, he said. Two hundred thirty lobster pots set and so far this month he had hauled them only four times. He could not go out. Too much fog. Three days ago he hauled 114 pots and brought in only sixty-six lobsters. His usual routine is to haul half the pots one day, half the next, and then spend the third day ashore, cutting bait, repairing gear, and working around the boat. He aimed to spend twenty to twenty-two days afloat in July, but the way things were going this summer. . . . The fog, he said, frays his nerves. He finds the fog creepy, crawly, disagreeable, and treacherous, and it softens the lobster bait. Everything in his shack was damp—including the old chair he keeps handy for callers. To those who know him, his shack is a center of sociability, maritime information, all manner of spare marine parts and fittings, island history, lore of the sea and whaling.

I mentioned, in passing, my longshore lumber. Salvage is, after all, sweet. "I hear there's a fair amount on the beach," Captain Poole said. He suspected a lot of it comes from naval and other government installations. "They never save anything in the Navy." Much of it, he said, is dunnage—pieces of wood laid on the bottoms of holds for cargo to rest on, or stowed among cargo to prevent motion and chafing. Cargo discharged, dunnage is often pitched overboard when the vessel puts to sea again.

"Gathering longshore lumber was a usual part of the way of life on the Vineyard fifty years ago. A man would hitch up a team of horses or oxen and spend a day, or an afternoon, combing the beach." Very few, he added, can now comprehend that bygone Yankee way of life. His uncle's house—a small sturdy dwelling that squats on a knoll within view of all who pass along the State Road—was framed and boarded with longshore lumber. The same uncle warned him that some day the last of the Yankees would be rounded up and placed on reservations like the Indians who preceded them.

Speaking of that reminded Captain Poole of a Chilmark man who inherited from his mother's brother on condition that he erect a suitable stone to the memory of his uncle. The uncle had been a money-lender, had amassed what was then thought to be quite a sum. After he died the nephew ordered a fine stone set up with these words incised.

Here lies Old Twelve and a Half Percent.
The more he lent the less he spent.
The more he had the more he craved.
O God, can Ichabod be saved?

The inscription, Captain Poole conceded, can no longer be found in Chilmark's burial ground. The oral tradition remains, however, a legend outlasting granite.

Although Captain Poole did not like the fog, there was much to be said in its favor. Boats tied up in the Basin—and the Basin itself achieved foggy picturesque strangeness. So did the grizzled sea dog, or copy thereof, sculling about in an orange dory. Fog wiped away houses, the farther shore; and fog warmed the water.

Lobstermen, yachtsmen, people with small children—all dislike it. But surfboard riders did not seem to mind, nor walkers.

Nor the dumpmaster. Foggy damp days are fine for burning. Only mid-July and the Chilmark dump trench was filling at an amazing rate. The dump said many people are here. And more herring gulls may have been prowling the dump, yellow-eyed and alert, than Menemsha harbor and basin.

The trench, deep enough to trap a tank, eighty-feet long and fifteen wide, slices into a twelve-acre tract of wooded land on Tabor House Road. Very few persons spend time in Chilmark without discovering where it is—between the North and Middle roads. Summers, the dumpmaster works at the dump about one day a week. Despite the generous size of the trench, ample space for driving in, unloading, and then driving out again, it is surprising how many people will miss. Some customers doubtless have poor aim, others may fear falling in. In either case, there it lies—where they discharge it. Using a burned down old hayfork—or is it a dung fork?—the dumpmaster puts it where it belongs, at $1.40 an hour.

Dump management is in his hands. When the middens rise, and the paper and garbage and brush piles need burning, and wind and weather seem right, the dumpmaster phones the Fire Chief; "I think I'll go to the dump today," he says. The chief knows what he means.

If, in the fire chief's judgment, setting the dump on fire would not be right—the surrounding woods too dry or the winds too strong—he may tell the dumpmaster no. But, said the latter, he never has.

Although the dumpmaster likes the fog, dump-pickers do not. Foggy days and consequent burnings seem to lessen their chances, not only in Chilmark, but in Gay Head, West Tisbury, and the down-island towns.

Bird notes. Three or four barnswallows have been objecting. Now that their young have reached a size that it makes it impossible for them not to be seen—they no longer can huddle below the rim of the nest—my presence, you might say next door, annoys the old birds. The annoyance is mutual. The old birds make nerve-rasping sounds and fast swooping gestures. They threaten. Yesterday one of them flew a short piece down meadow, then rounded on me. Zoom! Today, however, the campaign is over. The young have flown—must have taken off early. Yes, the young have departed and left the usual evidence that they were here. I got out the shovel for post-hatching-season clean-up.

The small wading birds that appeared on the beach and looked very much like sandpipers were in fact plovers; thicker-necked, shorter-coupled, heavier-billed, larger-eyed than the pipers. Were they semipalmated or piping plover? Or possibly Wilson's? At the time I did not know, and now I never will.

The persistent call of the towhee—what was he saying, repeating over and over? He twirked, hiccoughed, tremoloed, took quite a shaking up each time he surged. A brave vibrato, the sound of an outgoing personality, a velocity of assurance, a flight maybe not of music but of companionship, friendship, a reiteration that he was there.

Six wild swans in stringy formation flew low, their wings throbbing, over Squibnocket Beach. Deep-bellied birds like flying boats. How they stuck their slender necks out!

One of Martha's Vineyard's fairest beaches fringes the west-southwest shore of Gay Head. Halfway between the Head and Squibnocket Point you come to dunes called Zacks Cliffs. A happy accident of forms—or so it seems—these dunes, not really cliffs at all, are somehow very pleasing. Strange vehicles make their way along trails through the old reservation lands to this beach. The departed Gay Head Indian, Granville Belain, driver of the last Vineyard ox team, combed this shore with oxen and cart. For a few years after World War II, you would have seen him there.

What was this heaving into view? It stood as though mired in the soft sand, midway between the foot of the dunes and the rim of the water.

From a distance it looked like a retail delivery van, maybe for milk or for bread. An old van is what it turned out to be, high on an ancient truck chassis, an old GMC, and converted into a mobile camp. As I walked by I noticed the oversize tires—did not want to, but I could not help it—also the lack of four-wheel drive. I walked on—did not want to think about it—but then a question arose. How does that heavy job navigate in loose sand? I turned back and so met the owner-driver-proprietor, a big round-featured sociable man dressed in sneakers and swimming trunks, body and face mushroom white. He introduced himself, Ray Graboy, repairman, Waterbury. Also a welder, he said. He looked as though he had lived in the glare of the torch—and his vehicle, too—the latter a true fancywork of patches and welds.

Seems that some years ago Mr. and Mrs. Graboy and their young set out on a camping expedition. They had rented a cabin in Harwich, Cape Cod, but when they arrived it was already occupied—a misunderstanding—so they turned around and drove home again. The experience decided Mr. Graboy. Henceforth, they would take their camp with them. On wheels. And so he built this—not built, precisely, but rather adapted and welded, and camped in it many years. Now that the kids had grown up and gone off, he and the wife, he said, camp it alone.

How does he travel in sand? By deflating the tires. He lowers the pressure to twelve pounds in front, fifteen in the rear. It also depends on the kind of sand. If the walking is difficult, so is the driving. When he cannot make it on fifteen pounds, he drops to fourteen—one pound of air can make the difference. He pointed to a pump mounted on the front bumper, and connected to the crankshaft—where the old starting crank used to be. After the deflation comes the inflation. The workingman's version of the land rover.

While Mr. Graboy and I were talking, Mrs. Graboy, a big pale woman dressed in a homemade bathing suit, was frying potatoes and onions. It was two o'clock in the afternoon. Windows and doors of the camp were wide open. The smell of how many years of camping and frying wafted poignantly on the salt air.

"I'm no money man," Mr. Graboy said, "I'm a repairman, but I like to enjoy life. I try to enjoy part of every day." No day is complete, he said, until he has enjoyed at least a part of it. Enjoyment day by day, as though each day might be his last—a personal philosophy. A man who appeared to be his own man. Philosophers, like some kinds of bums, love the beach.

You go down to the beach and see it more crowded and yet discover fewer people you know. This is a thing my generation is learning. So the question arises naturally, are the new summer people as nice summer people as we were when we were new? They probably are—and different, too. They have made their way by different devices. Their equipment is different. We used to go down with a rag of a towel. They go with transistor radio. They have made their way by different devices, and their different devices, inevitably, have made their way to the beach.

If measurable change has been going on all along, why is change now so apparent? Because this summer you see the table is set. First someone puts a knife on the table—you hardly notice. Then someone else adds a fork—and another, a spoon. Comes a napkin, saltshaker, pepper grinder, plate. Then an airlines-type plastic glass. Suddenly the table is set, and suddenly you see the difference.

A persistent fog frosting. Wet flourishing greenery, white viburnum and wild pink roses shone on the moors. In the highlands of Chilmark, between Peaked and Abel Hills, near Fulling Mill Brook, and about 165 feet above sea level, I found what looked like lily-of-the-valley, but I knew it was not. It was waxy white, shinleaf, one of the wintergreen family, standing tall on scaly scape, its leaves half buried in woodland mulch. In old England, they say country people used the leaves as balm for barked shins and other bruises; shinleaf meaning shinplaster.

And close by the shinleaf, common St. John's-wort, yellow-dun-flowered and bushy. Rural healers will tell you it drives away evil spirits, evil eye, and melancholia. If so, this should have been a healthy place. I could see how St. John's-wort might also drive away farmers. Common, weedy, thirty-five species, and some of them six feet tall. Were blossoming branches of common wild brambles, blackberries, etc., less familiar and ordinary, their beauty might be more admired.

Wet sand of Squibnocket at low tide. Young men on beached surf boards sleeping in rain; wet towels—their flags—hanging from upended longshore lumber. They added a touch of human beauty. A woman wandering among the rocks at the water's edge bent down to gather mussels.

I settled against the contouring dune beside a half-burned campfire log. A great scantling six feet by six feet lay on the lower beach. Luck to the back that carries it home! Age-old rocks, the gray sea breaking, and fog banking over the sea. A clump of pale beach grass thriving in gray-white sand. Curving line of the littoral. Headlands with green meadows on them. Coast line of island and northern ocean.

Now in the foreground of the water, among the mortal stones and boulders, a brown object rolled. Or did it? Seaweed? Shadow? Wash of surf? No, no, it rode the dying waves. I waded out, picked up a round metal float with fag end of rope yarn and sea weed attached, rusted, sea-changed, beautiful.

Days and scenes not to tell about, but rather to be part of. Everything spoke. The piping plover—or was it the semipalmated?—sprinted down the strand, making short flights and sounding a beeping call. A cry of pleasure. The expert ornithologist may not agree but it sounded so to me.

An early morning fog burned off. Ragged streaks of blue showed through the unraveling clouds. In mid-afternoon the sky grew patchy, blue in the gray and white. Then sun broke through. Suddenly the day was fair.

The parking lot filled, the beach became crowded. Cyril Norton said, "I cannot please everybody." Some people bring their own bad weather.

Jewels of seaweed encrusted with seashells, lavender mussel and comb-shaped cockle shells thrown away by the outgoing tide lay on the beach in perfect arrangements, and fine-lined landscapes drawn on wet sand by receding waves told fathomless tales of the sea.

Hills rising as high as three hundred feet, and remnants of farms going down to the edge of salt water, seem to me the distinguishing features of Chilmark. The historian of Martha's Vineyard, Charles Edward Banks, M.D., says Chilmark was a farming town from the beginning, that is, since 1714. Writing in 1908, Dr. Banks summed up the way it was in his time. His inventory reads: acres of land assessed, 10,436; number of dwelling houses, 171; horses, 111; cows, 115; other cattle, 93; sheep, 2,145. The figures came from the annual town report. Today's resident voters no longer tabulate livestock. For good reason. In fact, the last round-up slipped by unnoticed.

In the very recent past, driving along South Road any mild weather evening, you could see in a certain Chilmark pasture, two or three cows standing on a knoll, waiting, silhouetted against sea and sky. But the cows are not there now.

An abandoned barn near Wellfleet

A sheep, a rare sight today: less and less livestock are kept on Martha's Vineyard

Former pasture studded with native junipers

Pearly everlasting (*Anaphalis margaritacea*) belongs to the sun-
flower family and grows in great abundance on Vineyard roadsides.
This is the cherished New England flower often dried and kept in tight
little bundles in the parlor all winter

A thick patch of fleabane daisy (*Erigeron annuus*) and among the tiny flowers, two kinds of goldenrod: Canadian goldenrod (*Solidago canadenis*) and the seaside goldenrod, (*Solidago sempervirens*). The latter, shorter, deeply golden and thicker, is found mostly along the seashore, and like scrub pine, thrives on practically nothing at all

Another view of Canadian goldenrod. In richer soils, it produces a proud, tall stem laden with flowers

The aim of all that dazzle: fertilized seedpods

Chapter 10

ELIZABETH ISLANDS

Dukes County, which includes Martha's Vineyard, also embraces an archipelago called the Elizabeth Islands. Sixteen in all, counting ledges and rocks, these islands form a tail end of Buzzards Bay-Sandwich moraine. Extending southwestward fifteen miles from Woods Hole, they divide the waters of Buzzards Bay from those of Vineyard Sound.

For almost two hundred years the Elizabeth Islands were tied to the town of Chilmark. In 1864, however, they won political independence. They became the Town of Gosnold, named in honor of the discoverer, Captain Bartholomew Gosnold.

Northeast to southwest, reading the map right to left, the main Elizabeth Islands are Nonamessett, Naushon, Pasque, Nashawena, and Cuttyhunk—all Algonquian names, or approximations.

From the beach at Menemsha on Martha's Vineyard, you see them standing in a line, paralleling the Vineyard's north shore. Although only five or six miles away, they nevertheless appear distant. In summer they often are shrouded in haze. Often they loom like a gray-blue continuous coast. Many days they vanish in fog. Seen on a clear day, however, when the wind breezes from the north, the Elizabeth Islands seem to move closer. At such times each link rises clean and abrupt like a chain of low mountains with watery rifts between. Rolling or hilly, some hillsides furrowed with valleys, the islands present sun-bleached concave faces, cliffs of pale yellow clay and sand. Big rocks and boulders lie scattered about. You can see a few landing beaches. At Tarpaulin Cove on Naushon, the longest and largest island, a black and white light tower rises. An old Lighthouse Service report refers to the place as a "small indent in the shores of Nashawn Island, where coasters frequently anchor when met by head winds." Like many Indian names, Naushon answers to various spellings. Except on Cuttyhunk, the outermost island, one discerns very few buildings. The fact that all except Cuttyhunk are not occupied in the usual way makes a pleasing contrast with the surrounding region. Settlement never gained much of a hold on these islands.

Naushon, the largest island—eight miles long and two wide—has long been a private preserve. In *The History of Martha's Vineyard*, Volume II, *Annals of Gosnold*, Charles Edward Banks, M.D. wrote that when Major General Wait Still Winthrop bought Naushon in 1682, "it became the suburban estate of a man of wealth and culture who made it his playground and proceeded to develop it as such." Winthrop's heirs sold Naushon and adjunct islands to the east to James Bowdoin, also of Boston. Bowdoin's descendants held on for more than one hundred years. Then in the middle of the 19th century John Murray Forbes (1813–1898) of Milton, Massachusetts, who made a fortune in the old China trade and later became a railroad builder, purchased the Bowdoin holdings. Early in the 20th century Forbes kinsmen bought Nashawena, second largest of the Elizabeths. Other relatives bought Pasque. Today, all Elizabeth Islands except Cuttyhunk and Penikese—the latter a Buzzards Bay refuge for nesting seabirds, property of the Massachusetts Division of Fisheries and Game—are owned by the Forbes family in association. So these islands have been spared. Neither private nor public development has as yet overtaken them. A joy to the eye, they remain a rare ornament to the country and coast.

~~~~~~

In August, 1968, I called on Joseph Howes at his home in West Tisbury village. Born in Harwich on Cape Cod, 17 December 1874, he was ninety-three when I saw him, a ruddy well-looking countryman, tall and large-framed. It was 1886, he told me, when he was twelve, that he went with his parents and an older brother to live at Tarpaulin Cove on Naushon.

Tarpaulin Cove, about midway through Vineyard Sound, was in those days a port of call for coasters carrying coal, lumber, lime, and cement. Joseph Howes said he could remember when "125 vessels lay piled up there, waiting for the tide to change." The coasters, he said, depended on tide as much as on wind.

Joseph Howes' older brother, Ensign E. Howes, leased Tarpaulin Cove Farm, 2,010 acres, from John Murray Forbes, the then master of Naushon. Although Naushon was owned by Mr. Forbes, the federal government kept a post office and a customs house at the Cove, as well as the beacon light. The Seamen's Aid Society of Boston maintained a reading room and chapel. Sometimes women went to Naushon to sing and pray with the sailors. Joseph Howes said it was not unusual to see one hundred persons ashore. The Howes family handled the mail, one or two bags of letters and papers a day addressed to ships calling there. They also ran a ship's store.

Concerning the farm, Joseph Howes recalled four or five horses, twelve cows, some young stock and one thousand sheep. He said there was a good well of water, "and everything we wanted—garden, fowl, sheep, beef—never lived better—and plenty of milk and cream." He and his brother sold fresh milk in the harbor. "There was always someone there," Joseph Howes said, "never a day without a boat." But there was no school. For two winters Joseph Howes went to class in his native Harwich. That was only a little less schooling than that received by the average American of his day.

When United States Coast and Geodetic surveyors came to plot the topography of the Elizabeth Islands, they hired Joseph Howes to assist. In 1892, when the present light tower was built, he and his brother carted the brick and cement for the tower wall, which was laid up five courses thick. They also tended the fog bell. Activated by weights, it required winding up every four hours. And weather signals had to be set on flag poles. Weather reports reached Tarpaulin Cove over a government telephone line.

"Naushon is a beautiful island," Joseph Howes said. Although the hurricane of 1938 took down many big trees—in his words, "cut swathes through the beech orchard"—some of the last virgin timber in the east still stands on Naushon.

A beautiful island, and also confining. "What kind of killed the monotony," Joseph Howes said, "was captains coming ashore." At such times there would be presents of Jamaica rum, and gin in square bottles, four to a box, for his father and brother. His father once bought one thousand cigars from a skipper. Joseph Howes smiled as he remembered that.

"Shipping was very busy when we went to Tarpaulin Cove," he said. But only nine years later, coastwise traffic through Vineyard Sound was dying. Railroads were killing it off. When the third three-year lease on the farm expired, the older brother did not renew. No one called for fresh milk any longer, or came to the store to buy. The great fleets of schooners and brigs had all but vanished. Joseph Howes and his family pulled out of Naushon in 1894. As the last of the wind-driven ships sailed away, the customs house shut its doors. The post office closed down later.

A light wind breezed from the north, and Naushon stood shining in the sun. In Menemsha with Captain Donald LeMar Poole, I boarded his 31-foot lobster boat. "It's a relief to get out on the water, particularly today," Captain Poole said as he stood at the wheel of the *Dorothy C.* and steered a northeasterly course across Vineyard Sound. We were bound for Tapaulin Cove. As the slow boat forged her way through the waves, none of them more than three inches high, and Menemsha fell further astern, Captain Poole continued, "It always makes me uneasy to be on the shore, particularly on a nice day. The Lord wouldn't have made the world three-quarters water if he hadn't meant man to be on it. The land is only a place to go to fit out for another trip." Captain Poole had fitted out for the trip he expected to make tomorrow. Two barrels of lobster bait, putrifying fish parts, were already on board. They exuded a heavy aroma. Captain Poole, long seasoned in the profession, said he does not notice the smell. Mercifully, hard rain fell during the night, washing down the *Dorothy C.* and sweetening her some.

Seen from Vineyard Sound, and close to the water, Martha's Vineyard shows a high skyline. Much of its coast is steep and beautifully lined. As the *Dorothy C.* drove eastward, we passed Paint Mill Bight on the Vineyard's north shore. Years ago a barn paint was made there from local red clay. The clay was ground and mixed with skim milk. We slid by the ruins of the brick yard chimney, remnant of another enterprise involving local red clay—and also a loser. In spite of the brick manufactory, brick houses and barns were always scarce on the Vineyard. As it came abeam, Captain Poole pointed out Great Rock Bight, once a lobsterman's landmark. "There used to be lobstering in the Sound," he said, "but the draggers broke up the mussel concentration. The bottom is all sand now, and lobsters won't stay on sand." And just as well, he philosophized, for the draggers would sweep up all the lobstermen's gear. He knocked out, refilled, and lit his pipe.

From Menemsha to Tarpaulin Cove is about seven miles. Coming closer to Naushon, I saw it looks much like the Vineyard, but smaller and lower. And when you stop to think about it, there is no reason for it to look very different.

"I haven't been here since I was married forty-three years ago," Captain Poole said as we ranged ahead. Naushon's hills softened in their aspect, and the foliage got bigger. It was going to be all right to go ashore, he added. He had permission. We might land—providing we went without guns and left no litter.

This was indeed good news, because as we made for the Cove, it seemed to me as lovely a harbor as a man might come into in all the region. There were others this day who perhaps thought so too. Coming across Vineyard Sound, Captain Poole had counted sixty-one pleasure craft. Inside the Cove he now found thirty-one more. "Makes you realize what leisure has done for people," he said while the *Dorothy C.*, turning her engine slowly, lay to.

Deeper than a basin, shaped more like a bowl, Tarpaulin Cove looks like a painting of a romantic and idyllic coast—charming, endearing, and intimating true good. To port, on the edge of the Cove, rises the little white light tower, trimmed in black. This is the tower for which Joseph Howes carted the brick. It turned out to be a masterpiece of its kind. There, further inside the Cove, stands the big weathered farmhouse, trimmed in barn red, where Joseph Howes and his family lived three quarters of a century ago; and where they minded the post office and the ship's store. The barns that once housed horses and cows stand close beside the dwelling. A couple of short bleached poles remain, relics of the government telephone line that carried weather news over two strands of bare and doubtless humming wire. An isolated old tupelo tree resignedly makes its characteristic gesture. "Cares roll off your shoulders in a place like this," Captain Poole said as he hauled an anchor from a locker forward, and after carefully choosing the spot, dropped it over the side.

Keeping tradition alive through usage, Captain Poole referred to the Cove by its older name, the French Watering Place. The French Watering Place, he said, is good holding ground. He untied the skiff he had towed astern and took me ashore.

On the beach at Naushon I stepped into a picture in which all the lines of landscape appeared remarkably luminous. Time seemed halted; the present, all. I felt neither idea of progress nor sentiment of nostalgia. But the real adventure had been the going rather than the arriving. Only a few feet back from the beach, the wire fence gestured halt. The island was private property and I, although harmless, was a trespasser.

Back on the fragrant *Dorothy C.*, and squaring away for Menemsha, Captain Poole explained why he picked a day when the wind was in the north. If the wind were south or southwest, the trip going home might be wet. Captain Poole, pleased and confident, pulled on his pipe. He allowed it had been the kind of day you might wait seven years for. "Never test the weather any more than you do a woman," he advised in a low twanging voice, the voice of Yankee pragmatism, the code by which seafarers live.

Westernmost of the Elizabeth Islands, two and one-half miles long, three-fourths of a mile wide, and shaped like a human embryo, Cuttyhunk was the scene of the first English colony in America, a very useful settlement although it lasted only three weeks.

To this day, Cuttyhunk remains lightly populated. Perhaps its chief importance—in addition to primitive loveliness—is its position for navigators along the New England coast. The light at the west end of Cuttyhunk, flashing every ten seconds, warns the sailor to steer clear of Sow and Pigs Reef.

You fly to Cuttyhunk or go by boat. The 51-year-old *Alert*, a 58-foot ferry, a little tramp steamer, works a regular schedule from Pier 3 in New Bedford. A white-hulled craft, trimmed in New Bedford buff, she sails Tuesdays and Fridays, September 16 to June 15. In summer, however, she makes the 28-mile round trip every day. June 15 to September 16, the population of the little island swells from about 125 persons year-round to something over 600. The *Alert* carries the mail, the food supplies, lumber, furniture, trunks, and sometimes a baby bound for an island home after having first seen the light on the mainland.

The vacation season also promotes an island-to-island route. In the summer months the *Que-tal*, a 39-foot World War II landing craft, long since decommissioned, sails twice a week from Menemsha. In summer, many travel to Cuttyhunk in their own boats.

On an August morning I boarded the *Que-tal* as she lay by the caplog at Dutcher Dock in Menemsha. A number of tourists, summer-comers, or call them pilgrims, had already embarked. The captain-owner, dressed in shorts and moccasins, paced the deck. We passengers settled ourselves on benches, some forward, others aft. "No Passengers on Mast, Wheelhouse or Pulpit—Per Order U.S. Coast Guard," read a small sign tacked at the rear of the wheelhouse. In due course a youthful crew cast off. The captain, taking the wheel, piloted the boat through the basin, the inlet, and into Menemsha Bight. Cuttyhunk lay seven miles away, about the same distance in the northwest as Tarpaulin Cove to northeast. After cruising west along Gay Head's Lobsterville shore, we bore north. Broadcasters said the day would be fair. It was not. Now fog closed in. We passengers sitting very close to the water presently dropped out of sight of land. The *Que-tal* throbbed on, the fog thickened, tension mounted. One becomes aware that Vineyard Sound, a broad band of seawater, reaches out to all oceans.

What a contrast with the trip to Naushon! On that day you felt you could reach out and touch the islands. Today you saw nothing. You do not know where you are or where anything is in this piece of water.

"Never test the weather," Captain Poole had said. The skipper of the *Que-tal* may have felt the same way. He had, however, some twenty-two fares at stake and so, understandably, pressed on, testing. His crew, deployed on pulpit and wheelhouse, listened hard for sound of the bell buoy outside the entrance to the channel betwen Nashawena and Cutty-hunk. The channel, as some of us knew, is narrow and lined with rocks. We passengers peaked our ears. The boy in the pulpit leaned over the water, eyes straining. The lad on the wheelhouse roof sounded the horn. A horn from an unseen but nearby boat suddenly answered. Lobster pot buoys appeared. The skipper clawed off: Lines from the buoys might foul the *Que-tal*'s propeller. By this time we noticed the sea was lumpy, that is, some of us did.

The knelling of the bell buoy sounded strangely muffled. The *Que-tal* made toward the sound. And there it was, emerging all at once—a floating steel tower rising black above us. In the dense fog we almost ran it down. Our skipper hove to beside the bell buoy and ordered the crew to drop anchor.

Riding at anchor, we waited for the fog to lift. The *Que-tal* rolled with the swell. Now she climbs on the crest; now she drops in the hollow. The sweet land although near, seemed far away. A young passenger smiled at the skipper, but feebly. She said she felt sick. The skipper replied that no one has ever been sick on his boat. There could be a first time, I thought. The boat wallowed, and we waited and waited till the skipper somehow knew that some of us could not wait longer.

The skipper made his decision. He would try to pick up the buoy, he said, inside the entrance to Canapitset Channel. The anchor was raised. The *Que-tal*, at reduced speed, pushed forward. Meanwhile the fog began to wear thin and some holes appeared in it. The *Que-tal* slid by boulder-strewn shores. Nashawena loomed close aboard. Rounding Cuttyhunk Coast Guard Station, our vessel entered Cuttyhunk Pond. The placid pond, an arm of the sea, forms a large harbor—perhaps a quarter the size of the land mass enclosing it—and is the one first-rate shelter for boats in the Elizabeth chain.

The *Que-tal* ranged across the harbor and nosed up to the wharf. The *Alert*, the ferry from New Bedford, was already there. We passengers, fully recovered, clambered ashore. We strolled past the shacks where the fishing guides hang out their shingles: Dick Cornell, Bob Smith, Jim Nunes, Lloyd Bosworth, Charles Tilton—Cuttyhunk names. Acting as guide to sportsmen is, and for some time has been, a chief occupation among Cuttyhunkers. Once the home of pilots up or down Vineyard Sound, or in and out of Buzzards Bay—and also of working fishermen— the island now serves the well-heeled parties whose power boats fill the berths in the large marina. I learned that only two of the islanders still lobster for a living; of the two, one is old.

Looking left over from an earlier time, Cuttyhunk makes you imagine the places heard of, as well as recall places seen. Does it resemble the fishing village called Robin Hood's Bay on the Yorkshire coast, or Irish villages off Londonderry? Or perhaps the Scots islands of Little Minch? Half-remembered scenes from touring the Azores, the fishing enclaves on São Miguel, mingle with memories of motion pictures and voyages read about. Cuttyhunk makes you think you have been here before. Fishermen's and ex-fishermen's houses squatting at random, close to the harbor, set no discernible pattern. Some have vegetable gardens; some boast a small flock of hens. Where the land is not tended or cultivated, the natural cover grows rank.

There crouches a house nearly hidden behind a wall of lobster pots, high as a man can reach. Scaled to the size of the island and its economy, most of the houses are tiny, not much bigger than some of the pleasure boats in the marina, and certainly less well equipped. In spite of the far-away, almost exotic, virtually automobileless flavor, this is, on looking closer, America. Cuttyhunk is a miniature paradigm of all the fishing resorts: sportsmen lounging in easy chairs, cheek to jowl on board bulging boats, drowsing in port on this day of uncertain weather, sleeping off the morning drinks. While a very few old-style fishermen hunt for a living, the rest of the seafaring population engages in summer business.

The air was hot, the atmosphere humid and heavy. We tourists, leaving the harbor and shore, took the road, the main street of the village, which led us uphill. The main cluster of settlement rises steeply. Tucked into the hillside, half-hidden behind its own sign, a small shedlike building houses the Cuttyhunk post office. Closed. Time for lunch. Nearby, the Bosworth House beckons. Its long dining room, garnished with anglers' trophies, felt cool as I entered, and looked inviting. I took a seat. A young woman came from the kitchen, and announced, "We have fish chowder or fish salad."

Refreshed and recruited, I returned to the street and the hill. Farther up, on the right, in a narrow lane, nestles the Cuttyhunk Store—groceries and general merchandise, the only store on the island. I walked in and bought an ice-cream cone, the tourist's comforter and friend. A stack of booklets on top of the meat case caught my eye, "The Story of Cuttyhunk," and so I bought a booklet as well. Compiled in 1952 by Louise T. Haskell, a Cuttyhunk schoolteacher for twenty-six years, her story aims to recount "the history, geography, and legends of the island for use in the schools and for sale to those who are interested." I tend my ice-cream cone and read further. "Is Cuttyhunk the scene of Shakespeare's *Tempest*?" the teacher asks—and also answers, "Who can be sure? It well might be, for Gosnold was a protegé of the Earl of Southampton as was Shakespeare: and who can tell whether or not the great playwright was enamored by the tales of the island visited by the great mariner. . . . We like to think so anyway. . . . "

Cuttyhunk abridges a long colonial history. The word "native," to the English explorer, meant a person living in the territory at the time of discovery, usually a nonwhite of less complex civilization. To the New England whaleman and seafarer, "native" carried the same connotation. City dwellers venturing along the coast later used the same word to describe the Yankee inhabitants.

Colonial overtones all down the line: At the hilltop and summit stands a 19-century American temple, the former Cuttyhunk Club, launched in 1864 by "a group of New York gentlemen," some of the elect of the era. As the finest and most expensive building by far, the clubhouse dominates the island, economically and doubtless psychologically. Land down the slope for Cuttyhunk's public buildings was donated later by the club.

In her booklet, Louise T. Haskell writes that "William Wood bought out the Cuttyhunk Club's interest in the island in 1921." Born in Edgartown on Martha's Vineyard in 1858, William Madison Wood joined the American Woolen Company, a merger of twenty-eight Massachusetts mills, in 1900. The Wood Mill of the Company became the largest single woolen mill in the world, and William Wood became the Company president. After acquiring the Cuttyhunk Club's real estate, Mr. Wood then "endeavored to buy all the property which was for sale, in an effort to make the island a summering place for himself and his friends."

But, said the former schoolteacher, writing in 1952, "many of the pilots and fishermen who had acquired property. . . wished to remain on the island. . . . " She adds that William Wood helped bring town water to Cuttyhunk, town sewage, and telephone.

Something in an acquisitive society makes a man want to be king of the mountain or, in this case, own the island. An island, even more than a mountain, stands entirely alone and complete. A domain, an undivided whole, it signifies sole rights and absolutes. In the hope of being paid off with an island, Sancho Panza left wife and children to serve the Ingenious Gentleman, Don Quixote.

But of course the real story of Cuttyhunk, or of any island, lies in the people's day-to-dayness, the restraints and freedoms of an insular way of life. This story remains to be told. Meanwhile the storekeeper, one of the friendly natives, supplied a few notes. Most of the thirty to forty families living on Cuttyhunk are related. At the present time, three children attended the school. Winters, when she is not in the store, the storekeeper said she stays at home. Were she to visit around, she added, wherever she went she would hear the same news. She suggests that while I was looking around I might like to see the church—down the alley, behind the store. "You will find the doors open. Walk in. The church serves all denominations."

I said good-bye and left the store with its crowded shelves and solacing smells. Only a few steps away stands the little wood church. I entered in ecumenical spirit, but the prospect inside was colorless, rather barren and bleak. Flanking the opposite side of the alley are three little brown buildings in a row—town hall, schoolhouse, and library. Totally absent is the village green. There is no central square. You have the feeling the dock is the place of meeting, a sort of downtown to which the men go. A village without a barroom, beauty shop, or launderette, it does, however, boast a bakery. Thirty to forty households share a group isolation: no doctor, dry cleaner, or dentist. In spite of boom times in the vacation business, Dukes County, which includes Cuttyhunk, shows the lowest median family income of any county in the state.

The road climbs to 150 feet above the surrounding sea. The fog reappears. Although it veils the view, you know nonetheless that the view is there. You can feel it. From time to time I got glimpses of Cuttyhunk Pond. By comparison with the surrounding land, it presented a vast harbor. The foreground showed a disorganized scene where wilderness elements still dominate.

I retraced my steps, descended the main street to a road near the base of the hill. This road, running along the south shore, leads to the island's West End Pond, and beyond, to Cuttyhunk Light. West End Pond, renamed Gosnold Pond, contains the islet on which, in the spring of 1602, Bartholemew Gosnold built the first house in New England, and where some of his men lived several weeks. A rough stone tower, a "Tercentenary Memorial to Bartholomew Gosnold and his Companions," marks the place, an infrequently visited monument to the navigator and pioneer of the first English settlement in America.

~~~~~~

The spotlight of history flicked at Gosnold. With more time in which to do his work, it might have focused on him. The oldest son of a Suffolk squire, he was born about 1572. He attended Cambridge University. In March, 1602, he sailed from Falmouth in Cornwall, England, with thirty-one men aboard the small bark *Concord*, seeking gold and also a passage through the continent to the south sea. Taking a short route across the Atlantic, he made a landfall on the coast of Maine. He then turned south, sailed into Cape Cod Bay, and discovered the foreland he named Cape Cod. He spent an afternoon ashore on the cape with John Brereton, a shipmate and fellow cantabrigian, who later wrote an account of the voyage. After skirting the Cape's outer shore and doubling Nantucket, Gosnold passed through Muskeget Channel between Nantucket and Martha's Vineyard. He explored Nantucket Sound, traversed Vineyard Sound, rounded Cuttyhunk, anchored and landed. Leaving some of his men to build the kind of house they thought they needed on the islet in what is now called Gosnold Pond, he cruised Buzzards Bay, probing for a westward passage. Failing to find it, he sailed back to Cuttyhunk. There he learned that none of his crew would stay on in the house they had built. Everyone wanted to go home to England. In the hope now of making a saving voyage, that is, one incurring no loss to the backers, Captain Gosnold cut and took in a cargo of sassafras, an expensive medicine in his country but plentiful on the island. He sailed from Cuttyhunk in June. Five weeks later he arrived in England, himself and all his men in good health. From London he wrote his father. Evidently the Suffolk squire was satisfied neither with the reports he received nor the sort of riches his son brought home.

Bartholomew Gosnold's letter to his father is one of three documents surviving pertaining to the voyage, written by men who made it. The other two are narrative accounts, one by John Brereton and the second by Gabriel Archer, "a gentleman of the said voyage." "Brereton's Relation," as the former is called, is considered the earliest English work on the region. The reader who wants to peruse these pieces—and they seem to me among the choicest yet written concerning the Cape and islands—will find them in the Appendix.

On returning to England, Bartholomew Gosnold is said to have had a run-in with Sir Walter Raleigh. Raleigh considered Gosnold a trespasser in what was then vaguely called "the north part of Virginia," and therefore included in Raleigh's patent. Just the same, Gosnold continued promoting settlement in America. When the Virginia Company of London sent out three ships late in 1606, Gosnold sailed as vice admiral of the fleet and also captain of one of the vessels. The fleet sighted Cape Henry, the southern promontory marking the entrance to Chesapeake Bay, late in April, 1607. The Company's sealed instructions were opened. Gosnold, named one of the seven-man governing council, which also included Captain John Smith, was charged with searching the country for minerals and for a passage through the American continent. As a member of the governing council, Gosnold opposed selection of the marshy island in the James River as the site for founding a colony. It was nothing like the salubrious islet he had chosen at Cuttyhunk five years earlier. Unfortunately, his experience and judgment were overruled. Less than four months after disembarking, more than half the colonists at Jamestown were sick of malaria and dysentery. Sixty died—among them, Bartholomew Gosnold, 1 September 1607, age about thirty-five.

Gosnold led the way for the Pilgrims, yet he remains one of the least known figures of New England exploration and settlement. I think almost any reader of the letter he wrote his father will feel certain qualities; strength, self-respect, intelligence, and an adventurous amiable spirit. In any case, Bartholomew Gosnold seems to have been the first European to get the overall picture of Cape Cod and the offshore islands.

Chapter 11

CHILMARK DIARY

SUMMER was dropping to leeward. Autumn drew abreast. Sixty degrees at 7:30 this morning. A hard and oddly warm norther was blowing. Diffused through thin rack and high-flying cloud, the light fell flat and even. Clouds driving south crumpled into long folds of dark gray, textured and streaked with white. On the opposite shore of Menemsha Pond, two red pennants flew from the Coast Guard flagpole—gale warning, the annual September word of a tropical hurricane heading this way. Another was said to blow east of Nantucket, an extensive cyclone accompanied by rain, thunder, and lightning, the kind the West Indies breed every year, late August to mid-October. Although hurricane is the highest term in the wind scales, winds of seventy-five miles an hour and over, the winds seldom exceed one hundred miles. If they did, they might be tornadic—that is, too violent to measure.

Summer falls away fast. Distractions and roadside debris had suddenly ended. Nights now were almost as long as days. At night, fewer lights shone out of the Chilmark hills. Each evening the pond shore loomed darker. Another equinox was approaching. The changing season began the return of the island to its native sons. Meanwhile, we who were slow to depart enjoyed the prospect. So did those who vacation against the traffic, and so did the striped bass derby people.

In jeeps and campers the striped bass fishermen, and their women, cruised by. They do not look like the islanders, nor do they resemble the summer people. They appear to be a separate layer in the social geology, another aspect of the island ecology. Courted by the local Chamber of Commerce, they have become a naturalized post-Labor Day phenomenon.

Although gale warning pennants still flew from the pole in Menemsha, there was no gale. By four o'clock the sun broke through. Clouds were in lavender tatters. A slanting sun spread across the meadow. Down in a corner, against a windbreak of stonewall and sumac now blending russet with green, five female pheasants were preening.

Watching them, each bird trimming and dressing her feathers, I realized preening is a group activity. Could a bird alone do a good job of preening? After much arranging and smoothing, the pheasants sprinkle themselves with dust scooped from thin sandy soil. Another phenomenon shaping up: With fewer people around, wildlife is more in evidence—wildlife that was here all along but understandably hidden. So various kinds of living things find greater elbowroom now.

Further fall phenomena: The towhee, at last, had no more to say. It flitted silently from viburnum to alder. The slate-gray catbird, slimmer than a robin, came out of the branches and made himself sociable close to the house—another reaction to seasonal changeover. Cobwebs festooning the Scotch pines were gaudy with diamond-bright dew. Islanders call this real Vineyard weather. I had often been told the real weather begins after Labor Day, now I saw it is so.

The wind hauled southwest. By noon the day was shimmering slightly, and horseflies were waking up. Only one small sailing boat roamed the pond, plowing watery acres. On the Quitsa shore you can drop your clothes and wade in naked as when you were born. Nude swimming is a kind of rebirth. Then lying on the bank in the sun, I noticed beside me a nest of dried grass with two gray and ghostly objects in it, skeletons of what burrowing mammals? Field mice, or maybe moles? Coming up from the pond, I passed touch-me-not, its deep-orange spotted blossoms hanging like jewels (some call it jewelweed), its seed pods ready to burst at a touch; and violet asters—fifty species grow here. The kind I met were tall-stemmed and hefty; also wooly white, matted down dusty miller. I found certain evidence in the path. Who had been here? A dog more than likely, but then why not a fox or a vixen?

As the colors faded in afternoon haze, as blues merged to grays, and greens drifted and seeped into yellows, the marvelous scene began to resemble an old, badly printed postcard.

Another September afternoon: loafing along the south shore dunes, face turned to the sun, ear to the waves, listening to the breakers swelling, advancing, retreating—perhaps an aftermath and affect of far-off and blown-out hurricanes—and then looking down the long clean stretch of surf-whitened unencumbered beach. A streak of serene self-satisfaction will out. I felt as smug as a Vineyarder after the tourists have gone.

Although Martha's Vineyard is no oceanic isle, it partakes of the mystery of all green islands. As the sun goes down and evening rises, and the afterglow suffuses the sky, ruby-reddening the pond's dark water, and very few lights peep out from the hills, an island feeling may overtake you.

"Ever since the settlement of the Vineyard, in 1642, Gay Head has remained an Indian reservation and town, and very little of its annals in two hundred and sixty-seven years of existence relates to the white man or the white man's customs and development," wrote Charles Edward Banks, M.D., in *The History of Martha's Vineyard, Annals of Gay Head*, first published fifty years ago. "Every attempt of the Caucasian to introduce himself with a view to permanent attachment has resulted in his withdrawal from the field, and today this peninsular and insular town is unquestionably Indian in the warp and woof of its very fibre," Dr. Banks continued.

The former Indian reservation of Gay Head, incorporated as a separate town in 1870, has for some time now been attaching Caucasians. Dividing and subdividing, as though separating warp from woof, Gay Head is probably changing faster than any town on the Vineyard.

In the past ten years, three new roads have been cut through the one-time tribal and common grounds. They are wide roads and paved. One slices through the old South Pasture, then follows along the south shore. Another parallels the north, the Vineyard Sound side. The third and newest, West Basin Road, breaks through the Lobsterville dunes to the west of Menemsha Creek. It barges into the breeding and nesting grounds of herring and great black-backed gulls. The birds now share the gullery with tourists and birders.

Who does not know the herring gull, the common sea gull, seen not only on every sea coast but also inshore beside ponds and rivers? A gray-mantled bird with black wing tips, white belly, yellow beak, and pink legs, it may be more widely known than the robin or sparrow. Big, and a strong graceful flyer, gregarious, predatory, a meat and fish and not a seed eater, this bird is very much in the picture. It seems to appeal to all manner of painters and shutter-snappers. Very fittingly, they show respect for the bird. Without the benefit of its scavenging, man would dwell by a more filthy shore.

Dumping of garbage and discharge of waste into coastal waters has been a great thing for the herring gull. Pollution expanded its food supply! Where in cleaner times some herring gulls starved in winter, the new environment feeds them all. Thriving on sewage and dying fish, their numbers increase—but not unchecked. Nature would not permit that. The great black-backed gull has been moving in on them.

An impressively large black-mantled, white-bellied bird—considerably larger than a herring gull—the black-backed has also been gaining in numbers and at the same time extending its breeding range south. You see them now in appreciable numbers on the Gay Head Lobsterville grounds, associating with the herring gulls, mixing with the smaller herring gulls and also dominating them. The great black-backed seems to be the scavenger's scavenger, eating whatever the herring gull eats *and* preying on herring gull eggs. On a spring visit to the gullery, I had seen how the black-backed gulls settled themselves on the higher ground in the dunes. They made their nests on the little hilltops. As for herring gull eggs, long overall as hen's eggs, nesting in shallow saucers of sand ringed by dried grasses, dependent on camouflage for protection, their olive drab color spotted with brown—seeing these deviant wild egg shapes proved to be one of the high great moments.

All was quiet on West Basin Road. The excitement and traffic of summer had died, as had several hundred herring gulls from causes as yet unknown. Some young brown dead ones lay by the roadside. A few of the living wheeled overhead. The last of the pale pink swamp and marsh roses were blooming, their fragrance enhanced by the taste of salt in the air. Rose hips, false and beautiful fruit of wild roses, dappled the moor with dots of orange and scarlet. Knotweed stood bushy beside the road. Entanglements of it, some of them four feet high, would soon provide a harvest of bird feed. West Basin Road led to little coves where Gay Head scallop boats swing at their moorings. At the end of the road, close to Menemsha Inlet, a Gay Header was overhauling his boat, preparing for winter fishing.

From West Basin Road to the Lobsterville Road, where small seaside camps are proliferating, and then out the North Road, Gay Head dunes meet the new wave of buying, selling, and building. Gay Head is wide open. So far, anything goes. See Gay Head now—and while you can, descendents of Wampanoags.

All roads in Gay Head lead to the lighthouse. Built of orange-red brick and unpainted, this is the only red-skinned tower in the region. So Gay Head boasts an Indian light, a chunky squawlike figure. After World War II ended, the Cape & Vineyard Electric Company wired the island's westernmost town. And after that the kerosene lamp bid farewell to the light on Gay Head. The great Fresnal lens with its thousand prisms, a museum piece of optical science and art, was sent down-island to Edgartown for display on the grounds of the Dukes County Historical Society, where it rests now. Gay Head Light—three white flashes and then one red repeated every forty seconds—converted to incandescent bulb while the last lightkeeper retired, switched over to a pension.

On a flawless fall day, such a one as this, you see the town's wild underlying sadness. Architectural atrocities are even more painful to the eye after the owners and renters have gone. These crimes of a rich and aggressive civilization where everybody tries desperately to be somebody add a new note of sorrow.

Another sad thing in Gay Head has been spoliation of the bright clay cliffs of the promontory from which the town takes its name. Summertime sightseeing buses unloading and loading again, lines of sightseers clogging the narrow paths, the locally staffed souvenir and refreshment stands, the Gay Headers whose job it is to look ethnic for descendants of those who destroyed the Indian folkways, environment, customs, and culture—these manifestations dim the color. They erode the headland's grandeur somewhat. Although the world, it is well understood, conspires to hide the vulgarity of this kind of overexposure, a few are willing to speak of it. "You can have the summer," said an islander, then added in words of one syllable, "Give me the fall." The clay cliffs of Gay Head, sixty feet high and variegated, drop abruptly to the water—they just became a

National Landmark, so one kind of exploitation may end. When seen again, if they do not in fact look different, you will look at them differently. And a new note of sadness will be added; namely, another bronze plaque.

The state road passes through Gay Head center, a center without store or post office but marked by a town hall and school. (The Chilmark post office and rural delivery handles the mail for Gay Head.) The center, however, seems to hold. Although recent years have seen the last barn collapse and the last team of oxen go on its long way, some new small houses built and some large cars abandoned in dooryards, the overall change in the center has not been destructive. Most of the year-round families live beside the state road. Some make their homes along trails leading into the heath. Very few reside close to the water the way the seasonal people do.

Along the new south shore road, however, the town is telling a different story. The new south road, penetrating the wildest scenery, pierces the heart of the old reservation, exposes new miles of duneland and beach and tupelo groves to suburbanization.

Much of the land between the road and the ocean remains unenclosed and unposted—a rare circumstance on the Vineyard. You can leave your car by the road, then go by foot over sandy paths to the water. Nevertheless, there are always some who believe they can drive where the ox carts traveled. As I walked to the beach I came on a visitor trying to jack up his car. It lay in sand to the bumpers. There was nothing either of us could do except exchange civilities.

A fair afternoon, warm sun and cool wind. Wheel tracks in the sand and an assortment of footprints indicated someone had been here before. Although the situation scarcely resembled Robinson Crusoe's on Juan Feranadez, just the same, there was no one as far as the eye could see up and down the beach. Solitude stretched. In the absence of people, all things became consciously clearer.

Beach grass waved long willowy arms. Its vividness does not reside in its color, for the grass is, in fact, bleached, faded, and pale. But it runs free, untamed, coarse-textured, and supple. You see it holding, you sense it stretching upward through many layers of sand. You can almost feel it doing its work, beach grass, also called sand reed, its rootstocks interlacing and binding the sand.

Walking southeast and passing the dunes called Zacks Cliffs, I picked up and examined and discarded stones as I went. To see what magic is in a stone, you must find it yourself, or be given it by someone you love.

I came on a platoon of thick-necked plover, solidly built birds, beautifully pied and patterned. They seemed to be golden plover. Running ahead, seldom getting their feet wet, some went on two legs, some whizzed on one. "Look," the latter seemed to be saying, "one leg!" As I gained on them, the retractable legs went down and the birds gathered speed. They made sure I kept my distance.

Castaway on white sand, or half buried in it, whatever washes onto the beach undergoes change and gains new interest. Some noble sticks of longshore lumber—I deeply regretted having to pass them up. Here were plastic containers, undented, undamaged, the new and indestructible terror—the beaches of the world could be buried beneath them. Beside them, tin cans rotting away looked benign. Food tins looked very old-fashioned, oil cans positively antique. Glass bottles appeared innocuous. Fused out of sand, the beach wears them down and returns them to the stuff they were made of. I passed great streamers of rubbery-looking seaweed left high and drying on the strand—God's plastic, one might call it, only some parasite probably feeds on it. But where is the parasite tough enough to digest the polystyrene product? I continued southeast until, when I faced the ocean, Nomans Land lay dead ahead.

Nomans, an irregular triangle one and one-half miles long by one mile wide situated three miles south of the southwest corner of the Vineyard, was the shore Bartholomew Gosnold first landed on in 1602 after touching Cape Cod. Nomans is the land Gosnold first called Martha's Vineyard. The origin of its later name is uncertain, but the historian, Dr. Banks, takes "Nomans" to be a short form of an Indian name, Tequenomans. "The status of this island up to 1714 was an anomalous one, though being practically unoccupied except by Indians, it gave little concern to the people of the Vineyard," Dr. Banks wrote. When Chilmark incorporated in 1714, Nomans was brought within its corporate limits. Thereafter Nomans remained part of Chilmark, although according to Dr. Banks, "it is scarcely mentioned in the proceedings of the annual meetings for years at a time." And yet there was a period when forty families lived on Nomans, farming, raising sheep, and fishing.

Writing in the first decade of the 20th century, Dr. Banks was contemporary with one Henry B. Davis, the last inhabitant of Nomans. In

1913 the island passed into absentee hands. For the next forty years it served as refuge and port in a storm for fishermen, yachtsmen, and rum runners. In 1952 the United States Government bought it and turned it into a practice target for bombers. As Captain Donald LeMar Poole, commercial fisherman and scion of one of Chilmark's founding families, put it, "The Navy blasted hell out of Nomans, though the soil is better there than on the Vineyard." Today the waters surrounding Nomans are marked on the charts, "Prohibited Area," but fishermen still resent the loss of its harbors. "Boat Off Noman's Hit by Bullet from Navy Plane," read a front-page item in a recent issue of the *Vineyard Gazette*. "Edward S. Amazeen of Oak Bluffs . . . arrived in Menemsha Basin . . . to report that his boat, *Duchess*, had been hit by a bullet fired from a plane as he fished off Noman's Land in company with several other craft. Capt. Walter Manning of Gay Head, who saw the man and his boat, told the *Gazette* that the bullet penetrated the craft about two feet above the water-line, and plowed through the structure, eventually lodging inside the hull. It was speculated that the bullet had ricocheted off the water. The damage to the boat was not described as serious, but that fact that it was hit at all spread alarm and indignation among the fishermen."

September 20. Sunny and warm. Barometer 30.35 and steady. Joe-pye-weed, dull purple-pink, was dying, and poison ivy was looking discouraged. It had been a poor season for poison ivy. But goldenrod! Fields, moors, and roadsides lay under a frosting of flowerheads ranging from chrome to pumpkin-coach yellow, from plumelike and clublike and rodlike to flat-topped or branching like elm. Goldenrod comes in varieties —each spray composed of how many tiny flowers—and in various fragrances. Sweet goldenrod on the stalk smells almost saccharin, but the flowers give off a spicy odor when crushed. Sweet goldenrod leaves, crushed, smell like cider. This is goldenrod one can brew. Seaside goldenrod, masses of it, splattered the sandy scape with most intense color, headings of yellow bursting from strong stems covered with long pointed, coarse dark-green leaves. A yellow from which you make dye.

Sea lavender, also called lavender thrift, undulated at the edge of the pond. Sea lavender, goldenrod, yarrow, Queen Anne's lace (wild carrot), fragrant Canada thistle, blue-eyed grass, pink-eyed grass, late purple aster—the commonest sorts of wildflowers bunched, while speaking of beauty, will also say something about truth and justice.

A September blue day, the kind of blue you never see in summer. Fifty degrees honed the edge of the morning. At 7 A.M. it was sharp.

Driving down-island, wheeling into North Tisbury, I saw a white oak couched alone in a field, its heavy old limbs hanging low. A great white oak surrounded by garnet-brown grass, breasting how many seasons. How many times had I seen it, yet not really seen it. When you see it couched instead of standing, you see it for the first time.

Down-island, in Edgartown, a carpenter knelt on the roof of a shed, tinkering with the cornice. Was he adding something or taking something away? The day was ideal for either. "Say, John," a passerby called out, "You're doing a damn good job—whatever you're doing."

A perfect early autumn day, brilliant and toward noon warming up. I drove around Edgartown in the sun, which lit up gray shingles, white clapboard, stone walls, rusting iron, tombstones and fences. The old settled part of Edgartown—should it not be a National Landmark fully as much as Gay Head? Everything here looks historic, some of it almost Old World. Stone walls glinting in sunlight look heavy with bygones; each stone is a reminder of life cycles lived. In sunlight you read the town's story as you ride by.

Edgartown had shucked off summer. Summer throngs tend to obscure the past, crowd it aside—and a good thing too—but now the durable past reemerged, seen in its realm of dead things. Many shops had gone dead, hotels the same. These, however, did not rest in peace. In another day they would rise again. Meanwhile, the viewpoint changed. Increasing awareness of the permanent dead heightens the consciousness of living. The pleasure of heightened consciousness is what one unexpectedly feels, here in another season.

In the north central part of West Tisbury town, not far from Indian Hill, sunlight percolating through branches fell on an oasitic place. The place is the burying ground of what early missionary whites, and the Society for Propagation of the Gospel, called praying Indians—although there is and was good reason to think all Indians, in their way, prayed. Guide books call it the Christiantown Memorial.

A wooded oasis, cool, reassuring, and tranquil, it emanates sense of place and long home. Above all, an expression of man in harmony with anonymous things. The stones in the Indian burying ground, nameless and dateless, and all more or less the same size, the same as they were when first picked up from the field. Homage to wealth, tribute to office, fear of being forgotten are absent. There is no loneliness of the tomb. All has returned to a warm-looking leaf-covered earth.

So the sandy slope in the semiclearing appears a quietly happy place. You wander along its irregular rows, down the little paths that seem to define family groupings, feeling in key and at ease.

Although these red men are said to have been praying converts, they lie here in Indian dignity, including the one who lies under the imported marble slab on which these words are inscribed: "Mary C/wife of John A Spencer/died Nov 14, 1847/AE 35." If I read it right, the marble slab is a white man's monument to an Indian wife.

After several sharp-whetted mornings, Indian summer set in. No fire was needed. The door stood open. Sweet air blew in on a southwest wind. An accumulation of smoke drifted out. I soon followed.

Turning away from the beach at Gay Head, a short tramp through loose sand will place you high on the dunes that separate Squibnocket Pond from the ocean.

Squibnocket Pond, straddling the line between the towns of Gay Head and Chilmark, is the largest fresh water pond on the Vineyard. Bought fifty years ago, lock, stock, and barrel by rich and far-seeing Boston men, the pond and surrounding area early became a protected enclave. Once again, money saved open space—or rather, has saved it so far. Looking out over Squibnocket Pond, you easily imagine, especially when seeing—as I did—scores of wild swans, each one stately and cruising apart from its fellows. The wild or common whistling swan is a smaller bird with less curve in the neck than the mute swan, the usual park variety. Still, it is characteristically swan; one would not mistake it. Does its long neck serve as a periscope, enabling the bird to see and fish in rough waters? To come on wild swans, or geese, ducks, or coots—to see many large birds of any wild kind—is somehow much more affecting than an equal number of small ones.

September ending. This was a day warm enough to swim. Cyril Norton says swimming in salt water cures a cold. Fresh water, no; but salt, yes. He vows he went in on a September day with 102 degrees of fever, and was fine after the immersion.

"Is it the salinity?" I asked.

"Yes," he said, "and a lot of other minerals, too."

Honor, then, to many minerals, and to the experience, strength, and wisdom of the uncommon native son who outswims most summer people.

Uplands of Chilmark, once grazed and farmed, provided pasturage now for wildflowers—blue chicory on high leafless stems and patches of low-stemmed deep purple heal-all, sometimes called carpenter's herb. Leaves coming down exposed dry stone walls, long enduring monuments to unknown persons, low wages, ownership, industry, and limited choice of materials. Stone barnyard walls built to keep livestock in, stone fences around fields to keep the stock out, miles of stone laid up through the slow seasons, stone foundations and stone gate posts, too—and all of these in this, our machine age, emerging as handcraft and art. Chilmark, with the passing years, becomes renowned for its walls.

September was ending and Captain Poole still was at it. Both price and supply are holding up. He said that as long as he could haul lobsters to the tune of $200 a week, he would leave his gear in. Today, however, he was coiling his plastic ropes. Where the old hemp lines hardly pulled through two years, the new plastic product lasts four. Captain Poole was also knitting funnels of bright green nylon cord. The funnels fit into the ends of the lobster pots. Every fisherman, Captain Poole says, knits his own. Working at the bench in his shack in Menemsha on Dutcher Dock, his door swung wide, he said it would not do to stand there knitting during the summer. If he did, he would not get his knitting done; he would be too busy answering questions. Captain Poole was using the hand-whittled shuttle he bought for a quarter when he was sixteen. Whittled artifacts, too, like Chilmark's stone walls, become transformed by latter-day eyes into art.

As September ended the barometer fell. The wind hauled northeast; rain drummed a tattoo. At the Chilmark dump, the dumpmaster matter-of-factly set the last loads on fire. Captain Swill, the private-enterprise garbage collector, laid up his truck. The very last of the season was done with and over.

Edgartown Harbor, a mysterious sight on an early September morning

Textures

Wellfleet Harbor

The famous Wellfleet bridge, built strictly for pedestrians

169

The dunes at Truro, a magnificent mountain range of sand; ever shifting and moving, no two days alike. Only jeeps or landrovers dare venture into this country. On the other side, the Atlantic has created fishing beaches where visitors come to enjoy the sun and sea

Another view of Truro. Sand, over a period of time, behaves much like water: only when grass grows on the "crest" of a dune does it stabilize and approach something like permanence

171

A window in Sandwich's glass museum

Moonlight on the waters off Edgartown dock

Chapter 12

WELLFLEET TO PROVINCETOWN

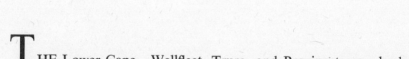

THE Lower Cape—Wellfleet, Truro, and Provincetown—beckoned.
I wanted to visit these towns in autumn. Now October arrived.

As I pulled out of Hyannis a full moon was rising. It cleared the tree-
tops—just barely (it seemed) at first—but then began climbing faster,
a pale yellow circle, round face and all. Our generation may be the last
to see the face. Even now it is getter harder to find the benign expression
after seeing the close-up photos. As you cruise east on an October evening, pitch pines black in the moony landscape, Cape Cod appears uninhabited— until you turn away from the highway and into village neon
lights.

The man working the evening shift was a recent arrival on Cape Cod.
He gave me a friendly hail. With a tourist like me, he felt an old-timer.
He said that this is the best time of year on the Cape. "The days are
warm, the nights cool, and the crowds have gone that way." He gestured
with both hands toward the door.

A warm sunny Indian-summer day. Looking around I felt a calm that I think was not here in spring. In spring one notes a bustle of preparation, a bracing for what is to come. Getting ready to open up; remodeling, painting, new plumbing going in. Days growing longer, expectations greater. All that had departed. Pilgrimizing and spending had had their hour. Everything was on the other tack now. A different breed of tourist was on the road; many older people, well groomed and coiffured, gray and lavender-haired couples looking like models for advertising annuities, driving big new automobiles, and wearing the newest in eyeglass frames and suede coats. There is something congenial between this season and people in the autumn of years.

Seventy-three, four, five degrees, and so warm I almost felt the barometer falling as I entered the Massachusetts Audubon Society's Wellfleet Bay Wildlife Sanctuary, lying just north of the Eastham town line. The Massachusetts Audubon Society, the oldest Audubon society and the largest conservation organization in the Commonwealth, was founded in 1896. "Take only pictures, leave only footprints," the Audubon Society sloganizes. In time, however, you may not be able to see the sand for the footprints, or the sanctuary for the pictures. Anything too much photographed will suffer from overexposure.

Increasing numbers of people, pictures, and footprints point up the high and growing importance of sanctuaries and refuges. The 650 acres of woodland and saltmarsh comprising the Wellfleet Bay preserve—and most of Wellfleet's north shore—do not fall within the authorized boundaries of the Cape Cod National Seashore. The sanctuary rest rooms indicate something too—that birdwatchers are the least vandalistic people. This may sound trifling, but sometimes it is the little things that reveal the big ones. The sanctuary provides space indeed, not only for wildlife but also for tourists. This is the place guided tours by beach buggy over Nauset Beach start from. And this is where you reserve a place on the day-long tour of the tidal flats of Monomoy Island off of Chatham, three towns away.

Goose Pond Trail: Goose Pond is a large shallow puddle lying back of the saltmarsh that stretches along the west shore of Wellfleet Harbor. Well out in the pond, the Audubon Society set up a blind on posts and built a plank bridge to it. After edging my way along the plank, I entered the blind, the concealing enclosure from which you observe the wildlife. It is lighted by two narrow slots in the wall through which the observer looks out. Inside I found two broken-down chairs well plastered with hardened dung. Small birds had evidently subverted the lookout slots into pigeon holes. Roosting on the backs of the chairs, they used the seats for dropping boards. But this is the way it is living with birds. Hauling a chair up to one of the slots in the wall, I balanced on the chair's forward edge. I gazed out on a covey of what appeared to be very large yellow-legged sandpipers standing and wading around in the mudflat. Now that I was concealed in the blind, they came closer: Greater Yellow-legs. As I emerged from my place of birdspying, a Greater Yellow-legs came flying in for a soft muddy-bottom landing. There was a sound of beating wings as the bird first raised them, then folded them slowly. Its body teetered as it put down.

In his 1912 book, *A History of the Game Birds, Wild-Fowl and Shore Birds of Massachusetts and Adjacent States,* Edward Howe Forbush, then the State Ornithologist, preferred the name "Winter Yellow-legs." He listed it as a bird hunted for food or sport. If the name is insipid, the bird is not. One of the sandpiper family, but rising some fifteen inches tall, with long bright black bill and long bright yellow legs, it assumes a teacherlike stance and expression. It does not look edible to me, and certainly not sport to hunt. Forbush said of the Winter Yellow-legs, "The bird is suspicious and noisy . . . but it is easily deceived by a good bird caller, and sometimes can be called back to the decoys after it has been shot at. . . . " He wrote that the Winter Yellow-legs "seems to be very fond of both land and water insects, and must do considerable good as an insect eater." These likeable, fallible, metaphorical traits tally with the visual experience.

After retreating from the blind, I picked up Goose Pond Trail again and continued along its damp circuit. Ribbons and streamers of marsh grasses waved in all manner of amber color. In a marshy channel, mallards were swimming, camouflaged and so naturally that I was surprised when I saw them. Doubtless I missed many others. I hope so. When not everything can or wants to be seen, then there is really seclusion. Then you get a feeling of space on the horizontal. How do birds know of this sanctuary? They seem to. Unmolested, some species are almost tame. I walked to within six feet of a chickadee. Audubon must have walked right up to many a bird. You learn that to do so among unfrightened wildlife is, after all, not remarkable.

Not far from where a small spring-fed stream, Silver Spring Brook, meets the Bay, stands a splendid patch of one of the three thousand species of sweet flags and sedges. All of them taken together have been of little importance economically speaking. Like the swamps and ponds, wet woods and wet meadows they grow in, they will become more valued. Some rushes appear in perfect condition—smooth, firm and compact, and a well-toasted brown. Others, aging and gray, are raveling out. The trail comes to a beautiful ending in a carpet of partridge berry, dark green and deep piled.

Little more than fifty years ago, no law protected the yellow-legs, or any game bird or wild fowl. At the time of its discovery by Europeans, North America enjoyed a denser game bird population than any other continent. The United States was incredibly rich in birds. Wildfowl pretty well held their own until the end of the Civil War, but then a change came. After 1865 an unparalleled exploitation of natural resources began. The nation gave predatory drives free rein. The most glorious home in the world for wild ducks was in large measure ruined and the vast flocks annihilated. Although the birds survive, the great winging throngs have gone.

Unlimited shooting and selling of game birds ended only in 1918. The Migratory Bird Treaty of that year between the United States and Canada prohibited the sale of game. The treaty protected waterfowl throughout its range of migration. After 1918 the market gunner quietly disappeared. From then on, duck shooting became the restricted seasonal pastime that it is now, the season varying according to place and supply.

In the days of ungoverned destruction, by far the greater number of birds shot were lured to ambush by decoys—wooden likenesses of birds —either by professionals with heavy guns and limitless ammunition, or by members of ducking clubs, or residents of coastal regions.

"From a quite unknown beginning, the making of decoys grew slowly to a stage of minor coastal industry," Joel Barber wrote in *Wild Fowl Decoys*, first published in 1934. "Beginning with gunners, it spread to scattered individuals having a peculiar knowledge and knack with tools. All work was done by hand. Practitioners went by the name of 'Stool-makers.' The years immediately following the Civil War saw the beginning of decoys made by machinery. . . .

"But the 'longshore stool-maker never ceased production. Handmade decoys were always the favorite of the experienced professional and fastidious sportsman. . . .

"Decoys were the tools of a grim profession."

Other specialists in decoy history say Indians were the first makers. Using mounds of seaweed or mud, or bark shaped and plastered with feathers, they lured mallards and black ducks away from the flyways and down from the passing migrations. If some individuals of the species could not tell a duck from a decoy, it made little difference. The Indian and the pioneer white who killed game only to eat, made no dent in the flocks of birds and no impression on decoy-making.

Like many handcrafts, decoys developed their regional variants. There was, for example, the bag decoy said by Joel Barber "to have originated on the marshes of Cape Cod and used principally in the gunning of Black Duck. Bag decoys are . . . literally bags made of unbleached cotton or light-weight duck, and stuffed with dry grass or granulated cork. . . . Five or six of them in a line make a most effective showing. . . . "

The author of *Wild Fowl Decoys* wrote that he once saw "a Cape Cod Sheldrake with a crest made of horse hair. It had come to rest in the window of an antique shop in the village of Chatham. . . . It was a drake, and a very gay old bird. . . . "

Few of the many who whittled and carved the decoys and stools and stool pigeons are known by name today. One hears of the Wrights of Osterville, and of Elmer Crowell and his son, Cleon. These men became professional carvers. They made miniatures, and birds for decorative purposes as well as working decoys.

The end came only recently. Among the last of the famous names, Henry Keyes Chadwick of Oak Bluffs, Martha's Vineyard, who in his lifetime made more than one thousand decoys and who carved and painted the native ducks, died in 1958. His brother-in-law, Frank Adams of West Tisbury, another whose decoys are sought by collectors, died in 1944. An Adams decoy came to rest in the Shelburne Museum in Shelburne, Vermont. Inasmuch as decoys were made to serve conditions no longer existing, the real art and craft of the real decoy-maker cannot—ever—come back.

Fortunately, the Wellfleet Bay Wildlife Sanctuary stays open year-round to people—as well as, of course, wildlife. Close by lies another refuge, the Wellfleet Drive-in and Trailer Camp. The trailer camp is one of several similar enclaves on Cape Cod overlooked by the guide books, but people with trailers know about them. Here most of the customers seem to own boats as well as automobiles. And why not? Wellfleet must be a fine town for boats. It provides a new large paved town pier and marina with boat-launch facilities for all tides.

A pinched land, only about three miles wide by about eight long, Wellfleet ranks tenth in size among Cape Cod's fifteen towns, twelfth in population, and eleventh in population density. It confronts a bay sixty miles wide. Part of it is composed of islands, and back of it lies the ocean. Physically, Wellfleet is open-spaced and exposed. Temperamentally it may be as unconfined as they say it was in Prohibition Days, now so proudly remembered.

"There seems to be general agreement that many a case of bootleg liquor came ashore . . . and that a goodly quantity was consumed here as well," writes Judy Stetson, author of *Wellfleet, A Pictorial History*, published by the Wellfleet Historical Society, Inc. "What is interesting," she says, "is the general attitude of the town toward this 'criminal' activity going on in their midst. Virtually everyone knew what was happening, of course. Even the school children knew what signals to watch for that meant a load coming in, and which lanes not to walk down after dark, because if you did a very un-birdlike 'bob-white' call would precede you all the way, but it impinged very little on the normal routines of the vast majority not actually engaged in rum-running. They weren't afraid of the bootleggers, they weren't especially indignant about them, they weren't particularly elated at being so close to the source of supply, and they went about their routine business in the usual way." A snug harbor for smuggling, drinking, and also everyday living.

Bounded by dangerous shoals and breakers, the town offers all comers asylum from the sea. Approaching by land, along Route 6, you presently reach another refuge, the Chapel of St. James the Fisherman. A church-in-the-round, its free-standing steeple rising above a grove of pines, the chapel presents a fresh appearance. Contemporary in design, it adds a note of vitality to a countryside still architecturally immature, fixated for the most part on what has been, and on real and unreal colonial.

I drove to the knoll the Fisherman's Chapel stands on. The church door was open. The Chapel's unconcealed framing timbers were like bare bones. Inside, a central sanctuary and a free-standing altar rise. Six rows of pews surround it. I sat down and contemplated a small sign, "Next Service June 23." Meanwhile, through the coming winter, would the door remain open?

The day dawned misty, hesitated, then advanced mild-eyed and somewhat unsettled. I noted a great change since yesterday. Unrestrained reds were coloring marshes and wetlands. Swamp maple, the most conspicuous tree of the lowlands, flamed in garish magnificence.

There was an Ocean View Drive in Wellfleet. On how many edges of the world, posted in how many different languages, would the words translated read, "Ocean View"? On the back side, at Wellfleet-by-the-Sea,

I came to the ocean whence I turned north. A high moorland, treeless but covered with low dense growth, was dotted with small camps and summer places, but an irregular topography provides many natural separations. The moor still seemed free. From Ocean View Drive, from heights of fifty to one hundred feet, you look down on the rolling Atlantic. To watch waves slanting in, then breaking below you—to stand high in the dunes and leave to the shore birds the sand that the waves are wetting —makes you feel good.

Although from Nauset Harbor in Orleans to Race Point in Province-town one unbroken beach stretches, each Lower Cape town along the way claims and names its own portions. At Wellfleet's Cahoon's Hollow Beach a couple of fishermen, surf casting, were trying their luck. Hollows are low places formed in the Lower Cape coastal cliffs where east-west valleys meet the shore. At Newcomb Hollow Beach, further north, a toothless old angler said to me, "These are the crumbs." Was he speaking of the end of the fishing season, or of one man's season of life?

Taking one road and then another, letting the car decide which turn to make, drifting and from time to time getting lost, I presently reached Gull Pond. On the shore of Gull Pond there is no way to tell, no hint that the ocean lies very close by. Serene and shallow, the pond is sur-rounded by pines, more a pond for birds than for people, I would guess. Just the same, the Town has built a fine stairway to it and set out benches and picnic tables along a brown sandy beach—another Wellfleet com-bination bird and people refuge. Wellfleet, good and beautiful place, with some of the finest high wooded land on the Cape, does not appear overcrowded.

The sight of bare tables can make you feel hungry. I set a course for Wellfleet Center and presently raised its steeples. The center is a New England hill village. Both its dignity and laissez-faire may derive from its stagy location. On Main Street, the proprietress of the lunchroom claimed that at this time of year, from Orleans to Provincetown, and exclusive of both, hers is the only place serving chowder. Hail, Wellfleet Main Street sanctuary.

~~~~~~

For some or no reason, *Wellfleet, A Pictorial History*, the bicentennial publication put out in 1963, does not speak of Winslow Lewis. Born in Wellfleet, 11 May 1770, the son of Winslow and Mary Knowles Lewis, kin to Edward Winslow, Pilgrim father, Winslow Lewis was perhaps the foremost lighthouse man of the 19th century.

Little is known of his early years. He certainly had some schooling. From its beginning, Wellfleet provided its children with schools. You cannot learn navigation, the prerequisite to higher ranks and command, unless you first learn to read, write, and figure. Like many boys of the town, Winslow Lewis was bred to the sea. He became a captain and made several voyages as commanding officer. Then around 1810, shortly before he turned forty, he quit seafaring. He moved to Boston and entered business.

He became a specialist in designing, building, and equipping lighthouses. The Lighthouse Service, then an arm of the Treasury Department, was new. Winslow Lewis saw the opportunities in selling goods and services to a not yet well-organized government.

In 1811 Winslow Lewis won a contract to install his newly patented lamps and reflectors in the forty-nine lighthouses then owned by the Lighthouse Service. His lamps used less oil than their predecessors. He became the Service's first Superintendent for Lighting. In 1815 he agreed to supply all lighthouses with high-grade sperm oil, visit each annually, and report its condition. For his services he received "one-half the oil consumed under the old plan," that is, by the former and now-replaced lamps. Seven years later the contract was renewed for a consideration of one-third the oil. Later, however, when the government asked for open bidding on whale oil, Winslow Lewis lost out.

He had other problems as well. Northeast coast lighthouses in those days had a peculiar difficulty. When temperatures dropped and oil in the lamps became cold, the lights might go out—in much the same way that a cold engine stalls on cold fuel. Some keepers attempted to warm the oil by heating the room that contained the lamps—an expensive procedure at best, and impossible at its frequent worst. An interesting development followed.

A certain David Melville, employed by the Lighthouse Service, claimed in a pamphlet that he had told Superintendent for Lighting Winslow Lewis about a device that he, Melville, had contrived for keeping the oil in the lamps warm. Melville said his contraption involved returning the heat from the flame to the oil in the reservoir by means of a copper tube passing through the reservoir and connected to a funnel suspended over the flame. He wrote that he sketched the thing for Lewis and that Lewis pocketed the sketch and presently patented it in his own name.

Eventually, after charges and countercharges and threatened litigation, Lewis assigned the patent to Melville in 1818. Not satisfied, however, Melville published his pamphlet, "An Exposé of Facts . . . Relating to the Conduct of Winslow Lewis . . . Respectfully submitted to the Government and Citizens of the United States . . . and the Secretary of the Treasury."

A riffle through the compendious *Compilation of Public Documents and Extracts from Reports and Papers Relating to Light-Houses, 1789–1871*, published in the latter year by the Government Printing Office in Washington, D.C., indicates that Winslow Lewis was a controversial figure, praised by some and denounced by others. In general it seems that the politicians liked him, that the technicians and inspectors —his nephew among them—did not. In any case this sea captain, self-taught engineer, and man of affairs had known where to take his talents. Before he died in 1850 at age eighty, he built about one hundred structures for the lighthouse establishment. Having got the job done by hook or by crook, his name may well outlast them.

North to Truro and Provincetown! Route 6, at this end called Grand Army of the Republic Highway, snakes its way among Lower Cape ponds—Ryder, Snow, Round, and Great. Whoever named Cape Cod ponds apparently had no great gift for the job, using English names without the pleasures of English poetry or invention. Route 6 is now the only way north unless you can find the path of the Old King's Highway, or the trail of the Old County Road. There are probably fewer roads today than existed one hundred years ago, as there are fewer people year-round to use them.

Ninth in size among Cape Cod's fifteen towns, Truro ranks fourteenth in population and in population density. When it comes to leeway and margin, however, Truro rates high: high plains, splendid wild startling scenes. I turned from the highway onto South Pamet Road and followed its looping course toward the sea. By a cattail marsh on the sheltered side of soaring dunes I heard waves breaking on Truro's back side. They filled the air with their booming. Here, among a whole series of hills, the most cleanly outlined series I ever saw, rose a fast-climbing high and treeless hill covered foot-to-foot with evergreen partridge berry, or was it some other creeping plant? In any case, count it a rare grand sight of these travels. I would like to have gone walking on that hill, but all paths leading upward were closed, chained, or barred. No matter. There was much to enjoy from the roadside—the settled look of the little gray houses for one thing, and also the random and suitable way they perch and nest in the hills.

South Pamet Road in this narrow land finds no place to go except back to Route 6, and in the process becomes North Pamet Road. On the way to Truro Center I passed by Snow Cemetery, a ubiquitous Cape name—among the quick as well as the dead. Close by stands a Catholic chapel. I had already seen in Wellfleet Center the church called Our Lady of Lourdes. In the 20th century, more than ever before, this is mixed Yankee, Azorean, and Nova Scotian country. I drove past Tom Hill and around the flats where the Pamet River spreads into Cape Cod Bay. From Corn Hill Road you look onto acres of cattails, good for beaver food, and anything else? Yes, good to look at. What appears to be an abandoned industrial enterprise, maybe a salt works, sits way back in the marsh. Along the river are reminders of the declines and disasters —ruined anchorages and silted harbors—which consistently down the years have saved Truro from becoming a thriving and standard success-ful place.

As a center, Truro seems widely dispersed. On one side of the sinuous Pamet River stands the post office, filling station, and store; on the oppo-site shore, the library. The church sits on a hill. On another hilltop, surrounded by second-growth woods, a combination town hall, police station, and office of selectmen hides out.

Timber, never plentiful in this town, went long ago. The farming and much of the fishing have gone. Although little is said, and even less written about it, failure has been widespread. Truro has the look of a town where failure without indignity has long been a way of life. The resulting simplicity of the social environment, as well as the bare beauty of the natural scene, gives the town a distinctive flavor. Truro's most difficult times may be over. Since most of it lies within the authorized boundaries of the National Seashore, a flow of tourists seems assured. Will success be harder to live with?

Continuing north, you pass the new school, the Truro Central School, but it looks decentralized and small. It is rated "A" by the Common-wealth.

Still further north, on the back side of town, on the highlands between the Highland and the Longnook Beaches, you come to the Cape Cod, or Highland, Light. It stands on a blue clay cliff just south of one of the most dangerous bars on the coast, its bull lenses flashing every five seconds. Rising 183 feet above the sea, the most powerful light on the New England shoreline, its four million candlepower beam is visible twenty miles away. Like most of the great examples of lighthouse architecture, the present Cape Cod light was erected in the middle of the 19th century. Constructed of long narrow bricks painted white and capped in black, it typifies the genre.

Opposite Cape Cod Light, on the Bay side of town, lies North Truro village. The Cape at this point is about one mile wide. From a road called Bay View you also can see the ocean, the moor between being treeless. From Bay View Road I turned left onto Priest Road. The point of these details is this: on the right-hand side going east, crouching on one of the Truro knobs like a sculpture on a pedestal, sits a remarkable ruined automobile and below it, on the slope of a hollow, the remains of a dwelling about the same size as the car. Sun-blackened and bleached, salt-air-rusted and pitted and isolated, this great living junk is framed in a vast clean setting of land, sea, and sky.

On the shore of North Truro village, or on the back side of Truro Town at Head of the Meadow Beach, you see that down-Cape no longer points north. The Lower Cape has begun trending west.

―――――――――――――――――――――――

" 'Plymouth Rock? That's the name of a chicken,' the proud old Cape Cod Yankee will snort," wrote the compilers of *Massachusetts, A Guide to Its Places and People.* " 'The spot where the *Mayflower* people first stepped on American soil is right here in Provincetown, and you ought to freeze onto that fact . . . for it's been rising 300 years now, and most off-Cape folks don't seem to know it yet!' "

The *Guide's* Cape Cod Yankee strawman is right on both counts. The rock the Pilgrims allegedly disembarked on when, in due course, they made Plymouth Bay, is not a very remarkable object. On the other hand, the Plymouth Rock breed of domestic fowl, especially the barred variety, is one of the most satisfying and natty. A medium-size bird with single comb and smooth yellow legs, each feather evenly barred with gray-white and blue-black, it formerly ran in virtually every New England village and farmyard.

The Pilgrims, say some historians, consisted of thirty-five members of an English Separatist church in Leyden, Holland, who sailed from Plymouth, England, with sixty-six sectarians and servants on the *Mayflower*, 16 September 1620. Others say the vessel carried eighty-seven passengers, fourteen servants and workmen, and a crew of forty-eight.

William Elder Brewster, and William Bradford were among the leaders. After a voyage concerning which little is known, and after avoiding the shoals and breakers off what is now Chatham, the *Mayflower* dropped anchor in Provincetown harbor, 11 November 1620. The first party of Pilgrims went ashore the same day. The ship lay at anchor in Provincetown harbor five weeks before her people decided to settle on the other side of Cape Cod Bay, at Plymouth.

Today, Pilgrim Beach on Provincetown Harbor, west of the Truro line, is plastered with barrackslike bungalows. Shocking? Not really. This is America, land where our fathers died, land where our fathers' world is dead. Just the same, I was dismayed to find row houses here. I turned from the long continuous strip that faces, and at this point all but blankets, the historic harbor. I kept my eyes on the mountainous dunes now rising grandly to starboard, and on the new road slicing through. Traveling between the harbor and Pilgrim Lake, you gain a wonderful rear view of Provincetown rounding out the hook with which Cape Cod ends. Stretched between a wide waterfront and a high-rising white sandy desert, Provincetown looks strangely foreign. Minareted by the Pilgrim Monument, 252 feet high, 352 feet above sea level, this New England atypical port seems exotic.

Going in at the end of a perfect fall afternoon, emerging from Route 6 onto Commercial Street, the sun was sinking dead ahead. Running one-way the length of the village, Commercial Street lies on a more or less east-west axis. Driving down it, narrowly clearing utility poles and pedestrians, and even store fronts debouching directly onto the street without benefit of sidewalk, Old World streets come to mind. I remembered the narrow defiles of Sienna. Inside as well as on the approaches, Provincetown strikes me as European, and more like a small city than a village, unless one means Greenwich Village. And indeed Provincetown is a satellite of the latter—and not only in summer, as everyone knows, but also in other seasons.

A painter with whom I am acquainted, and a poet whose path I have crossed before, have summer homes among the colonists close-packed under Telegraph Hill at the western end of Commercial Street. Although summer has passed, I found them lingering. The painter said his appealing little old house is "a pain in the neck," but he likes Provincetown very much, and so does his wife. One of the older art colonists, successful and now becoming set in his ways, he said he was opposed to the National Seashore's plan for bicycle paths through the Province Lands. The Province Lands, 4,400 acres of wildlands, marsh, and spectacular dunes at the tip of Cape Cod, have been public lands since colonial times. But now that the paths have been laid out and paved, the painter has changed his mind. He finds them splendid for walking. They take him to dunelands where he had not been before. His wife remarked that swimming at Herring Cove Beach, where the Atlantic meets the Bay, is like swimming in champagne: The waters bubble. The poet dropped in. He lives next door—six feet away. He entered as though in search of an interruption, a change of mind set, or maybe a beer. Provincetown this time of year, he said, is ideal for weather and work.

Near the eastern end of Commercial Street, between a deserted fish packing plant and St. Mary of the Harbor, a waterfront church, another painter, a tall well-framed man, built as large a house and studio as he could with the money in hand. It is a great three-story barn of a place with balconies overlooking the harbor. The big structure, rather physiognomic, reflects the man's physical characteristics. From the studio dwelling you see the Cape stretching southward. You can see the sun rise, and see it set. When wind and rain blow hard from the east, the house leaks where the balconies attach, but the painter is fatalistic about it. "They all leak on the east side," he said shrugging, smiling. He eats at a nearby restaurant until he finds money—that is, sells pictures enough to finish the kitchen. Provincetown, he said, is a great town for breakfasting out.

Smallest in size of Cape Cod's fifteen towns, ranking eighth in population, Provincetown heads the list in population density. The hook at the end of Cape Cod has been known since Gosnold's time and many historians think, long before. The hook is a sandpile. There is no sign of stone in Provincetown. Because the bedrock slopes seaward, it lies very deep this far out.

As the painter-colonist reported, bicycle paths have been laid through the old Province Lands. The black macadam paths crisscrossing white sand help define the desert wildness. They give it form. In spite of the paths, and the trails for sand buggies, the Province Lands look like a place you could wander in for days, stumbling in sand traps and through eddying dunes. With luck you might in time reach the shore of a pond, for ponds are found even here. In no part of the Cape is a pond far away.

By Race Point Road I reached Race Point Coast Guard Station. There Massachusetts Bay, Cape Cod Bay, and a gray-green-yellow frothing Atlantic spread themselves north, east, and west. A landsman, I stood on the rim of the land, and clung to it while I gazed at the mind-stealing sea.

A couple of pretzel bends in Province Land Road brought me back to the village, but not until I first passed a monstrous motel. It faces the Bay and one of the sand bars the Pilgrims avoided. A doorman, dressed in stereotype Pilgrim fashion, stood guard at the entrance. And still Provincetown Beach looks undisturbed and as fascinating as when Pamet Indians, walked it, all unsuspecting.

Gale winds blowing this mild mid-October day could blow you from the Town Wharf and into the harbor where dirty trawlers and picturesque draggers were riding and tossing at anchor. Other fishing craft, moored cheek to cheek at the caplog, chewed against old rubber tires. It is hard to imagine men, women, and children lying here five weeks in the three-masted, double-deck, bark-rigged *Mayflower*, 180 tons, Christoper Jones master—and harder still to picture her under sail, her normal speed two and a half miles an hour. For those making the voyage it must have been a highly condensed experience.

A funny thing how Provincetown missed in the school books. The great wonder is not that the Pilgrims landed at Plymouth but rather how they avoided shipwreck on the back side of the Cape, how they escaped the offshore sands and ocean bars—especially Peaked Hill Bars, the northerly shoals they had to clear before rounding Race Point and coming into Provincetown Harbor. Has the *Mayflower's* skipper received his due?

While the vessel lay at anchor in front of Provincetown before there was any town, Dorothy, wife of William Bradford, Pilgrim father and later governor of Plymouth Colony, drowned in the harbor. Did she fall overboard, or jump? Was she pushed? History does not say. Provincetown is only two streets wide—Commercial one way, Bradford the other. Does the latter recall Dorothy as well as William? The street names reflect the prevailing Western-world influences—enterprise (Commercial) and piety (Bradford)—acquisitiveness and simplicity, the democratic and divided life that generates struggle, tensions, values, and perhaps constitutional government.

The facade of the town, seen from Town Wharf, makes a fine long shallow panorama. On Commercial, the waterfront street, fishermen, draggers, sea skimmers mingle with those who prey on the longshore tourists. Using their wits, setting their lures, aiming to reap what they did not sow, the seasonal shopkeepers and the fishermen make a congenial mix.

Although some of the bars, bazaars, and restaurants on Commercial Street have closed down, many stay open for the post-season. Automobiles and motorcycles from far-away states were in evidence. A number of persons went walking by, looking—looking around, maybe looking for something. Like what? A man who is his own man, perhaps? Or for something believed in, something you feel very sure is there and that you have not yet found.

People do not walk up and down Bradford Street looking, because Bradford is where the everyday businesses are, the automobile showrooms, the gasoline stations, the dry-cleaning plants, and the laundries. Provincetown's year-round population is 75 percent Portuguese. Many all-weather residents live on Bradford, as well as up and down the short side streets between the two long transverse ones. Politically, Portuguese run the town, and probably the Madeira Club.

On Commercial Street, very fittingly, the Chrysler Museum occupies an abandoned Methodist Church, a Yankee church built in the 1880's. But in Provincetown, as in many a New England village, Yankee stock shows signs of losing out.

Looking at the fusty old clapboard church, one might say it tries to be reborn. Perhaps in its new incarnation it pays for its former 19th-century sins. It now houses the art collection of Walter P. Chrysler, Jr. How did the conglomeration that ranges from Luristan bronzes to Tiffany glass, that includes a Bernini marble, a Persian prayer rug, a Rembrandt etching, a Prendergast painting—how did it come to Provincetown? The answer is simply that Walter P. Chrysler, Jr. lives here. As for local and indigenous art, the Chrysler Museum gathers in Sandwich glass. This famous glass was made in the Upper Cape town of that name between 1825 and 1888 from secret and now lost formulas.

Sandwich, fronting on Cape Cod Bay, incorporated in 1639, is the oldest town on the Cape. The first settlers were drawn by riches of salt marsh hay. By the beginning of the 19th century the town, a prosperous farming community, had also become a sporting resort for Boston businessmen. In 1824 Deming Jarves (1790–1869), a wealthy and irascible glass manufacturer, a chemist and man of genius, came down from Boston by boat to enjoy the fishing and hunting. Looking straight down the barrel, he saw in the forests a seemingly inexhaustible supply of fuel for his furnaces. In front of him lay white sand, the bulkiest item in glassmaking. Cape Cod Bay offered cheap transportation, and the salt marsh grasses good packing material for his finished products.

The following year he set up shop in the town of Sandwich, and next door to the village, he built a company village of Jarvesville to house his workers, most of them imported from abroad. Studying his costs, he saw that his main expense was wages paid to glass blowers. He presently figured that if you poured hot glass into a mold and then pressed the glass down with a plunger shaped like the inside of whatever article you wanted to make, the glass would be forced into every part of the mold, and the plunger instead of the glass blower's breath would do the hollowing. Jarves's invention developed a new breed of artisan, the designer-moldmaker. Moldmakers such as Hiram Dilloway went on to evolve the lacy patterns and frostlike traceries that made the name of Sandwich glass. Thus Sandwich glass is the product of the moldmaker's rather than the glass blower's art, and also the mysteries of the Jarves "batch" mixed behind locked doors.

Besides collecting Sandwich glass, Mr. Chrysler buys from the local living artists. Thus P'town, as everyone calls it, appears to be twice blessed: the artist by the patron of the colony, the fisherman by the bishop at the annual Blessing of the Fleet in June. These blessings mean something. Artists and fishermen take great risks. Both confront the unknown.

In Provincetown the permanent residents and the seasonal seem to be hitting it off. The latest Provincetown Yacht Club list shows forty-seven family members, twenty-five of them in the resident class. Provincetown's yacht club cannot be called run-of-the-mill. The old myth about clubs is, I suppose, that if you cannot keep some people out, then you do not have a club. Provincetown Yacht Club, however, runs on a kind of joyful collective opposite principle. The club is open. Apparently anybody can join. For $10 if you own a boat, $5 if you do not. Lacking quarters and real estate, the club seems to be an association in the spirit. Meetings are held in restaurants or in private homes. You do not have to own a dock to be a yacht club. Full privileges are extended to members of other clubs. Provincetown Yacht Club is very reciprocal. A member asks, "Will you be in Provincetown next summer? Join us. It's a marvelous place."

Chapter 13

NANTUCKET

S HAPED rather like a pork chop, the island of Nantucket lies about twenty miles east of Cape Poge, the easternmost point of Martha's Vineyard. Many a resident of the latter has not yet set foot on the former. There are more than a few like my Vineyard friend who, when asked if he had been to Nantucket, replied, "Nantucket? Yes, I was there once —for about twenty minutes in 1921." And really there is little reason to go from island to island. Most people wanting a change of scene will choose to travel further.

Nantucket also lies about twenty miles from the southeastern tip of Cape Cod. From Woods Hole in Cape Cod's southwest corner, the distance is thirty-eight miles. Woods Hole is the mainland terminal for the Steamship Authority, whose vessels ply to Nantucket four times daily in summer, twice daily in winter. In summer, two additional boat lines ferry between Hyannis and Nantucket. Three airlines operate in and out of Nantucket Memorial Airport.

Nantucket is slightly less than half the size of Martha's Vineyard. Low-lying and sandy, fifteen miles long and about two and one-half wide, it embraces almost fifty square miles. It enjoys eighty-eight miles of coastline. For the past thirty-five years, year-round population has been static at 3,500. Summer population swells to about 16,000. No name in the region is better known than Nantucket, an Indian word said to mean "The Far Away Land."

Historians assert that Thomas Macy, a Quaker, was the first Englishman to settle on the island. With his family and a friend, Edward Starbuck, he sailed in an open boat from Salisbury on the coast north of Boston. He crossed Massachusetts Bay, rounded Cape Cod, traversed Nantucket Sound, and arrived on the island in the fall of 1659. Little more than one hundred years later, a Nantucket whaleship, rounding Cape Horn, was carrying the name of its home port to the Pacific Ocean. By 1840 Nantucket, with a population of 9,700 persons, had become the whaling center of the world.

Nantucket's golden age of whaling was, like most golden ages, brief. Presently whaleships became too large to clear the shallow bars outside the harbor. All departments of whaling began to move to New Bedford. In 1846 a great fire destroyed one-third of Nantucket Town. Three years later, Nantucketers by the hundreds left for the gold fields of California.

The Civil War took its toll of Nantucket men and ships. The last whaling vessel to sail from Nantucket put to sea in 1869, ten years after oil was struck at Titusville, Pennsylvania. Petroleum had arrived. At the same time, the westward movement of the American people continued. Nantucket's population decreased to four thousand.

Agriculture on Nantucket also declined. Sheep population, once as high as seventeen thousand head, dwindled and then all but disappeared. No longer was the island a base of trade. Connection with the mainland, and with off-islanders, became of prime importance. By the 1870's, Nantucket homes were being opened to visitors. "Tourists were no longer regarded with a tolerant eye," wrote a local historian. "They were welcomed with sincerity."

No general zoning ordinance exists on Nantucket. The entrepreneur and builder have done according to individual lights. Town, county, and island have identical boundaries. It is all one. In 1955 the town established two historic districts, Old and Historic Nantucket, and Old and Historic Siasconset, the latter a village at the east end of the island. Historic District regulations control exterior design of all buildings within the districts.

In spite of steep losses in resident population and a change in condition from a port of commerce and industry to a place of resort and recreation, Nantucket's dramatic days seem not to be over. Very recently, Walter Beinecke, Jr., a man with money and economic-esthetic ideas as to what Nantucket should look like and be, began to assemble real estate. Presently he owned 80 percent of the town's commercial property. He set to work remodeling old buildings, hotels, wharves, and storage facilities. He rented his remodeled properties, in some instances, to their former owners. He also spoke about what he was doing, and what he thought would be best for Nantucket.

"Buying Up an Island for Its Own Good," read a headline in a news magazine. "Restoration Is Making Some of the Natives Restless," proclaimed another. "What we want are fewer hot-dog and postcard people, and more who come in on their private boats and spend money on antiques, groceries, and quality gifts," said Mr. Beinecke, described as the heir to "a substantial portion of the Sperry and Hutchison Green Stamp fortune." Apparently he also had this to say. "To us, trippers are the people who come on the excursion boat and who leave within four hours. As the saying goes: 'They come with a dirty shirt and a five-dollar bill and don't change either.' "

Till I read these words, I did not believe that the day tripper—bashing around seeking recreation and travel, dropping his pop bottle by the roadside, and grousing about the cupidity of the islanders—was more sinned against than sinning. After reading, I was not sure.

The summer schedule of the Steamship Authority provides a one-day excursion between Woods Hole and Nantucket. It also offers a one-day trip from Martha's Vineyard to Nantucket and return, but not the other way around—a sore point I learned later when I called at the Nantucket Chamber of Commerce.

Suddenly I felt a great wish to be counted among the day trippers. Four hours in which to see Nantucket: the beauty of economy in the use of specific means to an end. Not to see it all—one never can—but to see, select, and respond, to pass judgment or reserve it. Perhaps to meet with the unexpected. And then the boat ride, a veritable cruise through Nantucket Sound.

At Oak Bluffs on Martha's Vineyard, on a morning in early July, the *Nobska* arrived from Woods Hole. She tied up at the pier. The oldest vessel in the Steamship Authority's fleet, the *Nobska* carried a load of excursionists who had embarked at Woods Hole. She had the look of a boat that has seen better days. We day trippers from Oak Bluffs swarmed aboard. The main deck was crowded, but there was space on the boat deck. A clear day and destined to be one of the season's warmest.

A packed steerage-class sort of boat was the *Nobska* as she put out to sea. And indeed this was a deep-water voyage. That was its beauty. The day trippers for the most part looked cheerful. Some seemed to be eating their way across. Presently we lost sight of land. Only steamer chairs and walkers around the deck are lacking to make things feel trans-oceanic. Were it not for the gulls and terns following, balancing over the updraft of the ship's stern, gliding with scarcely a wingbeat, we might be far out on a glassy ocean. But less than two hours after leaving Oak Bluffs, we raised Nantucket Cliffs, a low hazy mound on the north shore of the island.

The low edge of Nantucket's glacial accumulation comes down to the rim of the harbor. As the boat came in, between the east and west jetties, then rounded Brant Point Coast Guard Station, the harbor looks wide. Coatue Point and Beach on the east side seemed wild and uninhabited. Directly ahead, Nantucket Town rose on gentle morainal hills. It appeared long-settled, built up, commercial and bustling.

Day trippers and camera slingers disembarked. Three sight-seeing companies, gunning for us with buses and taxis, picked off a few. The rest of us, more than a little confused, began a drift toward Main Street. The crowd seemed to know where to find it. Stepping along Steamboat Wharf, then out Easy Street, is not unlike going ashore at Gibraltar, the downtown streets devoted to business and the shops to inducing tourists. Detaching myself from the throng, I entered the first fish market I saw and called for six little necks on the half shell.

Expensive and excellent little necks! They would taste even better if you could be sure that the quahog population is not being overfished. But Nantucket Town Reports indicate their abundance is diminishing. In spite of transplanting, restocking, and the watchfullness of the Shell-fish Constable, their numbers do not increase.

The quahog, Pequot Indian word for the attractive thick-shelled hard round clam, is an important commercial bivalve mollusk of the Atlantic coast from southern New England southward. Growing slowly in sandy and muddy bottoms, it may take three years to reach two inches, its legal size. Called "little neck" in its legal youth, the quahog, when larger and more mature, qualifies as a cherrystone. In its middle years, old age, and greater size—it may live to thirty or thirty-five—it is known as a chowder clam.

Inside Nantucket Town, on a broad well-known and cobblestoned Main Street, you do not feel as though on an island. This town has big trees and big handsome town houses. One street in from the waterfront and you could be inside one or another good-looking New England small town or village, or even a southern one. A rather self-conscious place with a certain pretentious simplicity along its streets, wide and narrow, and in the facades of its houses. The expression overall is not really simple but rather a frank unabashed appeal to money and people who have it or mean to get it. A beautifully stocked sporting goods-hardware store, a luxury food and liquor store—these could hold their own in any port of the world. And most of the summer glut of goods and all these automobiles had to come here by water, just as every cobblestone paving Main Street came as ship ballast from the beaches of Gloucester. Impressive logistics—to get the stuff onto the island. Impressive spirit of enterprise, trade. And impressive spirit of maritime peoples. At the top of Main Street on this small Atlantic island sits an institution called the Pacific National Bank.

It was hot work being a day tripper, pounding the cobblestones. I fell out of the ranks of heavy pedestrian traffic. On Fair Street I sat awhile on the ancient pew in the yard of the Friends Meeting House and Nantucket Historical Society. Sitting outdoors, getting a four-hours' feeling of street and town—on this warm day it seemed a winter town, houses close-packed and built for heating, and also to hold the heat. Not built for summer airiness. Not all the houses are good-looking. Possibly the majority are not. The fences are, however, as are the hedges, the topiary art, cutting and trimming shrubs into fancy shapes, and the screens of *Euonymus japonicus*, evergreen, dark and glossy.

Historical: a locked-in district. Past glories overshadowing present importance: symbols of death pangs. The day trippers are the life of the place. Summer residents pass by conservatively dressed. Conservatism all down the line. While I sat for half an hour or more, no one entered or left the Society museum. No cause for wonder, however: This was no day to be indoors. Furthermore, the town itself is a kind of outdoor museum of the whaling period.

A nice municipal feature of Main Street is the green benches. At the corner of Main and Center streets I joined a couple of old men, year-rounders, sitting watching the tourists go by. "I haven't taken down my storm windows yet," said one.

"I wouldn't bother then," says the other. "It'll soon be September first."
A short season, and to an old man even shorter, and a winter town.

There was time for an ice cream cone at the palace on Main Street,
a big lively emporium doing a good job of serving the public. From the
crowded but cool patio in the rear, you gaze up at steeples while licking
your cone. Again, the setting seemed European. I drifted with the human
tide going down Main Street—toward Steamboat Wharf—and came
again to the fine food and liquor store. It looked more inviting than ever.
I stopped and made a small purchase.

Further along, at the foot of Main Street, stands the Pacific Club.
Built by William Rotch, whale-oil merchant, in 1772 for an office and
warehouse, it was earlier called Rotch Market. Later it served as a clubhouse for masters who had hunted whales in the Pacific. A three-story
red-brick white-trimmed building now occupied by cribbage players, it
looks almost as noble and historic as it does on the postcards.

At the wharf I saw the vessel *Nantucket*. Built in 1956, she is the
Steamship Authority's finest, its queen of the fleet. Walking over her
gangway is pure traveling pleasure. When the whistle blows and she
gathers headway, she feels like a ship. Now it turns out that while some
trippers carry cameras, others tote portable bars stocked and equipped
with ice and glasses. It made me thirsty to see them. I brought forth
my Main Street purchase.

Enjoying a few early-evening drinks while sailing over a flat sea, into
the setting sun; accompanied by an escort of sea gulls and a gentle breeze
on the water, I found the two and a quarter hours to Oak Bluffs passed
too quickly.

Sailing from Woods Hole, on the fall schedule, I returned to Nantucket—and with automobile. Nantucket harbor no longer looked un-
familiar; Nantucket Town, as I drove up Broad Street and turned onto
Federal, no longer seemed strange.

"At my first landing I was much surprised at the disagreeable smell
which struck me in many parts of the town; it is caused by the whale
oil, and it is unavoidable; the neatness peculiar to these people can neither
remove nor prevent it." So wrote a lyric enthusiast for Nantucket, J.
Hector St. John de Crevecoeur, in his book *Letters from an American
Farmer*, published in 1782.

Did Crevecoeur land near Rotch's warehouse? In any case, there has
been an improvement. Nantucket smells fine, but you have to be a

colonial buff really to dig it. Again I saw magnificent hedges, beautiful varieties of fences, long wood door latches, and again I felt something southern about the town. A few tourists were sauntering—pleased-looking older couples, perhaps with their hard years behind them, and now not too badly off.

There are probably more old houses here than can be found in most small towns. Nantucket is where you get your fill of old houses. First, Nantucketers wrested the money to build them—many of them quite large. Not the houses of fishermen, but houses of the new seafaring rich. Then when the long decline set in and enterprising young men were going West, townspeople lacked means to keep them up, or even to tear them down. Then came the summer people, and with them came conservative wealth. In spite of off-island money, not all old houses have been restored. The same as in any old close-settled East Coast town, some are engagingly dilapidated. Some of the little historic streets are amazingly crowded. The old-time inhabitants huddled together within calling distance—just what one does not want now. As you walk street to street, looking at all the old houses, first to one side, then to the other, you work up a fine case of swivel-neck.

Nantucket Town contains old style summer hotels that could not compete or survive in a more active thriving resort. I had no trouble choosing among three availabilities: a genteel, furnished-with-antiques apartment; a room in the remodeled, all-Yankeed-up year-round hotel; and a room in a straight-forward new motel outside the Historic District, and down on the flats by the harbor. An unfashionable part of town, no doubt, but it offers light and air. Furthermore, the Jetties Beach is close by. I walked to it. Studying the map, I saw public beaches in every part of the island. Town and county appear to own about 2 percent of the shoreline.

"The development of Nantucket land has been a very unique and unusual process, substantially different from the development of real estate most anywhere else," say the authors of *Selected Resources of the Island of Nantucket, a Publication of the Cooperative Extension Service of the University of Massachusetts and the United States Department of Agriculture.*

"In 1670 the entire Island was owned by 27 men. They laid out their homesteads and a certain amount of land for house lots. They took from 20 to 40 acres each . . . and all the rest of the Island, about two-thirds or more, they decided to use for sheep pasturage.

"According to their estimates—1½ acres per sheep—this land would support 19,440 sheep, so each of the 27 men could have 720 sheep. Of course each man did not wish to have 720 sheep . . . so they bought and sold these sheep commons. . . ."

As the population of Nantucket increased, sheep commons changed hands. Owners of sheep commons were known as Proprietors, that is, Proprietors of the Common and Undivided Lands of Nantucket. The Proprietors held meetings at which each voted in accordance with the number of sheep commons he owned. Such was the system until the 19th century, when large holders of sheep commons, taking court action, forced the exchange of their sheep commons for specified pieces of land. That was the beginning of the end of the common and undivided lands. As late as 1957, however, the Town of Nantucket purchased a few sheep commons from an estate. Although little if any of the old common land is left, the peak of private ownership of Nantucket lands may be passing.

Today, 92 percent of the island is privately owned, including much undeveloped land, some of it in large tracts. But the first gifts of land—both small parcels and upland heath acreage—have been made to the Nantucket Conservation Foundation. The Foundation has also purchased land. The total acquired thus far adds up to more than two thousand acres. So a new kind of commons may be returning—without the Proprietors, or the sheep. The last will not be missed. Nantucket soils in general, are too sandy and drought-parched for agriculture. The old commons pasturage method was bad on two counts: It did not provide good feed for the stock, and it permitted overgrazing, a prime cause of soil erosion.

Agriculture in most times and places has been a destructive influence. Who, more than the farmer, pitted himself against nature and what grows naturally? Who cleared more land of forest and wildlife? You can beat swords into plowshares but they can still be tools of aggression and ruin. Farmers and part-time farmers once grazed or grew crops on 90 percent of Nantucket land. Today, the last island farming is disappearing. Groves, and perhaps even forests, are coming back. In his *History of Nantucket*, published in 1835, Obed Macy says that when the first settlers reached Nantucket in the fall of 1659, "They found the island covered with wood, and inhabited by about 1500 Indians, who depended for subsistence on fishing, fowling, and hunting. Game was remarkably plenty, and continued so many years afterward. . . ."

The island covered with wood—the words are hardly more than a supposition. There was no way for Obed Macy to know; he had no first-hand accounts to draw on. Of those earlier times, he writes, "the records . . . are nearly silent . . . the number of inhabitants was yet small . . . they were so illiterate that the little of their writings that have come to us, is hardly legible or intelligible."

When Crevecoeur arrived on Nantucket, one hundred years behind the first settlers, he described the island as "not being possessed of a single tree." He found it, however, "covered here and there with sorrel, grass, a few cedar bushes, and scrubby oaks. . . ." Sometimes it is hard to tell a scrubby tree from a shrub. Now, almost two hundred years after Crevecoeur wrote, there is evidence of "a gradual increase in the growth of shrubs, scrubby type wind-shaped trees, many groves of thriving up-growing trees including Tupelo, Sassafras, and some better shaped oaks and pines." So say the authors of *Selected Resources of the Island of Nantucket*.

~~~~~~

September weather lingering into October. Tourists could not ask for better days. Sixty-five degrees at ten in the morning under a silver-gray sky. Nantucket claims to be, and is, a gray town—which heightens the colors of its flowers. The yellowest roses bloom in fenced yards, and enormous bright dahlias. Only a closely structured settlement could produce, or would have practical use for, all these exceptional privet hedges.

Walking into town from North Beach Street you see examples of the real Colonial, and the real Federal Period. Also many an imitation, and conformity. Every shop, it seems, and some houses as well, carry a black-and-gold–lettered scrollwork nameboard, purportedly resembling those that displayed the name on the hull of a whaleship. Worst of all is the uncontrolled cuteness.

I strolled down to Straight Wharf, one of the properties bought and remodeled by Walter Beinecke, Jr. I had read that he says he is trying to keep Nantucket the way it used to be. I suppose that means the way that he thinks it was. Of course, Nantucket never had a shopping center and marina complex such as the one now abuilding. While tripling the number of berths for yachts, the new owner also imposes his fake gas-lamp and candle-dipping esthetic. He hopes to keep Nantucket safe from banana peelers. Will he also save it from improper oil disposal, misuse of marine toilets, and dumping of raw sewage into the harbor? For one man to own so much of Nantucket can hardly be good for the town. This sort of control adds to the spiritual stultification that tends to beset all islands.

Do not confuse the Jethro Coffin House with the Jared Coffin House. The latter is a restored hotel, the former, the oldest house on Nantucket. The Jethro Coffin House, 1686, stands on Sunset Hill Lane. The hill, a low mound, lies well up from the harbor, a good place to watch for a ship coming in. It looks like a splendid site to me, but those who built up the town built further south and east. So the oldest house stands isolated from other old dwellings, and in fact among everyday new ones. Jethro's art-lessness is good, Jared's affectation bad.

Time to buy lunch, and I was determined: not one cent for tribute, or for instant colonial. I looked for a place still independent and with its own style, where I could eat, nonconforming and apart from the restoration monopoly.

Allen's Diner with its red and green running lights may become the last unrestored antique in the town. The true diner resembles in shape and appearance a railroad dining car. Passengers Not Allowed to Stand on the Platform. Allen's is a true diner, for it was in fact a railroad car. Once it ran the rails from Nantucket east to Siasconset, "Sconset" as it is called. The short-haul railroad, built in the 1880's, closed down many years ago. The counterman in the low-ceilinged, crowded, bright var-nished wooden diner remarked, "We do things differently in Nantucket."

"What does that mean?" I asked.

He replied, "With this saying we solve our problems."

Nantucket Town approximates the island's geographical center. The former railroad to Sconset, eight miles away, ran south of the present level and straight Milestone Road with its new blacktop bicycle path beside it. Road and path traverse Nantucket's outwash plain, the flattest part of the island. Thirty years ago three Nantucket shops rented bicycles. Among them they mustered three hundred machines. Today Nantucket has seven shops with three thousand bicycles to rent, all told. At this time of year you see few cyclists. What one notices instead are four-wheel drive vehicles, which suggests that beaches are open to them. This raises a question. How many vehicles of this kind can an island this size withstand?

From Nantucket Town west to Maddaket you ride over a moorland covered with ground-hugging growth, a scene close-cropped as though trimmed by the wind. Although the country is lonely looking, it does not seem wild—the growth is not rank enough for that. The moors appear tamed by the winds. No real trees grow here, only patches of thickets and shrubs amid the prevailing coverage of beach heath, lichen, and bear-berry. Not a warm countryside, nor inviting: nothing pastoral at Ram Pasture, nor around Sheep Pond. Not only trees are absent but also stone walls, fences, meadows, and barns. Everyone has fled to Nantucket Town, or settled there in the first place. Nantucket appears to be a centralized island.

At Maddaket, at the island's west end, I drove to the edge of the dunes along a public way. Below is the beach—and it is available without trespass. So are the dunes available, not only to walkers but also to four-wheel drive vehicles. At Maddaket, between Hither Creek and Long Pond, the beach grass is getting badly cut up. Wheeled traffic could do more damage than sheep: It could turn these low bluffs into barren sand. Meanwhile, a developer's sign at this point exhorts you to choose an ocean or harbor view lot.

Traveling east from Nantucket Town, the road leads to Quaise, Polpis, Wauwinet, Quidnet—old names of perhaps old sites of Indian villages, but today simply neighborhoods and localities, no more than clusters of houses. There is only one post office outside Nantucket Town and that is at Sconset.

The moors eastward loom higher and wider than those to the west. They are wilder, less kempt by the wind, and to my eye, more inviting. As I passed Polpis Harbor, I stopped for the view of the wetlands.

In wetlands you compass both land and water. You enjoy in wetlands —and it depends on mood—the best, or worst, of both worlds. Wetlands often offer surprises and this, at the edge of Polpis Harbor, turns out to be no exception. I was not aware of breaking into the solitude of a little blue heron, but apparently I did. Or was it an eastern green, a more common bird and often more blue than green? With slow beat the heron lifted off—what a lot of wing spread for so skinny a body!

On Wauwinet Road, wires between the utility poles sagged under a weight of birds. How many, I wondered, and what, in sum, do they weigh.

These flocks were dense. Dark clouds of them circled and whirled, then perched. Brown-backed birds with spotted breasts—olive-backed thrush, or maybe gray-cheeked? These would be uncommon transients, not the four-hour kind.

Topographical variations run a gamut from slight to subtle. Again, the difference depends on mood. I went down to the beach at Wauwinet —for the pleasure of finding it open to me—to anyone—and I did it again at Quidnet. One of the very best things about Nantucket is frequent occurrence of public beaches. From the western end of Cape Cod to the eastern end of Nantucket, my concern was not wholly the natural environment, nor unalloyed social history, but rather the way men live. When you take man out of natural history, then you dehumanize it, and him.

Polpis Road takes you down the east coast of Nantucket Island to New England's most southeastern headland, Sankaty Head. From these cliffs, New England beams its second strongest beacon, Sankaty Head Light, built in 1849, a giantess standing 170 feet above the Atlantic and in power second only to Cape Cod (or Highland) Light at Truro. Sankaty Head's white light flashing every fifteen seconds blazes far out to sea by night. By day, the gleaming white tower girdled with one wide band of red makes a distinctive land and marine mark. Tall and serene, a constant guide in the midst of impersonal and dangerous natural forces, Sankaty Head Light helps humanize the scene.

From the cliff on which Sankaty Head Light stands you see, looking south, the knobbiest parts of Nantucket's morainal landscape—Altar Rock, Shawaukemo, Saul's and Folger hills. These are low hills—nothing exceeding one hundred feet—covered with low-lying vegetation, monotonous-looking and bleak. What warms the panorama are the fairways and greens of the Sankaty and Siasconset golf clubs.

Siasconset—Sconset—lies a mile and a half away. When you arrive there you find an east-pointing sign: "To Spain and Portugal, 3,000 miles." On the beach at Sconset you come full circle, back to the point of no beginning. You feel the energy of currents, sand piles shifting from land to sea. Above all, you feel the ocean presence, mindless and unphilosophical. Small talk, verities, and eternal clichés blow away.

Sconset lanes and rambler roses. Cottages overcome by roses. Summer houses and summer hotels. Closed for the season to be sure, but why did they look so prim-mouthed? The motley former fishermen's shanties, however, wore a different expression, low-lived and zesty. I think they must be the oldest American down-to-earth houses I ever saw that are still unfiddled with.

From Sconset to Nantucket Town by the aforementioned Milestone Road, you cross a landscape where sea-wind subdued elderberry and heather and plum vines cover a deep wash of gravel and sand, a landscape of low intensity, almost entirely stripped of its rocks and boulders. There is no bedrock. Can the passing traveler feel the lack of it? Why not? One responds with more than one's eyes. Whatever stone the glacier bestowed —and stone was never abundant on Nantucket—has long since been carted and hauled away, buried in wharf, building foundations and roads. I found the absence of stone disenthralls.

In search of stone I drove to Nantucket's highest point, Altar Rock, in the east-central part of the island. Here, even on a quiet day, the wind never stops. A bronze plaque nailed to the rock explains that a man named Henry Coffin gave the surrounding land to his native county. Had he not, this small boulder too might have vanished. In a gravelly land, even an ordinary rock is a monument.

After a day on the moors and sheep commons, and in the back country, I began to understand better why almost all the people settled in Nantucket Town. You can huddle together for practical reasons, and also for quite primitive ones—for efficiency in matters of business, and to satisfy human and household needs.

Nantucket is where you get your fill of mawkish representations of whales—on weather vanes, paper napkins, bookends, and ashtrays. And these manifestations are, perhaps, a logical sequel to a by and large sordid story. Although in the 18th and 19th centuries whaling was a staple industry that provided oil for the lamps of the nation and spermaceti for its candles, and although it played a part in American territorial expansion, no one emerges who was connected with it. Whaling was like mining in its exploitation of the working man. Fortunes were made by the few. In spite of lip service, sentimentality, and of course genealogy, there may be no whaling individual whom the world cares about. Herman Melville was, after all, only a casual whaleman.

Nantucket shares honors with New Bedford in the occult novel in which Herman Melville stowed a good deal of whaling matter. Although Nantucket was the great whaling port of the world until superseded by

New Bedford, other small ports in the region were also furnishing whale-men and outfitting ships. Melville drew his fictitious whalers from the then foremost nurseries of seafaring men—Nantucket, Cape Cod, Martha's Vineyard.

"The chief mate . . . was Starbuck, a native of Nantucket, and a Quaker by descent," Melville wrote in *Moby Dick*. Starbuck is charac-terized as "uncommonly conscientious for a seaman." He carried "far-away domestic memories of his young Cape wife and child. . . ."

Melville's second mate was Stubb, "a native of Cape Cod. . . . A happy-go-lucky. . . . When close to the whale, in the very death-lock of the fight, he handled his unpitying lance cooly and off-handedly, as a whistling tinker his hammer."

Flask was the name of Melville's third mate, "a native of Tisbury, in Martha's Vineyard . . . very pugnacious concerning whales. . . . So utterly lost was he to all sense of reverence for the many marvels of their majestic bulk and mystic ways . . . that in his poor opinion the wondrous whale was but a species of magnified mouse, or at least water-rat, requir-ing only a little circumvention and some small application of time and trouble in order to kill and boil. . . ."

The boatsteerers in *Moby Dick* reflected the polyglot cosmopolitan crews found on board world-ranging Yankee whaleships. Boatsteerers guided the thirty-foot whaleboats (perfected rowboats) launched from the ship in pursuit of whales once they were sighted. Boatsteerers also struck the whales, that is, threw the harpoons. For his three boatsteerers Melville created Queequeg, a Polynesian prince; Tashtego, "an unmixed Indian from Gay Head, the most westerly promontory of Martha's Vine-yard . . . which has long supplied the neighboring island of Nantucket with many of her most daring harpooneers"; and Daggoo, " a gigantic coal-black" native of an African coast.

In spite of Melville's personal experience and his knowledge of whaling lore, it would be a mistake to base one's impressions of whaling on read-ing *Moby Dick*.

When whaling began in small coastal places such as Nantucket, it was at first a communal activity. In the early days a whaleship skipper knew every man in his crew, and he knew the man's family. But by the time Melville shipped on the whaler *Acushnet* in January, 1841, the whaleship had become a factory, and whaling a sweated industry. By then it was every man for himself—owners, captains, and mates. Crews were being dredged from the bottom ranks of all races and nations. Half the men were green hands. Two-thirds deserted every voyage. Melville himself was a case in point—he jumped his first whaleship at the Marquesas. On his second he became a mutineer. Although *Moby Dick* appears to be about whaling, it actually is about something else, perhaps a fable of vengeance, or symbolic of something even Melville did not know.

One of the trustworthy true accounts of whaling is a little Nantucket book Melville knew. Written by or for Owen Chase of Nantucket, first mate on the whaleship *Essex*, it tells how the vessel was rammed and sunk by a whale in the Pacific Ocean in 1820. Chase, with the others who survived, spent ninety-three days at sea in open boats. They lived by eating their shipmates who died—all simply and matter-of-factly recounted in *Narrative of the Most Extraordinary and Distressing Shipwreck of the Whaleship* Essex.

Another reliable whaling book that Melville read was the work of two young forecastle hands. One of them, Cyrus M. Hussey, was a Nantucketer. The authors were the only survivors of a whaleship's company killed on a South Seas island by natives. It too has a long 19th-century title, *A Narrative of the Mutiny, on board the Ship* Globe, *of Nantucket, in the Pacific Ocean, Jan. 1824.*

In his *History of Nantucket*, Obed Macy included the testimony of whaling captains. Their plain statements tell a good deal. Captain Benjamin Worth said, "I began to follow the sea in 1783, being then 15 years of age, and continued till 1824. . . . During this period of 41 years, I was a shipmaster 29 years. From the time when I commenced going to sea till I quitted the business, I was at home only seven years."

Captain George W. Gardner told Obed Macy, "I began to follow the sea at 13 years of age, and continued in that service 37 years. . . . During 37 years I was at home but 4 years and 8 months."

While the men were away on voyages of thirty and forty months and even longer, whaling was a way of life for the women, too. Wives raised the children and managed all manner of business. When he visited Nantucket, Crevecoeur noted, "A singular custom prevails here among the women. . . . They have adopted these many years the Asiatic custom of taking a dose of opium every morning; and so deeply rooted is it, that they would be at a loss how to live without this indulgence. . . ." Crevecoeur said he was greatly surprised and wholly unable to account for, or guess at, the cause. Why surprised?

The money and glory of whaling came from a brutal and bloody business exploitative not only of men but also of natural resources, that is, the whales that it slaughtered, especially the sperm whale. The sperm whale had the finest oil. Doubtless the 19th-century discovery of petroleum saved this whale from extinction.

The whale is so beautifully adapted to an aquatic life that for a long time men thought it a fish. Even today these giant and largest of animals —they weigh about a ton a foot—remain mysterious in many ways. Sperm whales may reach 60 feet in length. The fantastic figures reported by old-time whalemen are not considered reliable. The largest whale, the blue, may measure more than 80 feet and weigh well over 100 tons. For comparison, an average-sized elephant weighs five tons. The almost mythical white whale is exceedingly rare. Whales have a four-chambered heart, warm blood, lungs, and affectionate instincts. The cow whale feeds her young on milk by squirting it into the calf. A mother will not desert a wounded calf, a tie which whalemen have often used to their own advantage. Whales hear rather than see the objects in the world they move in. They are the only seagoing mammals able to withstand vast oceanic pressures and plunge into abyss. They have two enemies, the killer whale and man.

The killer whale, the most dangerous dweller in the seas, even more terrible than the shark, is found from the Arctic to the Antarctic. Being only 30 feet long, whalemen have not wasted their harpoons on it. It hunts in packs and picks off the larger whales traveling in pairs or alone. The fact that whales, having lungs, must surface to breathe, makes them vulnerable to their second and far deadlier enemy. Many people other than whalemen find whales highly intelligent, inoffensive, social and likeable beasts.

Nantucket whalemen, like the Indians who first showed them how to whale alongshore, have vanished. The whales they pursued are hunted now by whalemen of other islands and nations. Zoologists say that whales are on the decline, that as a group they may be approaching the end. International efforts to regulate whaling began thirty years ago. But since modern whaleships are terribly efficient instruments of destruction, the disquieting question remains whether or not the International Whaling Commission can save the whale. Naturalists of whatever degree consider the extermination of a species an irretrievable crime and disaster.

Nantucket Harbor on a calm autumn day

Old pavement in Nantucket Town

Latch and door of Nantucket's oldest house

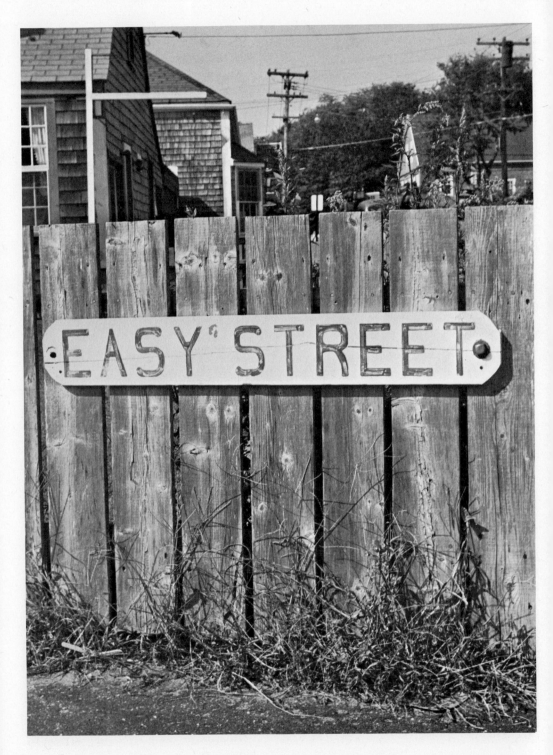

An insider's in-joke: but why shouldn't there be such a place?

Nantucket graveyard

Ball playing on the sands of Maddaket Harbor

Two fisherwomen crabbing in a canal

The summer ended, only one boat remains asail in Pleasant Harbor

Chapter 14

THE VINEYARD YEARS

T HE Vineyard years of Joshua Slocum concern his decline and disappearance. They hold particular interest for persons who know the
island and region.

Of all American sailing-ship captains, Joshua Slocum is the most
legendary. When, at age fifty-four, he brought the 37-foot homemade
Spray into harbor on the morning of 27 June 1898, he completed a feat
of seamanship never before accomplished. For the first time a man had
sailed around the world entirely alone.

As the first single-handed circumnavigator, Slocum made his mark
in history. He then went on to achieve a sure place in literature. With
the same sense of pride and professionalism he brought to manning his
craft on great waters, he wrote the story of his solo voyage and gave it
a simple descriptive title—*Sailing Alone Around the World.*

Serialized in the *Century* magazine, his story appeared in book form in 1900. Two years later, with earnings from writing and lecturing, Joshua Slocum bought what he thought he wanted—certainly what his wife, Hettie, wanted—a home. His youngest son recalled his father saying that if he settled down, it would be in the Hawaiian Islands. But when the time came, Slocum chose a New England island instead—Martha's Vineyard, where some of his sisters and a brother lived, and which he had visited several times.

On 1 March 1902, the *Vineyard Gazette* made a matter-of-fact announcement. "Capt. Joshua Slocum," it reported, "who has the fame of going around the world in a sail boat, has purchased the residence and lot formerly owned by the late John Manter. Also other land of Samuel E. West, so as to have enough for a small farm." The property lay on the Takemmy Trail, the Edgartown Road, a short distance east of West Tisbury village, not far from where Nancy Luce had written her poems and died twelve years earlier.

Farthest inland of the island's settled places, West Tisbury was favored by retired whaling captains and whalemen seeking to forget past voyages. Although Slocum also appeared to be quitting the sea, he did not, could not, give up the sloop in which he had sailed around the world. So while he farmed in West Tisbury, the *Spray* waited in Menemsha harbor in the adjoining town of Chilmark.

"When I was a very small boy, I went aboard the *Spray* when she lay in Menemsha," Captain Donald LeMar Poole said as he showed me his first-edition of *Sailing Alone Around the World*. "But," added Captain Poole, "not much fuss was ever made here over Slocum. To begin with, he was an off-islander, a foreigner. He was, or had been, a merchantman, and no love was ever lost between merchantmen and whalemen, and probably 90 percent of the Vineyard seamen were whalers. In those days there were probably a score or more shipmasters living at this end of the island. Slocum was in no way any more remarkable or outstanding for what he had done than many of his contemporaries."

Although Slocum may have seemed a familiar type to Vineyarders of his day, it nevertheless is unlikely they knew much about him. His books tell little about his life story. Contemporary assessment, furthermore, is a very difficult thing. In due course, time and the world decide. A few years ago the Dukes County Historical Society sponsored the placing of a bronze plaque in front of the house that the off-island ex-merchant captain once lived in.

"I was born in a cold spot, on coldest North Mountain, on a cold February 20th," Joshua Slocum wrote. Chilling was the scene, and sea-haunted. It overlooked the worn coast and tremendous tides of the Bay of Fundy bordering the west coast of Nova Scotia. The year was 1844.

Joshua Slocum's father was a farmer, and it was on a farm that he spent his early years—although he could hear the roaring of the tides in the distance. His mother, Sarah Jane Southern, was the daughter of a lighthouse keeper. She is said to have been a fine-featured gentlewoman whom her son resembled. Joshua was the fifth of eleven children.

In those days Nova Scotia was a shipbuilding center, a place dedicated to the sea and to the modes of life peculiar to seafaring men. "The wonderful sea charmed me from the first," Joshua Slocum wrote. By the age of eight he had, in his own words, "already been afloat along with other boys on the bay, with chances greatly in favor of being drowned." Like most 19th century country boys and professional sailors, he could not swim! He never learned. He was fatalistic about the sea. He knew it would claim him if it meant to, and in a sense he was willing to accept death in it. So from the beginning he was not afraid, but was drawn to the sea.

After a couple of years of one-room schooling, ten-year-old Joshua went to work helping his father. Having failed in farming, the father now tried to support his family by making fishermen's leather boots. Young Josh hated the work. Father and son did not get along. As long as his mother lived, however, the boy made only one attempt to escape. But when she died at age forty-six, he left for good.

The future circumnavigator made his first voyage at sixteen. By the time he was eighteen he had advanced to second mate. Although he had little schooling—he never learned to spell or punctuate—he had a taste for reading and learning.

For a number of years he sailed on British ships. Then in 1869, in San Francisco, he was offered command of an American coasting schooner. At age twenty-five he became Captain Slocum. He also became an American citizen.

Slocum's next command, a larger ship, was another step upward. With a mixed cargo he sailed from San Francisco to Sydney, Australia. There, while the vessel was unloading and loading again—a matter of two or three weeks—he met Virginia Albertina Walker, and married her in 1871. He was twenty-seven, she twenty-one. Born in New York but raised in Australia, Virginia (judging by photographs of her) was a regal-looking young woman. She loved the outdoors—was a splendid horsewoman and an excellent shot. Only a rarely strong and courageous wife accompanied a captain husband on more than one voyage. The cabin of a freight-carrying sailing ship was a confining home. There would be no other woman on board to help. But Virginia, for the rest of her life, sailed wherever Joshua went.

A voyage from the South Pacific far into the North, from Australia to Alaska for a cargo of salmon, made an unusual honeymoon trip. Although his ship foundered on a sandbar, Slocum rescued his bride and also the catch of fish. The owners, despite the loss of the ship, gave Slocum another command.

The following year Joshua's and Virginia's first child, a boy, was born in San Francisco harbor. A second son, also born on board, was named for the ship his father commanded. Then came a daughter, born while Slocum's vessel lay in Philippine waters. When Slocum was cruising for cod in the Okhotsk Sea, Virginia bore twins on shipboard, but they died in infancy. The youngest arrived in Hong Kong harbor on board the ship *Northern Light*.

Command of the *Northern Light*, a ship Slocum called as beautiful as her name, set the high-water mark of his merchant marine career. "I had a right to be proud of her," he wrote years later, "for at the time—in the eighties—she was the finest American sailing vessel afloat." Slocum's dream had not been to go around the world in a small boat alone. His dream had been to be a master of great merchant ships. What he had dreamed of, he now had won. But even while he was reaching a personal zenith, the sun was setting on the long day of sail. Winddriven ships like the *Northern Light* could not compete with steam. The *Northern Light* lost money, and as a part-owner, Slocum lost too. Presently, the tall-masted ship was sold and cut down for a coal barge.

Had Slocum continued merely successful he might be unknown today, like most masters in sail. He was destined, however, to go on losing, and on that course descend to fame.

A time when owners and masters were turning to steam seemed hardly the moment to invest the last of one's savings in a sailing ship, but Slocum was determined to go on in the way he had begun. He now bought the *Aquidneck*, in his words, "a little bark which of all man's handiwork seemed . . . the nearest to perfection of beauty, and which in speed, when the wind blew, asked no favors of steamers."

Slocum's oldest son recalled the bark was "as close to a yacht as a merchantman could be." The son remembered the square piano bolted to the deck, the handsome saloon, the livestock in pens on the roof of the deckhouse, the canary, and many books. Carrying freights, and with the Slocum family on board, the *Aquidneck* sailed from Baltimore for South America. By the time the bark reached the coast of Brazil, Virginia was ailing.

Virginia lay sick as the vessel approached Buenos Aires and anchored in the Plata River. She longed to see her people again. Slocum hurried ashore to try to get cargo for Sydney. Not many hours later, however, he saw the flag letter *J* flying from the masthead of the *Aquidneck*—J for Joshua—the signal that meant he was needed. He returned at once. That evening, 25 July 1884, in the presence of her husband, her children kneeling beside her shipbound bed, Virginia, not yet thirty-five, died. "When she died," her youngest son summed up years later, "then father never recovered. He was like a ship with a broken rudder."

Two years later, in Boston in 1886, Slocum married Henrietta Elliott, a first cousin just down from Nova Scotia. Hettie was a seamstress, twenty-four and pretty; Slocum, forty-two and lonely. Accompanied by his oldest and youngest sons, Slocum and his new wife set out in the *Aquidneck*, tramp-freighting along the east coast of South America. Things did not go well. One mishap seemed to lead to another until finally, the following year, in Paranagua Bay, Brazil, the *Aquidneck* "stranded broadside on, where, open to the sea, a strong swell came in that raked her fore and aft, for three days, the waves dashing over her groaning hull the while till at last her back was broke and—why not add 'heart' as well! for she lay now undone." Although Slocum did not say so, she also lay uninsured.

At this point a distressed mariner might have asked the American consul for a lift home, but not Captain Slocum. Saving what he could from the wreck, he went to work on the beach and, with a kit of hand tools built a 35-foot craft which he called a canoe. *Liberdade* he named it, because he launched it the day Brazilian slaves were freed. In the *Liberdade,* wearing the sails Hettie sewed, Slocum, Hettie, and the two boys sailed 5,500 miles in fifty-three days, from Paranagua Bay to Washington, D.C., where they arrived at the end of 1888.

In the space of three years Slocum lost his sea wife, Virginia, his ship the *Aquidneck*, and his profession as well. He could not get another command. The long age of sail was over.

At rock bottom now, Slocum turned to himself. He still had all his resourcefulness. Earlier sailing ship masters of little schooling had processed their logs into narratives of voyages. Slocum would turn out to be the last in a New England sea captain-writer tradition. He sat down and wrote *Voyage of the Liberdade* with, as he said, "a hand, alas! that has grasped the sextant more often than the plane or pen." Printed in 1890 at his own expense, sold by himself at $1 a copy, it brought neither money nor recognition. Even today, few of the many who know Slocum's name have read this remarkable book.

Then on a winter day in 1892, at loose ends on the Boston waterfront, Slocum met an old friend, Eben Pierce, a prosperous retired whaling captain. "Come to Fairhaven, and I'll give you a ship," the ex-whaler said to the ex-merchant captain. "But," Captain Pierce added, "she wants some repairs."

When Slocum arrived in Fairhaven on the eastern shore of New Bedford harbor, he found that his friend had, as he later wrote, "something of a joke" on him. The ship in question was a derelict oyster sloop called *Spray*, lying high and dry in a pasture along the Acushnet River. A Yankee shipmaster does not wear his heart on his sleeve, and Slocum did not say what he felt when he saw the old sloop whose sailing days, like his own, seemed finished. From that hour, however, Slocum and the *Spray* were never to be parted.

In *Sailing Alone Around the World*, Joshua Slocum tells how he rebuilt the sloop plank by plank. The job took thirteen months and $553.62. When launched, the *Spray*, in his words, "sat on the water like a swan." Just as he finished the rejuvenation, he unexpectedly received an offer—his first in almost six years—not a captain's berth nor on board a merchant vessel, but rather as "navigator in command" of an untested gunboat. Although the extremely hazardous trip he began in 1893 provided the subject for his second book, the brief *Voyage of the Destroyer*, it proved a digression from the main current of his life.

"I was born in the breezes," Joshua Slocum wrote, "and I had studied the sea as perhaps few men have studied it, neglecting all else." Just when or how he got the idea of sailing alone around the world can only be guessed at. Both his inner need to achieve, and his outward appearance of failure, seemed to be driving him toward it. But a pretext was needed to satisfy the world, and possibly his more conventional self. He announced he would undertake the voyage in order to make money by writing and syndicating travel letters. Newspaper-sponsored accounts of travel were in vogue in the 1890's. Two of his favorite authors, Robert Louis Stevenson and Mark Twain, had pointed the way.

So Captain Slocum got ready. Well-wishers supplied him with stores and the rather primitive equipment he took along, also with books—one of his first considerations in planning a voyage alone. He had carried freights around the world five times as ship's captain. He still had his charts, compass and sextant, rifles, revolvers, and medicines. He described to reporters the route he proposed to take. It was very different from the one he actually took. He thought he might be away two years. His calculation proved conservative by fourteen months.

Slocum set sail from Boston, 24 April 1895, alone in the *Spray*, without power, radio, ship-to-shore phone, money, or life insurance. Fifty-one years old, brown-bearded and bald-headed, he was, according to a reporter on the scene, 5 feet 9½ inches tall, 146 pounds in weight, "spry as a kitten and nimble as a monkey."

A southward course had been plotted, but the sloop sailed eastward instead. Hugging the familiar Massachusetts coast, Slocum went as far as Gloucester, twenty miles away, where he asked himself again "whether it were best to sail beyond the ledges and rocks at all." He moved on to Nova Scotia, his native land, which he had not seen for many years. He lingered there six weeks. Finally, on July 2, he let go, as he said, his last hold on America.

Slocum crossed the Atlantic to Gibraltar where British naval officers warned him of pirates in the Mediterranean. They advised him not to head for the Suez Canal. So Slocum recrossed the Atlantic, this time taking a southwestward course. He skirted the coast of South America. Alone, he survived the vicissitudes of the Strait of Magellan. He traversed the vast South Pacific on a pilgrimage to Australia, where in palmier days he had met and married Virginia. From Australia he sailed the Coral Sea north, passed through Torres Strait and into the Indian Ocean. After rounding the Cape of Good Hope, he crossed the Atlantic a third time. Three years, two months, two days, and 46,000 miles after starting out, Slocum dropped anchor at Newport, Rhode Island. Still he had a strong urge to return to the place of beginning, and apparently the *Spray* did, too. A few days later, "not quite satisfied . . .," he wrote, "she waltzed beautifully round the coast and up the Acushnet River . . . where I secured her to the cedar spile driven in the bank to hold her when she was launched. I could bring her no nearer home."

With publication of *Sailing Alone Around the World*, the unheard-of became an accepted fact. Some still questioned, however, Slocum's statement that with wheel lashed, the *Spray* steered herself while the captain sat below, cooking, reading, mending his sails or clothes, or sleeping. But no man could sail around the world and remain at the wheel day and night.

People understand now that the *Spray* with wheel lashed was able to hold her course. Yachtsmen, however, are still debating her points. Some think she must have been nearly ideal for going around the world; others, that she was dangerous and that Slocum succeeded in spite of her, not because of her. All agree that the 37-foot *Spray* was a very large beamy boat for one man to handle.

Since Slocum's day, a dozen men and more have sailed single-handed around the world but none has made a voyage like his. Those who came later took other routes, and after 1915 went through the Panama Canal. No one has repeated his passage through the Strait of Magellan among the icy crags and terrifying rocks, and although many have written about their exploits, none has produced a book the equal of *Sailing Alone Around the World*.

From circling the world, where does a man go next? The captain did not know which way to turn. Presently, by sail and tow, he guided the *Spray* up the Hudson River and through the Erie Canal to Buffalo. There, at the Pan American Exposition of 1901, the *Spray* rode the fair grounds lake while the captain sold souvenirs and books and answered the tourists' questions. The years of decline had set in.

When Joshua Slocum arrived at Martha's Vineyard the following spring, that is, 1902, and moved into his newly acquired farmhouse, Captain James Cleaveland, a native son and retired whaling master, lived in the big house next door. A Cleaveland granddaughter recalled that the Slocum place was "a very old, small Cape Cod house," and that Slocum "put a curving Japanese-temple type of roof over the front, and beside the door the usual shells and chunks of coral of the seafaring man. . . ." Her grandfather, she said, "used to entertain a great many interesting men in the kitchen. I remember his bringing Captain Slocum into the front part of the house and my aunt greeting him. As I remember, he was a small wiry man, bald, with a pointed beard and very bright, small piercing eyes. . . . Mrs. Slocum," she added "used to stay with us occasionally. She was quite firm in her determination never to go to sea with her husband again. . . ."

Slocum's first West Tisbury summer was ending when a letter came from Clifton Johnson (1865–1940) of Hadley, Massachusetts. Johnson, a photographer, illustrator, and writer, wanted to visit and interview Slocum. In his reply, the captain did not send Johnson the ferry schedule. Instead, he called on the mainland for him.

"The *Spray*, as I first saw her," Clifton Johnson wrote later, "lay gently rocking in a little cove . . . near Woods Hole . . . she had an attractive air of domesticity and was evidently built for a sea home. . . . It was a pleasure to set foot on her . . . to eat with Captain Slocum a rough and ready lunch that he deftly prepared in the little galley, and . . . when night came to bunk under a deck awning. . . . But, best of all, was a sail the next morning . . . from the mainland across to Martha's Vineyard. . . .

"His house is one of the most ancient on the island—an oak-ribbed ark of a dwelling with warped floors and tiny window panes and open fireplaces. Its aspect is at present rather forlorn and naked, but the captain knows how to wield the hammer and saw. . . . In a single season he has become an enthusiastic agriculturist. . . . Martha's Vineyard looks to him like Eden, and it is likely the sea will know him no more. . . ."

Travelogues then, as now, were a staple of the cultural life in West Tisbury. "Do not forget the lecture at Agricultural Hall on Thursday evening by Capt. Slocum." the *Vineyard Gazette* exhorted its readers in the fall of 1902. "A rare treat is in store for our people."

The next spring, Slocum bought more ground. "I have about 160 acres of beautiful land," he wrote Clifton Johnson. "On some of these acres are stumps which I shall endeavor to hoist out putting in a hill of potatoes in its stead."

As is often the way with an enterprising but untested farmer, the captain tried growing something new—in this case, hops. Mrs. Donald Campbell of West Tisbury recalled picking hops for Slocum when she was a girl—but only once, for he did not repeat the experiment. She said he was "tall, spare, courteous, and reserved."

In his second summer as a farmer, Slocum, instead of making hay, was sailing in Vineyard and Nantucket Sounds. At harvest time the *Vineyard Gazette* reported him in Buzzards Bay waters.

Now sixty, Slocum found island winters uncomfortably cold. "I became so interested in trying to keep warm these winter days," he wrote in a letter in March, 1904, "that I forgot all except the wood-pile. I have an oak grove, fortunately, near my house."

After 1904 Slocum spent little time on the farm. George G. Gifford, storekeeper and town clerk of West Tisbury during those years, described him as "not extremely tall nor extremely short, but a quite pleasant chap who talked with everybody. It was the general opinion," Mr. Gifford said, "that Slocum and his wife had separated—nothing legal—but just that he went his way and she went hers."

Joseph Chase Allen, newspaperman, author of *Tales and Trails of Martha's Vineyard* and *The Wheelhouse Loafer*, said that he knew Slocum the way a boy knows a man. During the captain's Vineyard years, a then-young Joe Allen lived in Chilmark with his uncle, Fred A. Mayhew, driver of the up-island stage, the same whose death Cyril D. Norton wrote the last word about. Mr. Allen recalled driving down-island one evening with his uncle to meet the boat. "The stage was just like a box," he said, "and not too well made—all windows and doors. For the return trip, a rather well-dressed woman took the middle seat and then a man got aboard and took the seat clear aft in the doggone box. I was up on the front seat with my uncle—we were headed up-island in the usual way—when all of a sudden I heard a hell of a rustle of paper. The man leans forward and says to the woman, 'I hope you don't object to the smell of salt codfish.' I looked around and he had the biggest jack-knife I ever saw in my life, and he was hewing chunks off the fish, and eating, and he ate a good deal of the way to West Tisbury. That was Slocum.

"He looked a lot like other men of his generation who had been to sea—whiskery, very quick in his movements, and inclined to be snappy in his speech as men will be who are accustomed to give orders. He was not the kind of man one would be tempted to take liberties with. Only the women didn't think too highly of a man who stayed away from home so much without any particular objective."

In the summer of 1905, after three seasons of farming, Hettie began taking paying guests while the captain lived a more private life on board the sloop at Menemsha. One of his friends in Menemsha was a young trap fisherman, Ernest J. Dean. Many years later the fisherman said he and Slocum spent hours together, on the *Spray* or on Dean's own boat. The ex-merchant captain who had sailed many seas talked with his insular friend about a new voyage. "It was most interesting and educational," Dean said, "to lay out the proposed courses with him, and also amusing to see him run his index finger—I think every finger and thumbs on both hands were knuckle busted, set back or crooked—they looked worse than the fingers of an old-time ball player—over miles and miles of ocean chart, and listen to his running chatter of his experiences in different parts shown on the chart."

When November came, Slocum weighed anchor. Alone in the *Spray*, he left Menemsha, headed south, and spent the winter in the Caribbean. By the time he was ready to sail north again, he had shipped a cargo of shells and other curiosities; also—at the request of local admirers of Theodore Roosevelt—a few rare orchid plants for the President.

Lives of lonely men are beset with peculiar perils. Sailing north, bound for home, Slocum detoured up the Delaware River in order to visit Leslie W. Miller, a Vineyard acquaintance who wintered in Philadelphia. He tied up at the Riverton, New Jersey, Yacht Club, opposite northeast Philadelphia, where he had been invited to lecture. At Riverton, a twelve-year old girl came aboard the sloop. A few hours later, the girl's father claimed she had been attacked. The authorities charged Slocum with rape.

When medical examination showed there had been no rape, the charge was changed to a misdemeanor, apparently indecent exposure. Slocum said he had no recollection of the matter. He was reported as saying that if anything occurred, it must have been during one of his mental lapses. In the course of the voyage around the world, he had received hard blows on the head, once from a heavy line heaved from a dock, and again from the *Spray*'s mainsail boom.

Whether from indifference, inability, or unwillingness to raise the $1,000 bail, Slocum spent forty-two days in prison. What forces of disintegration were overtaking the brine-burnt seafarer?

After quitting the jail in New Jersey and rejoining the *Spray* waiting in the Delaware River, Slocum steered for Long Island Sound. He sailed into Oyster Bay, delivered the one surviving orchid, met the President, then took the President's youngest son, Archie, and a sailor from the Presidential yacht, for a week's cruise on the *Spray*. Summer was waning when Slocum, at last, made Menemsha.

Came another autumn. Slocum was wandering again. In reply to a letter from a genealogist, he wrote, "My mails have not reached me on time of late. . . . I regret that I have not been able to be, myself, a better subject among my kin—to have added an interesting line. . . ."

Slocum sailed south, alone as usual, and spent a second winter in the West Indies. When spring returned he set his gray wings for the north.

He made a side trip up the Potomac River to call on Theodore Roosevelt. Summer found him cruising in Vineyard waters, and selling his books and shells. When cold weather came, he sailed south alone and spent the winter in Nassau.

The following spring, 11 May 1908, Hettie wrote her husband's publisher, The Century Company. She said she had read the *Spray* had been lost. "Personally have not heard from Captain Slocum since Nov. 1st 1907," she wrote. "Will you kindly let me know if you have heard." But the publisher had no word, either.

A month later Slocum sailed into New York harbor with a two-ton chunk of coral on board for the American Museum of Natural History. At the end of July the *Vineyard Gazette* reported, "Captain Joshua Slocum of the sloop *Spray* is on the Island and has been a recent guest of Mrs. Slocum at West Tisbury." The captain, in his adopted town, was evidently considered a transient. Ten years had passed since he returned from sailing around the world. Since then he had tried more ordinary living but found it no longer possible.

West Tisbury now lost all its charms for him. In September, 1909, Slocum wrote his oldest son he "would sell if a purchaser should turn up." Sixty-five years old and still determined to sail, Slocum proposed to embark on a voyage of single-handed exploration. His plan was to sail the *Spray* to Venezuela and up the Orinoco River. From the Orinoco, he would enter the Rio Negro, and proceed to the headwaters of the Amazons. He would then sail down the greatest of rivers to the ocean, and that way home.

Vineyarders watched the preparations. Captain Ernest Mayhew of Chilmark said he thought Slocum had been getting slack; that just before Slocum sailed, the *Spray* had been moored by two stakes; that high tide had lifted her bowsprit onto one of the stakes, and that when the tide fell, the bowsprit was hung up on the stake and lifted several inches. Later, he saw Slocum take an ax and drive it back into place. Captain Donald LeMar Poole said the *Spray*'s rigging was slack and in need of tarring. Ernest J. Dean, the trap fisherman, said that when he first met Slocum and the *Spray*, "they were both neat, trim, and seaworthy, but as the years rolled along, [Dean] noticed signs of wear and exposure."

On 14 November 1909 Joshua Slocum set sail. Captain Levi Jackson of Edgartown said he was coming in from codfishing off the Muskeget Shoals between Martha's Vineyard and Nantucket when he saw the *Spray* bound out. He said that at the time he remarked it looked bad for a boat without power to be heading southeast. The wind was coming from that direction and by evening blowing a gale.

Joshua Slocum vanished. Boat, logs, letters, papers—all disappeared with him and, one might say, his era, too.

Hettie's petition to the Probate Court of Dukes County filed 22 April 1912 said that Joshua Slocum "disappeared, absconded, and absented himself on the 14th day of November A.D. 1909; that said absentee . . . a Master Mariner by occupation . . . disappeared on the date above named under the following circumstances, to wit: He sailed from Tisbury Massachusetts in the Sloop *Spray* of about nine tons burden only . . . encountered a very severe gale shortly afterwards, and has never been heard from since. . . ."

There were and perhaps will always be many theories concerning what may have happened. The gale as Captain Levi Jackson described it, and the dangerous Muskeget Channel shoals on which the sloop could have tripped and foundered, must be considered. There is evidence that the long sea-voyaging finally told on the *Spray* as well as her consort. When Slocum first rebuilt the *Spray*, his inexpensive and local materials clearly included green timber; and although a boat built of well-seasoned wood may enjoy a long life, one built of green may have a quite short one— especially a boat that spends much time in warm climates, as the *Spray* had. The question arises, did the *Spray* lose a plank? Did she fall apart and break up? Or did the inevitable weak spots in her often-renewed sails and rigging cause her loss? Or did Slocum with his dim oil-burning running sidelights collide with a larger vessel? Then there is always the possibility of a fire at sea, or of the man at the wheel falling, or being washed over the side. Or did Slocum suffer another spell, and perhaps black out?

"No man ever lived to see more of the solemnity of the depths than I have seen," Slocum wrote in a letter. The words mean more now than when he penned them. Years passed before his last voyage legally ended. On 15 January 1924 the court granted Hettie whatever her husband had left. Joshua Slocum, the court declared, was dead as of the day he sailed from Vineyard Haven.

～～～～～～～～～～～～～～～～～～～～～～～～～～～～～～～

Victims of the changing world go unrecognized until they begin to fall. As far back as 1839, it is said, the heath hen, or eastern pinnated grouse, had disappeared from all places where it had lived except on the island of Martha's Vineyard.

The heath hen—heth'n, earlier generations of Vineyarders called it— was considered a fair table bird in the fall of the year. About eighteen inches in size, a ground dweller scratching for a living, it resembled the ruffed grouse or partridge, and even more, the prairie chicken of the West. Ornithologists guess that a common ancestor of both heath hen and prairie chicken once ranged the country from the East Coast to the plains this side of the Rockies. In time, however, separate races emerged—the prairie chicken West, the heath hen East.

Over a period of time the heath hen of the east dwindled until there were none anywhere except on Martha's Vineyard. As the bird made its last stand, the state began passing laws to protect it. State regulations, however, meant little to island towns. Local ordinances, from time to time, authorized hunting of the vanishing bird. The heath hen is said to have been an easy target on the ground or in the air. Its numbers dwindled steadily until in 1905, John E. Howland of Vineyard Haven, and George W. Field, chairman of the state fish and game commission, led a movement to save the remnant. Private money was raised, state money appropriated, and a heath hen reservation established on Martha's Vineyard's central plain. The heath hen seemed to respond to the conservation approach, and by 1916 the flock was thought to be two thousand strong. At that time many believed the struggle to save the bird had been won.

But in May of that year, at the height of the heath hen's nesting season, a brush fire swept the central plain. Beginning near West Tisbury, the fire burned to the outskirts of Vineyard Haven, Oak Bluffs, and Edgartown, almost the entire reservation area. Females incubating their eggs sat covering them until they themselves died. A few broods of chicks escaped, and a number of males. The following year there seemed to be fewer than one hundred birds, the males greatly outnumbering the females.

"In 1918 I was appointed . . . Superintendent of the heath hen reservation," Allan Keniston wrote in an article, "The Last Years of the Heath Hen." "It was my job to see that all plans for the care and protection of the birds were carried out. That meant planting fields of corn, sunflowers, clover, and other crops to provide a food supply for the whole year. . . . Mrs. Keniston and I occupied the house in the center of the reservation. . . ."

Allan Keniston died early in 1968. When summer came I got in touch with Mrs. Keniston. I wanted to confer with the woman who had lived ten years on the reservation and known the birds.

Late in July, in Edgartown, I called on her. On South Water Street, the giant pagoda tree an Edgartown sea captain brought in a flower pot from China in 1837 towers above a row of white clapboard former sea captains' houses. I met Mrs. Keniston on the porch of her sister's house, almost directly across the way. An alert, gray-haired woman, tatting an antimacassar, she retained a sturdy and gracious New England look.

Elizabeth Mayhew Keniston, daughter of Meltiah Mayhew and his wife, Rebecca Marchant, was born in Edgartown in 1888. She said she would not care to give her age but did not mind telling the year of her birth. When she was a girl she had known a woman who, when asked how old she was, replied, "Eighty, dammit." Mrs. Keniston's father had been a contractor and builder. She had heard him say people fed their help on heath hen. In those days, she said, "you'd go along and see them, part of the Vineyard, you know—just like the robin."

She was thirty when she and her husband, whom she had married three years earlier, went to live on the heath hen reservation. While Mr. Keniston patroled in a Model T Ford, "an old crank job" Mrs. Keniston called it, she kept watch from the fire tower. From the tower, she said, "you couldn't see anything but birds and bushes." Sand roads led to the Kenistons' house. Although they had no electric light, they had a telephone.

"I feel like the heath hen was part of my family," Mrs. Keniston said. "They are pretty things. You could hear them cackling and talking from the house to the blind—about a mile." She would hear them in the afternoons, around four, "sounding like mourning doves but not so doleful." Then about five or six o'clock "they came out like a flock of crows—quite punctual at certain hours, and then you wouldn't see them again till the sun rose the next morning."

Allan Keniston wrote that "when it became generally known that the heath hen was extinct everywhere else in the world but on Martha's Vineyard, they were hunted and killed to be sold to collectors and museums."

Mr. Keniston placed man first among the enemies of the heath hen. "Man hunted the heath hen for food, for money, and for sport," he wrote. "Then the summer people came, and they got kittens . . . to catch mice and amuse the children. When the summers were past the summer people returned to the city and the kittens, now cats, were left behind, and took to the woods. This was no hardship to the cats. . . . Without doubt they ate many heath hens. . . ."

Then came the automobile and new hazards. "In those days," Mr. Keniston noted, "our Island was crisscrossed in every direction by wagon roads. . . . The wagon roads crossed heath hen country and the mother heath hen and her brood of chicks used the road too. Along came a car, and the mother bird fluttered on the ground and in the air . . . the chicks running along in the deep ruts were ground into the earth. And so a whole brood would be destroyed."

And quite possibly man caused the great fire of 1916. Mr. Keniston wrote that "almost every year there would be two or more fires. Many started by accident. But some were set to burn off the brush so that a bumper crop of blueberries would grow. . . . The sad part of that was that spring was the time of burning. Also it was the breeding season."

Mrs. Keniston described the final years as "a long drawn-out thing." She said that "as the birds got fewer, and there were none anywhere else, the interest increased. Bird clubs came down, and the Audubon crowd— so many of them you could have hung them on hooks." Most of the interest was from off-island. Mrs. Keniston recalled that at one point the state sent a "special warden who didn't know a heath hen from a partridge." The state footed the bill, "and maybe some individuals contributed." Island towns put up nothing.

Toward the end there could have been more bird watchers than birds on the reservation. When the last heath hens quit the guarded fields and the tended grain, a small flock held out on the James Green farm, close to the Edgartown Road, a mile or so east of where Joshua Slocum had lived. People driving by would stop to watch the heath hens gleaning in Mr. Green's fields. The *Vineyard Gazette* called the last heath hens "public characters."

So the flock failed and faded until it ran down to a single bird, a male, the last of its race, scratching on the outskirts of West Tisbury. The last bird, photographed in 1930, trapped and banded in 1931, was seen again in 1932, and then no more. "After they were gone, everyone saw them—usually a quail—imagination run wild—everyone wanted to see the last one," Mrs. Keniston said.

The sand road that led to the home on the reservation has become Airport Road, and the house itself is headquarters for the Martha's Vineyard State Forest. During the years the heath hen was slipping downhill, Allan Keniston and his assistants were planting trees as well as feed for the birds, and these trees, red and white pine and white spruce, have become a forest. The airport built during World War II occupies a large tract on the old reservation. On one side of Airport Road, planes come down and take off where the last heath hens called. On the other side, a path leads into the pines.

Walking the silent corridors on pine-forest duff, in woodsy light, you could hear a bird move. You step lightly, and you listen. Eerie— the whole thing, the cycle of change; of death, decay, life, and disappearance. A blessed thing to be and feel part of, and never ask what it is.

Appendix

IN Volume Three of the Third Series of its *Collections, Boston, 1843*, the Massachusetts Historical Society reprinted from Samuel Purchas, the 17th-century English author of *Purchas his Pilgrimes*, three documents relating to Captain Bartholomew Gosnold's voyage in 1602, and the first settlement in New England.

The three, given below in full, are Gosnold's *Letter to his Father*, Gabriel Archer's *Account*, and M. John Brereton's *A Brief and True Relation*.

Bartholomew Gosnold's Letter to his Father

My duty remembered, & c. Sir, I was in good hope that my occasions would have allowed me so much liberty, as to have come unto you before this time; otherwise I would have written more at large concerning the country from whence we lately came, than I did: but not well remembering what I have already written (though I am assured that there is nothing set down disagreeing with the truth,) I thought it fittest not to go about to add anything in writing, but rather to leave the report of the rest till I come myself; which now I hope shall be shortly, and so soon as with conveniency I may. In the mean time, notwithstanding whereas you seem not to be satisfied by that which I have already written, concerning some especial matters; I have here briefly (and as well as I can) added these few lines for your further satisfaction: and first, as touching that place where we were most resident, it is the latitude of 41 degrees, and one third part; which albeit it be so much to the southward, yet is it more cold than those parts of Europe, which are situated under the same parallel: but one thing is worth the noting, that notwithstanding the place is not so much subject to cold as England is, yet did we find the spring to be later there, than it is with us here, by almost a month: this whether it happened accidentally this last spring to be so, or whether it be so of course, I am not very certain; the latter seems most likely, whereof also there may be given some sufficient reason, which now I omit: as for the acorns we saw gathered on heaps, they were of the last year, but doubtless their summer continues longer than ours.

We cannot gather, by anything we could observe in the people, or by any trial we had thereof ourselves, but that it is as healthful a climate as any can be. The inhabitants there, as I wrote before, being of tall stature, comely proportion, strong, active, and some of good years, and as it should seem very healthful, are sufficient proof of the healthfulness of the place. First, for ourselves (thanks be to God) we had not a man sick two days together in all our voyage; whereas others that went out with us, or about that time on other voyages (especially such as went upon reprisal,) were most of them infected with sickness, whereof they lost some of their men, and brought home a many sick, returning notwithstanding long before us. But Verazzano, and others (as I take it, you may read in the Book of Discoveries,) do more particularly entreat of the age of the people in that coast. The sassafras which we brought we had upon the islands; where though we had little disturbance, and reasonable plenty; yet for that the greatest part of our people were employed about the fitting of our house, and such like affairs, and a few (and those but easy laborers) undertook this work, the rather because we were informed before our going forth, that a ton was sufficient to cloy England, and further, for that we had resolved upon our return, and taken view of our victual, we judged it then needful to use expedition; which afterward we had more certain proof of; for when we came to an anchor before Portsmouth, which was some four days after we made the land, we had not one cake of bread, nor any drink, but a little vinegar left: for these and other reasons, we returned no otherwise laden than you have heard. And thus much I hope shall suffice till I can myself come to give you further notice, which though it be not so soon as I could have wished, yet I hope it shall be in convenient time.

In the mean time, craving your pardon, for which the urgent occasions of my stay will plead, I humbly take my leave.

7th September, 1602.   Your dutiful son,
                                         BARTH. GOSNOLD.

The Relation of Captain Gosnold's Voyage begun the six-and-twentieth of March, Anno 42 Elizabethae Reginae, 1602, and delivered by Gabriel Archer, a gentleman in the said voyage.

The said captain did set sail from Falmouth the day and year above written accompanied with thirty-two persons, whereof eight mariners and sailors, twelve purposing upon the discovery to return with the ship for England, the rest remain there for population. The fourteenth of April following, we had sight of Saint Mary's, an Island of the Azores.

The three-and-twentieth of the same, being two hundred leagues westward from the said island, in the latitude of 37 degrees, the water in the main ocean appeared yellow, the space of two leagues north and south, where sounding with thirty fathoms line, we found no ground, and taking up some of the said water in a bucket, it altered not either in color or taste from the sea azure.

The seventh of May following, we first saw many birds in bigness of cliff pigeons, and after divers others as petrels, coots, hagbuts, penguins, mews, gannets, cormorants, gulls, with many else in our English tongue of no name. The eighth of the same the water changed to a yellowish green, where at seventy fathoms we had ground. The ninth, we had two-and-twenty fathoms in fair sandy ground, having upon our lead many glittering stones, somewhat heavy, which might promise some mineral matter in the bottom, we held ourselves by computation, well near the latitude of 43 degrees.

The tenth we sounded in 27, 30, 37, 43 fathoms, and then came to 108. Some thought it to be the sounding of the westernmost end of Saint John's Island; upon this bank we saw sculls of fish in great numbers. The twelfth, we hoisted out hawser of our shallop, and sounding had then eighty fathoms without any current perceived by William Strete the master, one hundred leagues westward from Saint Mary's, till we came to the aforesaid soundings, continually passed fleeting by us sea-oare, which seemed to have their movable course towards the north-east; a matter to set some subtle invention on work, for comprehending the true cause thereof. The thirteenth, we sounded in seventy fathoms, and observed great beds of weeds, much wood, and divers things else floating by us, when as we had smelling of the shore, such as from the southern Cape and Andalusia, in Spain. The fourteenth, about six in the morning, we descried land that lay north, &c., the northerly part we called the north land, which to another rock upon the same lying twelve leagues west, that we called Savage Rock, (because the savages first showed themselves there); five leagues towards the said rock is an out point of woody ground, the trees thereof very high and straight, from the rock east-north-east. From the said rock, came towards us a Biscay shallop with sail and oars, having eight persons in it, whom we supposed at first to be Christians distressed. But approaching us nearer, we perceived them to be savages. These coming within call, hailed us, and we answered. Then after signs of peace, and a long speech by one of them made, they came boldly aboard us, being all naked, saving about their shoulders certain loose deer skins, and near their wastes seal skins tied fast like to Irish dimmie trowsers. One that seemed to be their commander wore a waistcoat of black work, a pair of breeches, cloth stockings, shoes, hat and band, one or two more had also a few things made by some Christians; these with a piece of chalk described the coast thereabouts, and could name Placentia of the Newfoundland; they spoke divers Christian words, and seemed to understand much more then we, for want of language could comprehend. These people are in color swart, their hair long, uptied with a knot in the part of behind the head. They paint their bodies, which are strong and well proportioned. These much desired our longer stay, but finding ourselves short of our purposed place, we set sail westward, leaving them and their coast. About sixteen leagues south-west from thence we perceived in that course two small islands, the one lying eastward from Savage Rock, the other to the southward of it; the coast we left was full of goodly woods, fair plains, with little green round hills above the cliffs appearing unto us, which are indifferently raised, but all rocky, and of shining stones, which might have persuaded us a longer stay there.

The fifteenth day we had again sight of the land, which made ahead, being as we thought an island, by reason of a large sound that appeared westward between it and the main, for coming to the west end thereof, we did perceive a large opening, we called it Shoal Hope. Near this cape we came to anchor in fifteen fathoms, where we took great store of cod fish, for which we altered the name, and called it Cape Cod. Here we saw sculls of herring, mackerel and other small fish, in great abundance. This is a low sandy shoal, but without danger, also we came to anchor again in sixteen fathoms, fair by the land in the latitude of 42 degrees. This cape is well near a mile broad, and lieth north-east by east. The captain went here ashore and found the ground to be full of pease, strawberries, whortleberries, &c., and then unripe, the sand also by the shore somewhat deep, the firewood there by us taken in was of cypress, birch, witch-hazel and beech. A young Indian came here to the captain, armed with his bow and arrows, and had certain plates of copper hanging at his ears; he showed a willingness to help us in our occasions.

The sixteenth, we trended the coast southerly, which was all champaign and full of grass, but the island somewhat woody. Twelve leagues from Cape Cod, we descried a point with some breach, a good distance off, and keeping our luff to double it, we came on the sudden into shoal water, yet well quitted ourselves thereof. This breach we called Tucker's Terror, upon his expressed fear. The point we named Point Care; having passed it we bore up again with the land, and in the night came with it anchoring in eight fathoms, the ground good.

The seventeenth, appeared many breaches round about us, so as we continued that day without remove.

The eighteenth, being fair we sent forth the boat, to sound over a breach, that in our course lay of another point, by us called Gilbert's Point, who returned us four, five, six and seven fathoms over. Also, a discovery of divers islands which after proved to be hills and hammocks, distinct within the land. This day there came unto the ship's side divers canoes, the Indians apparelled as aforesaid, with tobacco and pipes steeled with copper, skins, artificial strings and other trifles to barter; one had hanging about his neck a plate of rich copper, in length a foot, in breadth half a foot for a breastplate, the ears of all the rest had pendants of copper. Also, one of them had his face painted over, and head stuck with feathers in manner of a turkey-cock's train. These are more timorous than those of the Savage Rock, yet very thievish.

The nineteenth, we passed over the breach of Gilbert's Point in four or five fathoms, and anchored a league or somewhat more beyond it; between the last two points are two leagues, the interim, along shoal water, the latitude here is 41 degrees two third parts.

The twentieth, by the ship's side, we there killed penguins, and saw many sculls of fish. The coast from Gilbert's Point to the supposed isles lieth east and by south. Here also we discovered two inlets which might promise fresh water, inwardly whereof we perceived much smoke, as though some population had there been. This coast is very full of people, for that as we trended the same savages still run along the shore, as men much admiring at us.

The one-and-twentieth, we went coasting from Gilbert's Point to the supposed isles, in ten, nine, eight, seven, and six fathoms, close aboard the shore, and that depth lieth a league off. A little from the supposed isles, appeared unto us an opening, with which we stood, judging it to be the end of that which Captain Gosnold descried from Cape Cod, and as he thought to extend some thirty or more miles in length, and finding there but three fathoms a league off, we omitted to make further discovery of the same, calling it Shoal-Hope.

From this opening the main lieth south-west, which coasting along we saw a disinhabited island, which so afterward appeared unto us: we bore with it, and named it Martha's Vineyard; from Shoal-Hope it is eight leagues in circuit, the island is five miles, and hath 41 degrees and one quarter of latitude. The place most pleasant; for the two-and-twentieth, we went ashore, and found it full of wood, vines, gooseberry bushes, whortleberries, raspberries, eglantines, &c. Here we had cranes, stearnes, shoulers, geese, and divers other birds which there at that time upon the cliffs being sandy with some rocky stones, did breed and had young. In this place we saw deer: here we rode in eight fathoms near the shore where we took great store of cod,—as before at Cape Cod, but much better.

The three-and-twentieth we weighed, and towards night came to anchor at the north-west part of this island, where the next morning offered unto us fast running thirteen savages apparelled as aforesaid, and armed with bows and arrows without any fear. They brought tobacco, deer-skins and some sodden fish. These offered themselves onto us in great familiarity, who seemed to be well-conditioned. They came more rich in copper than any before. This island is sound, and hath no danger about it.

The four-and-twentieth, we set sail and doubled the Cape of another island next unto it, which we called Dover Cliff, and then came into a fair sound, where we rode all night; the next morning we sent off one boat to discover another cape, that lay between us and the main, from which were a ledge of rocks a mile into the sea, but all above water, and without danger; we went about them, and came to anchor in eight fathoms, a quarter of a mile from the shore, in one of the stateliest sounds that ever I was in. This called we Gosnold's Hope; the north bank whereof is the main, which stretcheth east and west. This island Captain Gosnold called Elizabeth's isle, where we determined our abode: the distance between every of these islands is, viz. from Martha's Vineyard to Dover Cliff, half a league over the sound, thence to Elizabeth's isle one league distant. From Elizabeth's island unto the main is four leagues. On the north side, near adjoining unto the island Elizabeth, is an islet in compass half a mile, full of cedars, by me called Hill's Hap, to the northward of which, in the mouth of an opening on the main, appeareth another the like, that I called Hap's Hill, for that I hope much hap may be expected from it.

The five-and-twentieth, it was that we came from Gosnold's Hope. The six-and-twentieth, we trimmed and fitted up our shallop. The seven-and-twentieth, there came unto us an Indian and two women, the one we supposed to be his wife, the other his daughter, both clean and straight-bodied, with countenance sweet and pleasant. To these the Indian gave heedful attendance for that they shewed them in much familiarity with our men, although they would not admit of any immodest touch.

The eight-and-twentieth we entered counsel about our abode and plantation, which was concluded to be in the west part of Elizabeth's island. The north-east thereof running from out our ken. The south and north standeth in an equal parallel. This island in the westernside admitteth some in creeks, or sandy coves, so girded, as the water in some places of each side meeteth, to which the Indians from the main do oftentimes resort for fishing of crabs. There is eight fathoms very near the shore, and the latitude here is 41 degrees 11 minutes, the breadth from sound to sound in the western part is not passing a mile at most, altogether unpeopled and disinhabited. It is overgrown with wood and rubbish, viz. oaks, ashes, beech, walnut, witch-hazel, sassafras, and cedars, with divers other of unknown names. The rubbish is wild pease, young sassafras, cheery-trees, vines, eglantines, gooseberry bushes, hawthorn, honeysuckles, with others of like quality. The herbs and roots are strawberries, raspberries, ground-nuts, alexander, surrin, tansy, &c. without count. Touching the fertility of the soil by our own experience made, we found it to be excellent for sowing some English pulse; it sprouted out in one fortnight almost half a foot. In this island is a stage or pond of fresh water, in circuit two miles, on the one side not distant from the sea thirty yards, in the centre whereof is a rocky islet, containing near an acre of ground full of wood, on which we began our fort and place of abode, disposing itself so fit for the same. These Indians call gold wassador, which argueth there is thereof in the country.

The nine-and-twentieth, we labored in getting of sassafras, rubbishing our little fort or islet, new keeling our shallop, and making a punt or flat-bottom boat to pass to and fro our fort over the fresh water, the powder of sassafras, in twelve hours cured one of our company that had taken a great surfeit, by eating the bellies of dog fish, a very delicious meat.

The thirtieth, Captain Gosnold, with divers of his company, went upon pleasure in the shallop towards Hill's Hap to view it and the sandy cove, and returning brought with him a canoe that four Indians had there left, being fled away for fear of our English, which we brought into England.

The one-and-thirtieth, Captain Gosnold, desirous to see the main because of the distance, he set sail over; where coming to anchor, went ashore with certain of his company, and immediately there presented unto him men, women and children, who, with all courteous kindness entertained him, giving him certain skins of wild beasts, which may be rich furs, tobacco, turtles, hemp, artificial strings colored, chains, and such like things as at the instant they had about them. These are a fair-conditioned people. On all the seacoast along we found mussel shells that in color did represent mother-of-pearl, but not having means to dredge, could not apprehend further knowledge thereof. This main is the good-liest continent that ever we saw, promising more by far than we any way did expect: for it is replenished with fair fields, and in them fragrant flowers, also meadows, and hedged in with stately groves, being furnished also with pleasant brooks, and beautified with two main rivers that (as we judge) may haply become good harbors, and conduct us to the hopes men so greedily do thirst after. In the mouth of one of these inlets or rivers, lieth that little isle before mentioned, called Hap's Hill, from which unto the western-most end of the main, appearing where the other inlet is, I account some five leagues, and the coast between bendeth like a bow, and lieth east and by north. Beyond these two inlets we might perceive the main to bear up south-west, and more southerly. Thus with this taste of discovery, we now contented ourselves, and the same day made return unto our fort, time not permitting more sparing delay.

The first of June, we employed ourselves in getting sassafras, and the building of our fort. The second, third and fourth, we wrought hard to make ready our house for the provision to be had ashore to sustain us till our ship's return. This day from the main came to our ship's side a canoe, with their lord or chief commander, for that they made little stay only pointing to the sun, as in sign that the next day he would come and visit us, which he did accordingly.

The fifth, we continued our labor, when there came unto us ashore from the main fifty savages, stout and lusty men with their bows and arrows, amongst them there seemed to be one of authority, because the rest made an inclining respect unto him. The ship was at their coming a league off, and Captain Gosnold aboard, and so likewise Captain Gilbert, who almost never went ashore, the company with me only eight persons. These Indians in hasty manner came towards us, so as we thought fit to make a stand at an angle between the sea and a fresh water; I moved myself towards him seven or eight steps, and clapped my hands first on the sides of mine head, then on my breast, and after presented my musket with a threatening countenance, thereby to signify unto them, either a choice of peace or war, whereupon he using me with mine own signs of peace, I stepped forth and embraced him; his company then all sat down in manner like greyhounds upon their heels, with whom my company fell a bartering. By this time Captain Gosnold was come with twelve men more from aboard, and to show the savage seignior that he was our Captain, we received him in a guard, which he passing through, saluted the seignior with ceremonies of our salutations, whereat he nothing moved or altered himself. Our Captain gave him a straw hat and a pair of knives; the hat awhile he wore, but the knives he beheld with great marvelling, being very bright and sharp; this our courtesy made them all in love with us.

The sixth, being rainy, we spent idly aboard. The seventh, the seignior came again with all his troop as before, and continued with us the most part of the day, we going to dinner about noon, they sat with us and did eat of our bacaleure and mustard, drank of our beer, but the mustard nipping them in their noses they could not endure: it was a sport to behold their faces made being bitten therewith. In time of dinner the savages had stole a target, wherewith acquainting the seignior, with fear and great trembling they restored it again, thinking perhaps we would have been revenged for it, but seeing our familiarity to continue, they fell afresh to roasting of crabs, red herrings, which were exceeding great, ground nuts, &c. as before. Our dinner ended, the seignior first took leave and departed, next all the rest saving four that stayed and went into the wood to help us dig sassafras, whom we desired to go aboard us, which they refused and so departed.

The eighth we divided the victuals, namely, the ship's store for England, and that of the planters, which by Captain Gilbert's allowance could be but six weeks for six months, whereby there fell out a controversy, the rather, for that some seemed secretly to understand of a purpose Captain Gilbert had not to return with supply of the issue, those goods should make by him to be carried home. Besides, there wanted not ambitious conceits in the minds of some wrangling and ill-disposed persons who overthrew the stay there at that time, which upon consultation thereof had, about five days after was fully resolved all for England again. There came in this interim aboard unto us, that stayed all night, an Indian, whom we used kindly, and the next day sent ashore; he showed himself the most sober of all the rest, we held him sent as a spy. In the morning, he filched away our pothooks, thinking he had not done any ill therein; being ashore we bid him strike fire, which with an emerald stone (such as the glaziers use to cut glass) he did. I take it to be the very same that in Latin is called *smiris*, for striking therewith upon touch-wood that of purpose he had, by means of a mineral stone used therein, sparkles proceeded and forthwith kindled with making of flame. The ninth, we continued working on our storehouse, for as yet remained in us a desired resolution of making stay. The tenth, Captain Gosnold fell down with the ship to the little islet of cedars, called Hill's Hap, to take in cedar wood, leaving me and nine more in the fort, only with three meals meat, upon promise to return the next day.

The eleventh, he came not, neither sent, whereupon I commanded four of my company to seek out for crabs, lobsters, turtles, &c. for sustaining us till the ships returned, which was gone clean out of sight, and had the wind chopped up at south-west, with much difficulty would she have been able in short time to have made return. These four purveyers, whom I counselled to keep together for their better safety, divided themselves, two going one way and two another, in search as aforesaid. One of these petty companies was assaulted by four Indians, who with arrows did shoot and hurt one of the two in his side, the other, a lusty and nimble fellow, leaped in and cut their bow strings, whereupon they fled. Being late in the evening, they were driven to lie all night in the woods, not knowing the way home through the thick rubbish, as also the weather somewhat stormy. The want of these sorrowed us much, as not able to conjecture anything of them unless very evil.

The twelfth, those two came unto us again, whereat our joy was increased, yet the want of our Captain, that promised to return, as aforesaid, struck us in a dumpish terror, for that he performed not the same in the space of almost three days. In the mean we sustained ourselves with alexander and sorrel pottage, ground-nuts and tobacco, which gave nature a reasonable content. We heard at last, our Captain to 'lewre' unto us, which made such music as sweeter never came unto poor men.

The thirteenth, began some of our company that before vowed to stay, to make revolt: whereupon the planters diminishing, all was given over. The fourteenth, fifteenth and sixteenth, we spent in getting sassafras and fire-wood of cedar, leaving house and little fort, by ten men in nineteen days sufficient made to harbor twenty persons at least with their necessary provisions.

The seventeenth, we set sail, doubling the Rocks of Elizabeth's Island, and passing by Dover Cliff, came to anchor at Martha's Vineyard, being five leagues distant from our fort, where we went ashore, and had young cranes, herneshowes, and geese, which now were grown to pretty bigness.

The eighteenth, we set sail and bore for England, cutting off our shallop, that was well able to land five and twenty men or more, a boat very necessary for the like occasions. The winds do range most commonly upon this coast in the summer time, westerly. In our homeward course we observed the foresaid floating weeds to continue till we came within two hundred leagues of Europe. The three-and-twentieth of July we came to anchor before Exmouth.

Some historians think the island Archer called Martha's Vineyard was the islet now known as Nomans Land. Some believe Dover Cliff meant Gay Head. All agree Elizabeth's Island was the present-day Cuttyhunk.

∿∿∿∿∿∿∿∿∿∿∿∿∿∿∿∿∿∿∿∿∿∿∿∿∿∿∿∿∿∿∿∿∿∿∿

Scarcely known when Gosnold sailed, the region that became New England was considered part of the "remote, heathen, and barbarous lands" included in Raleigh's Patent from Queen Elizabeth. Brereton called it the "North Part of Virginia." *Purchas his Pilgrimes, A Brief and True Relation of the Discovery of the North Part of Virginia . . . by M. John Brereton, one of the voyage . . .* was first published in London in 1602.

To the Honorable Sir Walter Raleigh, Knight, Captain of her Majesty's Guards, Lord Warden of the Stanneries, Lieutenant of Cornwall, and Governor of the Isle of Jersey.

Honorable Sir,—Being earnestly requested by a dear friend, to put down in writing, some true relation of our late performed voyage to the north parts of Virginia; at length I resolved to satisfy his request, who also emboldened me to direct the same to your honorable consideration; to whom indeed of duty it pertaineth.

May it please your Lordship therefore to understand, that upon the five-and-twentieth of March 1602, being Friday, we went from Falmouth, being in all, two-and-thirty persons, in a small bark of Dartmouth, called The Concord, holding a course for the north part of Virginia: and although by chance the wind favored us not at first as we wished, but enforced us so far to the southward, as we fell in with Saint Mary, one of the islands of the Azores, (which was not much out of our way) but holding our course directly from thence, we made our journey shorter (than hitherto accustomed) by the better part of a thousand leagues, yet were we longer in our passage than we expected, which happened, for that our bark being weak, we were loth to press her with much sail; also, our sailors being few, and they none of the best, we bear (except in fair weather) but low sail; besides, our going upon an unknown coast, made us not over bold to stand in with the shore, but in open weather; which caused us to be certain days in sounding, before we discovered the coast, the weather being by chance, somewhat foggy. But on Friday, the fourteenth of May, early in the morning, we made the land, being full of fair trees, the land somewhat low, certain hammocks or hills lying into the land, the shore full of white sand, but very stony or rocky. And standing fair along by the shore, about twelve of the clock the same day, we came to an anchor, where eight Indians in a Basque-shallop with mast and sail, an iron grapple, and a kettle of copper, came boldly aboard us, one of them apparelled with a waistcoat and breeches of black serge, made after our sea-fashion, hose and shoes on his feet; all the rest (saving one that had a pair of breeches of blue cloth) were naked. These people are of tall stature, broad and grim visage, of a black swart complexion, their eyebrows painted white; their weapons are bows and arrows. It seemed by some words and signs they made, that some Basques or of St. John de Luz, have fished or traded in this place, being in the latitude of 43 degrees.

But riding here, in no very good harbor, and withal, doubting the weather, about three of the clock the same day in the afternoon we weighed, and standing southerly off into sea the rest of that day and the night following, with a fresh gale of wind, in the morning we found ourselves embayed with a mighty headland; but coming to an anchor about nine of the clock the same day, within a league of the shore, we hoisted out the one half of our shallop, and Captain Bartholomew Gosnold, myself and three others, went ashore, being a white sandy and very bold shore; and marching all that afternoon with our muskets on our necks, on the highest hills which we saw (the weather very hot,) at length we perceived this headland to be parcel of the main, and sundry islands lying almost round about it: so returning towards evening) to our shallop (for by that time the other part was brought ashore and set together) we espied an Indian, a young man, of proper stature, and of a pleasing countenance, and after some familiarity with him, we left him at the sea side, and returned to our ship; where in five or six hours' absence, we had pestered our ship so with codfish, that we threw numbers of them overboard again: and surely, I am persuaded that in the months of March, April, and May, there is upon this coast better fishing, and in as great plenty, as in Newfoundland: for the sculls of mackerel, herrings, cod, and other fish, that we daily saw as we went and came from the shore, were wonderful; and besides, the places where we took these cods (and might in a few days have laden our ship) were but in seven fathoms water, and within less than a league of the shore: where, in Newfoundland they fish in forty or fifty fathoms water, and far off.

From this place we sailed round about this headland, almost all the points of the compass, the shore very bold: but as no coast is free from dangers, so I am persuaded, this is as free as any. The land somewhat low, full of goodly woods, but in some places plain. At length we were come amongst many fair islands, which we had partly discerned at our first landing; all lying within a league or two one of another, and the outermost not above five or seven leagues from the main: but coming to an anchor under one of them,* which was about three or four leagues from the main, Captain Gosnold, myself, and some others, went ashore, and going round about it, we found it to be four English miles in compass, without house or inhabitant, saving a little old house made of boughs, covered with bark, an old piece of a weare of the Indians to catch fish, and one or two places, where they had made fires. The chiefest trees of this island are beeches and cedars, the outward parts all overgrown with low bushy trees, three or four feet in height, which bear some kind of fruits, as appeared by their blossoms; strawberries, red and white, as sweet and much bigger than ours in England; raspberries, gooseberries, whortleberries, and such an incredible store of vines, as well in the woody part of the Island, where they run upon every tree, as on the outward parts, that we could not go for treading upon them; also, many springs of excellent sweet water, and a great standing lake of fresh water, near the sea-side, an English mile in compass, which is maintained with the springs running exceeding pleasantly through the woody grounds which are very rocky. Here are also in this island, great store of deer, which we saw, and other beasts, as appeared by their tracks; as also divers fowls, as cranes, hernshaws, bitterns, geese, mallards, teals, and other fowls, in great plenty; also, great store of pease, which grow in certain plots all the island over. On the north side of this island we found many huge bones and ribs of whales. This island,

* The first island called Martha's Vineyard. Note in original.

as also all the rest of these islands are full of all sorts of stones fit for building; the sea sides all covered with stones, many of them glistening and shining like mineral stones, and very rocky: also, the rest of these islands are replenished with these commodities, and upon some of them, inhabitants; as upon an island to the northward, and within two leagues of this; yet we found no towns, nor many of their houses, although we saw many Indians, which are tall big-boned men, all naked, saving they cover their private parts with a black towed skin, much like a black-smiths apron, tied about their middle and between their legs behind: they gave us of their fish ready boiled, (which they carried in a basket made of twigs, not unlike our osier,) whereof we did eat, and judged them to be fresh water fish: they gave us also of their tobacco, which they drink green, but dried into powder, very strong and pleasant, and much better than any I have tasted in England: the necks of their pipes are made of clay hard dried, (whereof in that island is great store both red and white,) the other part is a piece of hollow copper, very finely closed and cemented together. We gave unto them certain trifles, as knives, points, and such like, which they much esteemed.

From hence we went to another island, to the northwest of this, and within a league or two of the main, which we found to be greater than before we imagined, being sixteen English miles at the least in compass; for it containeth many pieces or necks of land, which differ nothing from several islands, saving that certain banks of small breadth do, like bridges, join them to this island. On the outside of this island are many plain places of grass, abundance of strawberries and other berries before mentioned. In mid May we did sow in this island (for a trial) in sundry places, wheat, barley, oats, and pease, which in fourteen days were sprung up nine inches and more. The soil is fat and lusty, the upper crust of grey color; but a foot or less in depth, of the color of our hemplands in England; and being thus apt for these and the like grains; the sowing or setting (after the ground is closed) is no greater labor, than if you should set or sow in one of our best prepared gardens in England.* This island is full of high timbered oaks, their leaves thrice so broad as ours; cedars, straight and tall; beech, elm, holly, walnut trees in abundance, the fruit as big as ours, as appeared by those we found under the trees, which had lain all the year ungathered; hazle-nut trees, cherry trees, the leaf, bark and bigness not differing from ours in England, but the stalk beareth the blossoms or fruit at the end thereof, like a cluster of grapes, forty or fifty in a bunch; sassafras trees, great

* Here begins the extract in Purchas.

plenty all the island over, a tree of high price and profit; also, divers other fruit trees, some of them with strange barks of an orange color, in feeling soft and smooth like velvet: in the thickest parts of these woods, you may see a furlong or more round about. On the north-west side of this island, near to the sea-side, is a standing lake of fresh water, almost three English miles in compass, in the midst whereof stands a plot of woody ground, an acre in quantity or not above: this lake is full of small tortoises, and exceedingly frequented with all sorts of fowls before rehearsed, which breed, some low on the banks, and others on low trees about this lake in great abundance, whose young ones of all sorts we took and eat at our pleasure: but all these fowls are much bigger than ours in England. Also, in every island, and almost in every part of every island, are great store of ground-nuts, forty together on a string, some of them as big as hen's eggs; they grow not two inches under ground: the which nuts we found to be as good as potatoes. Also, divers sorts of shell-fish, as scallops, muscles, cockles, lobsters, crabs, oysters, and wilks, exceeding good and very great.

But not to cloy you with particular rehearsal of such things as God and nature hath bestowed on these places, in comparison whereof the most fertile part of England is (of itself) but barren: we went in our light-horseman from this island to the main, right against this island some two leagues off, where coming ashore, we stood awhile like men ravished at the beauty and delicacy of this sweet soil; for besides divers clear lakes of fresh water, (whereof we saw no end) meadows very large and full of green grass; even the most woody places (I speak only of such as I saw,) do grow so distinct and apart, one tree from another, upon green grassy ground, somewhat higher than the plains, as if nature would show herself above her power, artificial. Hard by we espied seven Indians, and coming up to them, at first they expressed some fear; but being emboldened by our courteous usage, and some trifles which we gave them, they followed us to a neck of land, which we imagined had been severed from the main; but finding it otherwise, we perceived a broad harbor or river's mouth, which ran up into the main; and because the day was far spent, we were forced to return to the island from whence we came, leaving the discovery of this harbor, for a time of better leisure. Of the goodness of which harbor, as also of many others there-bouts, there is small doubt, considering that all the islands, as also the main (where we were) is all rocky grounds and broken lands. Now the next day, we determined to fortify ourselves in a little plot of ground in the midst of the lake abovementioned, where we built our house, and covered it with sedge, which grew about this lake in great abundance; in building whereof we spent three weeks and more: but the second day after our coming from the main, we espied eleven canoes or boats, with fifty Indians in them, coming toward us from this part of the main, where we, two days before landed; and being loath they should discover our fortification, we went out on the sea-side to meet them; and coming somewhat near them, they all sat down upon the stones, calling aloud to us (as we rightly guessed) to do the like, a little distance from them: having sat awhile in this order, Captain Gosnold willed me to go unto them, to see what countenance they would make; but as soon as I came up unto them, one of them, to whom I had given a knife two days before in the main, knew me, (whom I also very well remembered) and smiling upon me, spake somewhat unto their lord or captain which sat in the midst of them, who presently rose up and took a large beaver skin from one that stood about him, and gave it unto me, which I requited for that time, the best I could; but I pointing towards Captain Gosnold, made signs unto him, that he was our captain, and desirous to be his friend, and enter league with him, which (as I perceived) he understood, and made signs of joy: whereupon Captain Gosnold with the rest of his company, being twenty in all, came up onto them; and after many signs of gratulations (Captain Gosnold presenting their lord with certain trifles which they wondered at, and highly esteemed,) we became very great friends, and sent for meat aboard our shallop, and gave them such meats as we had then ready dressed, whereof they misliked nothing but our mustard, whereat they made many a sour face. While we were thus merry, one of them had conveyed a target of ours into one of their canoes, which we suffered, only to try whether they were in subjection to this lord to whom we made signs (by shewing him another of the same likeness, and pointing to the canoe) what one of his company had done: who suddenly expressed some fear, and speaking angrily to one about him (as we perceived by his countenance,) caused it presently to be brought back again. So the rest of the day we spent in trading with them for furs, which are beavers, luzernes, martins, otters, wild-cat skins, very large and deep fur, black foxes, coney skins, of the color of our hares, but somewhat less; deer skins, very large, seal skins, and other beasts' skins, to us unknown. They have also great store of copper, some very red, and some of a paler color: none of them but have chains, ear-rings or collars of this metal: they head some of their arrows herewith much like our broad arrow heads, very workmanly made. Their chains are many hollow pieces cemented together, each piece of the bigness of one of our reeds, a finger in length, ten or twelve of them together on a string, which they wear

about their necks: their collars they wear about their bodies like ban-
deliers a handful broad, all hollow pieces, like the other, but somewhat
shorter, four hundred pieces in a collar, very fine and evenly set together.
Besides these they have large drinking cups made like skulls, and other
thin plates of copper, made much like our boar spear blades, all which
they so little esteem, as they offered their fairest collars or chains for a
knife or such like trifle, but we seemed little to regard it; yet I was
desirous to understand where they had such store of this metal, and
made signs to one of them (with whom I was very familiar) who taking
a piece of copper in his hand, made a hole with his finger in the ground,
and withal pointed to the main from whence they came. They strike fire
in this manner; every one carrieth about him in a purse of tewed leather,
a mineral stone (which I take to be their copper,) and with a flat emery
stone (wherewith glaziers cut glass, and cutlers glaze blades,) tied fast
to the end of a little stick, gently he striketh upon the mineral stone,
and within a stroke or two, a spark falleth upon a piece of touchwood
(much like our sponge in England,) and with the least spark he maketh
a fire presently. We had also of their flax, wherewith they make many
strings and cords, but it is not so bright of color as ours in England:
I am persuaded they have great store growing upon the main, as also
mines and many other rich commodities, which we, wanting both time
and means, could not possibly discover.

Thus they continued with us three days, every night retiring themselves to the furthermost part of our island two or three miles from our
fort: but the fourth day they returned to the main, pointing five or six
times to the sun, and once to the main, which we understood, that within
five or six days they would come from the main to us again; but being
in their canoes a little from the shore, they made huge cries and shouts
of joy unto us; and we with our trumpet and cornet, and casting up our
caps into the air, made them the best farewell we could: yet six or
seven of them remained with us behind, bearing us company every day
into the woods, and helped us to cut and carry our sassafras, and some
of them lay aboard our ship.

These people, as they are exceeding courteous, gentle of disposition,
and well conditioned, excelling all others that we have seen; so for
shape of body and lovely favor, I think they excel all the people of
America; of stature much higher than we; of complexion or color, much
like a dark olive; their eyebrows and hair black, which they wear long,
tied up behind in knots, whereon they prick feathers of fowls, in fashion
of a coronet; some of them are black thin bearded; they make beards
of the hair of beasts: and one of them offered a beard of their making

to one of our sailors, for his that grew on his face, which because it was of a red color, they judged to be none of his own. They are quick-eyed, and steadfast in their looks, fearless of others' harms, as intending none themselves; some of the meaner sort given to filching, which the very name of savages (not weighing their ignorance in good or evil,) may easily excuse: their garments are of deer skins, and some of them wear furs round and close about their necks. They pronounce our language with great facility; for one of them one day sitting by me, upon occasion I spake smiling to him these words: How now (sirrah) are you so saucy with my tobacco? which words (without any further repetition,) he suddenly spake so plain and distinctly, as if he had been a long scholar in the language. Many other such trials we had, which are here needless to repeat. Their women (such as we saw) which were but three in all, were but low of stature, their eyebrows, hair, apparel, and manner of wearing, like to the men, fat, and very well favored, and much delighted in our company; the men are very dutiful towards them. And truly, the wholesomeness and temperature of this climate, doth not only argue this people to be answerable to this description, but also of a perfect constitution of body, active, strong, healthful, and very witty, as the sundry toys of theirs cunningly wrought, may easily witness. For the agreeing of this climate with us (I speak of myself, and so I may justly do for the rest of our company,) that we found our health and strength all the while we remained there, so to renew and increase, as notwithstanding our diet and lodging was none of the best, yet not one of our company (God be thanked,) felt the least grudging or inclination to any disease or sickness, but were much fatter and in better health than when we went out of England.

But after our bark had taken in so much sassafras, cedar, furs, skins, and other commodities, as were thought convenient, some of our company that had promised Captain Gosnold to stay, having nothing but a saving voyage in their minds, made our company of inhabitants (which was small enough before) much smaller; so as Captain Gosnold seeing his whole strength to consist but of twelve men, and they but meanly provided, determined to return for England, leaving this island (which he called Elizabeth's Island) with as many true sorrowful eyes, as were before desirous to see it. So the 18th of June being Friday, we weighed, and with indifferent fair wind and weather, came to anchor the 23d of July, being also Friday, (in all, bare five weeks) before Exmouth.

Your Lordship's to command,

JOHN BRERETON.

A brief Note of such commodities as we saw in the country, notwithstanding our small time of stay.

Trees.   Sassafras trees, the roots whereof at 3*s.* the pound, are 336*l.* the ton; cedars, tall and straight, in great abundance; cypress trees; oaks; walnut trees, great store; elms; beech; holly; hazlenut trees; cherry trees; cotton trees; other fruit to us unknown. The finder of our sassafras in these parts was one Master Robert Meriton.

Fowls.   Eagles; hernshaws; cranes; bitterns; mallards; teals; geese; penguins; ospreys and hawks; crows; ravens; mews; doves; sea-pies; blackbirds, with carnation wings.

Beasts.   Deer, in great store, very great and large; bears; luzernes; black foxes; beavers; otters; wild-cats, very large and great; dogs like foxes, black and sharp-nosed; conies.

Fruits, Plants and Herbs.   Tobacco, excellent sweet and strong; vines, in more plenty than in France; ground-nuts, good meat, and also medicinable; strawberries; raspberries; gooseberries; whortleberries; pease, growing naturally; flax; iris florentina, whereof apothecaries make sweet balls; sorrel, and many other herbs wherewith they make salads.

Fishes.   Whales; tortoises, both on land and sea; seals; cods; mackerel; breames; herrings; thornbacks; hakes; rockfish; dogfish; lobsters; crabs; muscles; wilks; cockles; scollops; oysters; snakes, four feet in length, and six inches about, which the Indians eat for dainty meat, the skins whereof they use for girdles.

Colors to dye with, red, white, and black.

Metals and Stones.   Copper, in great abundance; emery stones, for glaziers and cutlers; alabaster, very white; stones glistering and shining like mineral stones; stones of a blue metalline color, which we take to be steel ore; stones of all sorts for buildings; clay, red and white, which may prove good terra sigillata.

Notes

CHAPTER 1

Paragraphs from this chapter appeared in "Off Season," my article in *The American Scholar*, Vol. 37, No. 3, Summer, 1968.

Pages 12–13. *These Fragile Outposts—A Geological Look at Cape Cod, Martha's Vineyard, and Nantucket* by Barbara Blau Chamberlain, The Natural History Press, 1964. The best natural history background book on the region.

CHAPTER 2

Page 37. The WPA Federal Writers' Project operated from 1935 to 1942 in forty-eight states. *Massachusetts—A Guide to Its Places and People* was written and compiled by the Federal Writers' Project of the Works Progress Administration for Massachusetts, copyright 1937, Houghton Mifflin.

Page 37. Thanks to Houghton Mifflin for permission to quote from *Cape Cod: Its People and Their History*. Henry C. Kittredge's book is one of three fine works on the Cape written by men with the given name Henry. The others are *Cape Cod* by Henry David Thoreau, and *The Outermost House* by Henry Beston.

251

CHAPTER 3

A variant of this chapter appeared in *The American Scholar*, Vol. 38, No. 2, Spring, 1969. I called it, "Pages from a Chilmark Diary."

I thank William H. King of North Tisbury and Albion A. Alley of West Tisbury for joining in.

CHAPTER 4

Page 62. The edition of *Cape Cod* published by W. W. Norton & Company, 1951, with Introduction by Henry Beston, includes Thoreau's fourth and last trip to Cape Cod. Thoreau visited the Cape in 1849, 1850, 1855, and 1857.

Pages 64–65. John Hay tells of the annual migration of the alewife in a little book called *The Run*, first published in 1959, The Natural History Library Anchor Books edition, 1965. A good book.

Page 68. *The Heart of Emerson's Journals*, edited by Bliss Perry, various editions.

Page 68. In his book *A Trip Around Cape Cod, Nantucket, Martha's Vineyard, South Shore, and Historical Plymouth*, published by the author at Monument Beach, Mass., copyright 1898, E. G. Perry, "A Cape Cod Boy" as he calls himself on his title page, writes, p. 128, ". . . on another neck of land, running into Town Cove . . . the house of Capt. Edward Penniman, that Arctic whaleman's chief of his clan—himself a history, with his house full of Arctic bear robes, he himself hunted down, and a man whose record Cape history will not willingly let die . . ." Perry includes a black and white photograph of the Penniman house. Indeed, his book is notable for its turn-of-the-century pictures.

CHAPTER 5

This chapter draws on my essay, "Speaking of Books: *The Outermost House*," published in *The New York Times Book Review*, July 31, 1966 reprinted in *Page 2—The Best of Speaking of Books . . .* , edited by Francis Brown. Holt, Rinehart and Winston, 1969.

Page 76. From an unpublished letter by Henry Beston to Martha Brookes Hutcheson. I thank Martha Hutcheson Norton of Princeton, New Jersey, owner of the letter, for bringing it to my attention and for permission to quote.

Page 76. From unpublished correspondence, Henry Beston to Richard W. Hatch, formerly of Vineyard Haven, Massachusetts. Many thanks to Mr. Hatch for use of these items.

CHAPTER 6

I am very grateful to Donald LeMar Poole, friend and correspondent through many years. And to Cyril D. Norton for the pleasure of his company.

CHAPTER 7

A first-hand description of Cape Cod houses as he saw them in Yarmouth early in the 19th century is given by Timothy Dwight (1752–1817), Congregational minister and one-time president of Yale, in his *Travels in New England, 1821–22*.

CHAPTER 8

In my article on Nancy Luce, "The Time and the Place," published in *The American Scholar*, Vol. 35, No. 3, Summer, 1966, I paid respects to five earlier pieces written about her by others. I said, "For the first comprehensive scholarly as well as fascinating account of the poet, Ben C. Clough wins the laurel." Ben C. Clough's essay, "Poor Nancy Luce," appeared in *The New Colophon*, Vol. 2, No. 7, September, 1949.

Benjamin Crocker Clough was born in Vineyard Haven in 1888. His grandfather, Benjamin Clough, had been third officer on the whaleship *Sharon*, (Captain Howes Norris) which sailed from Fairhaven, Massachusetts, in May, 1841, bound for the Pacific. An account of a mutiny on board the *Sharon*, and the heroic part played by Third Officer Benjamin Clough, then twenty-one, appeared in "Anatomy of a Mutiny," an article by Philip F. Purrington, *The American Neptune*, April, 1967.

Ben Clough's grandmother, Sarah Ames Crocker, had defended Nancy Luce in the years when the poet was being harassed. As a boy, Ben C. Clough heard about Nancy from his grandmother.

After schooling in his home town, Ben Clough went to Harvard where he received his A.B. in 1911 and later his Ph.D. In 1913 he joined the faculty of Brown University. By the time he became Professor Emeritus of Greek and Latin Classics, he had taught at Brown thirty-five years.

Page 121.   Nancy Luce's literary remains, sold by the town to pay her burial expense, eventually landed in Goodspeed's Book Shop, Boston. *Vide Yankee Bookseller* by Charles E. Goodspeed, Houghton Mifflin, 1937. In 1941 Professor Clough bought the Luce-ana from Charles E. Goodspeed. In 1963 he gave it to the Harris Collection of American Poetry in the John Hay Library, Brown University. It is a pleasure to acknowledge Ben Clough's generous help.

Page 123.   Thanks to Henry Beetle Hough, editor and for many years publisher of the *Vineyard Gazette*, for access to the files of the newspaper.

I am indebted to Daniel Manter of West Tisbury, son of the late George W. Manter, for making available what I have called the Manter Memorabilia inherited from Nancy Luce.

CHAPTER 9

The History of Martha's Vineyard, Dukes County, Massachusetts, in three volumes, by Charles Edward Banks, M.D., was published in 1911, reissued in 1966 by Dukes County Historical Society.

Curators and Librarians of Dukes County Historical Society, I appreciate your helping hands.

CHAPTER 10

In addition to *Annals of Gosnold*, included by Banks (see preceding note), three privately printed books recount the history of the privately owned Elizabeth Islands: *Early History of Naushon* by Amelia Forbes Emerson, 1935; *Naushon Data* by the same author, 1962; *Three Islands—Pasque, Nashawena and Penikese* by Alice Forbes Howland, 1964. Mrs. Howland is also the author of a chapter on the Elizabeth Islands published in *Martha's Vineyard, A Short History and Guide*. John Murray Forbes' *Letters and Recollections*, edited by his daughter, Sarah Forbes Hughes, Houghton Mifflin, 1900, two volumes, tells of squirely family life on Naushon in the 19th century, and also documents a noteworthy mercantile and public career.

CHAPTER 11

The full title of the *Short History and Guide* (preceding note) is *Martha's Vineyard, A Short History by Various Hands together with A Guide to points of interest, with maps and pictures*, edited by Eleanor Ransom Mayhew, Dukes County Historical Society, 1956—a valuable book. For further reading about the Vineyard, see *Sketches of Martha's Vineyard and Other Reminiscenses of Travel at Home* by Samuel Adams Devens, James Munroe & Co., 1838; *Martha's Vineyard—Summer Resort, 1835–1935* by Henry Beetle Hough, Tuttle Publishing Company, 1936, reissued by Avery's, Edgartown, 1964; *An Island Summer* by Walter Teller, Knopf, 1951; *The Wheelhouse Loafer* by Joseph Chase Allen, selected and edited by Colbert Smith, Little, Brown & Co., 1966; *An Introduction to Martha's Vineyard* by Gale Huntington, sponsored by Dukes County Historical Society, 1969. This is a careful job documented with old photographs from the Society's archives.

CHAPTER 12

Page 177.   *Wild Fowl Decoys* was reissued in hard cover by Peter Smith, in soft cover by Dover.

Page 179.   Published in 1963, *Wellfleet, A Pictorial History*, honored the 200th anniversary of incorporation of the town.

Page 182.   I thank my brother-in-law, William J. Block of New York and West Tisbury, for fraternal encouragement all down the line. Specifically, he put me onto Winslow Lewis, and ran down in the New York Public Library a copy of an *Exposé of Facts Respectfully submitted to the Government and Citizens of the United States Relating to the conduct of Winslow Lewis . . .*

Addressed to the Hon. The Secretary of Treasury by David Melville, A Citizen of the United States, Providence, R.I., 1819.

Page 189.   Deming Jarves was the father of James Jackson Jarves (1818–1888), author and critic, editor of the first newspaper published in the Hawaiian Islands, and pioneer art collector. The son found little to admire in either the father's factory or its product. In 1881 James Jackson Jarves gave his collection of Venetian glass to the Metropolitan Museum of Art in memory of his father.

Sandwich, the Town that Glass Built, by Harriot Buxton Barbour, Houghton Mifflin, 1948, is a useful, well-illustrated book on the subject.

CHAPTER 13

The Nantucket Atheneum devotes four shelves to books about Nantucket. The collection includes many unuseful volumes. There are, however, four good histories: *History of Nantucket and of the Whale Fishery* by Obed Macy, Boston, 1835; *History of the American Whale Fishery from Its Earliest Inception to the Year 1876* by Alexander Starbuck, Waltham, 1878, (first published as Part IV of the Report of the U.S. Commission on Fish and Fisheries, Washington, 1878), reprinted in two volumes with new preface by Stuart C. Sherman, Argosy Antiquarian, New York, 1964; *Nantucket: A History* by R. A. Douglas-Lithgow, Putnam's, 1914; *The History of Nantucket County, Island and Town*, Including Genealogies of First Settlers by Alexander Starbuck, Boston, C. E. Goodspeed, 1924, reprinted by Charles E. Tuttle Co., Rutland, Vermont, 1969.

Page 195.   William Rotch (1734–1828), Quaker whaling merchant, born in Nantucket, died in New Bedford. In his *Memorandum Written . . . in the Eightieth Year of His Age*, but not published until 1916 (limited edition, 450 copies), he defended the position he took in the War of Independence. "When the Revolutionary War began in 1775," he wrote, "I saw clearly that the only line of conduct to be pursued by us, the Inhabitants of the Island of Nantucket, was to take no part in the contest, and to endeavor to give no occasion of offence to either of the contending Powers. . . .

"A great portion of the Inhabitants were of the Denomination of Friends, and a large number of the considerate of other Societies united in the opinion that our safety was in a state of Neutrality. . . . Our situation was rendered more difficult by having a few restless Spirits amongst us, who had nothing to lose, and who were often thwarting our pacific plan, and subjecting us to danger, not caring what confusion they brought upon us, if they could get something in the scramble. . . .

"It was about the year 1778 when the current in the Country was very strong against us at Nantucket . . . that the people who thought we ought to have joined in the War (not Friends) began to chide and murmur against *me*. They considered me the principal cause that we did not unite in the War (which I knew was measureably the case,). . ."

Page 195. Four editions of *Letters from an American Farmer* are in print at this time, two in hard cover, two in soft. Crevecoeur's chapters on Nantucket and Martha's Vineyard as he saw them in the late 18th century make enjoyable reading today.

Pages 202–4. Herman Melville's (1819–1891) great book, *Moby Dick, or The White Whale*, was published in 1851.

Page 204. Owen Chase's 1821 *Narrative* was reissued in 1963 by Corinth Books. The same publisher reprinted the 1828 book by William Lay and Cyrus M. Hussey under the title, *Mutiny on Board the Whaleship Globe*.

Page 204. The invaluable work on whaling is *The American Whaleman, A Study of Life and Labor in the Whaling Industry* by Elmo Paul Hohman, Longmans, Green and Company, 1928. Written forty years ago, it remains the outstanding book on the subject. Among its many virtues are excellent illustrations and bibliography.

Page 204. *The Voice of the Whaleman with an Account of the Nicholson Whaling Collection* by Stuart C. Sherman, Providence, R.I., 1965. A scholarly and readable guide to source materials including those in the Providence Public Library.

CHAPTER 14

Pages 214ff. *The Search for Captain Slocum: A Biography*, Scribners, 1956, presented the results of my research on Joshua Slocum to that date. Publication of the biography brought further material to light. I put it into *The Voyages of Joshua Slocum*, Rutgers University Press, 1958, an omnibus volume including Slocum's three books, *Voyage of the Liberdade*, *Voyage of the Destroyer from New York to Brazil*, and *Sailing Alone Around the World*, as well as a biographical introduction and commentaries. *Voyage of the Liberdade* also appeared in my book *Five Sea Captains*, Atheneum, 1960, a collection of voyages under sail written by some notable sea captain-writers of New England.

In addition to publication in *The Voyages*, *Sailing Alone* is in print in several editions; *Liberdade*, in one.

Page 222. From an unpublished letter datelined, West Tisbury, 17 April 1903.

Pages 222–223. From a letter to William H. Tripp, datelined West Tisbury, 18 March 1904. This letter was published in full in my article, "50th Anniversary of Start and Probably End of Epic Voyage," the *Vineyard Gazette*, 26 June 1959.

Page 227. "The Last Years of the Heath Hen" by Allan Keniston, The Dukes County *Intelligencer*, Vol. 7, No. 4, May, 1966, published by Dukes County Historical Society, Inc., Edgartown.